Risk and the Rupee in Pakistan's New Economy

In a world of open markets and global trade, current development thinking seeks stability and prosperity for the world's poor by expanding access to financial products. By bringing credit and savings facilities to those who have historically enjoyed little access to formal finance, the 'financial inclusion' agenda promises to spark bottom-up growth at the same time as it offers a safety net. Yet by tooling-up households with access to finance in order to secure financial and economic stability amidst the instabilities of open markets, the financial inclusion agenda overlooks how new risks that are generated by the globalisation of money and markets ultimately undermine money and the financial inclusion agenda itself.

Cast against fundamental change in the monetary environment that has accompanied the globalisation of markets, this book examines the rapid liberalisation of money and markets in Pakistan, itself a pioneer in the promotion of financial inclusion and a 'frontier economy' for global investment. It argues that liberalisation has generated substantive problems not only for the central bank as guardian of national currency, but for ordinary households in everyday transactions. By exposing jarring contradictions between free markets and financial inclusion, the book contributes to important emerging debates about how poor people engage money and finance, setting this micro-scale analysis in a comprehensive framework that scales right up to the heights of global finance. This construction generates a set of meaningful links between the abstraction of 'globalisation' and the experience of everyday economic engagement in the periphery that challenges money theory and the development sector's embrace of financial inclusion alike, by posing substantive and empirically-grounded monetary contestation that demonstrates a burden of risk imposed on ordinary people that is only exacerbated by financial inclusion.

Antonia Settle holds a McKenzie Postdoctoral Fellowship at the University of Melbourne, Australia. She was a Research Associate at the Sustainable Development Policy Institute in Islamabad and has lectured in political economy at La Trobe University and the University of Melbourne.

Risk and the Rupee in Pakistan's New Economy

Financial Inclusion and Monetary Change in a Frontier Market

Antonia Settle

CAMBRIDGE
UNIVERSITY PRESS

CAMBRIDGE
UNIVERSITY PRESS

University Printing House, Cambridge CB2 8BS, United Kingdom

One Liberty Plaza, 20th Floor, New York, NY 10006, USA

477 Williamstown Road, Port Melbourne, vic 3207, Australia

314 to 321, 3rd Floor, Plot No.3, Splendor Forum, Jasola District Centre, New Delhi 110025, India

79 Anson Road, #06–04/06, Singapore 079906

Cambridge University Press is part of the University of Cambridge.

It furthers the University's mission by disseminating knowledge in the pursuit of education, learning and research at the highest international levels of excellence.

www.cambridge.org
Information on this title: www.cambridge.org/9781108489935

© Antonia Settle 2020

First published 2020

Printed in India by Nutech Print Services, New Delhi 110020

A catalogue record for this publication is available from the British Library

ISBN 978-1-108-48993-5 Hardback

Cambridge University Press has no responsibility for the persistence or accuracy of URLs for external or third-party internet websites referred to in this publication, and does not guarantee that any content on such websites is, or will remain, accurate or appropriate.

Contents

Figures

Figures

Acknowledgements

This book owes a great to deal to Professor Emeritus Dick Bryan from the University of Sydney. Dick's ideas and support have fuelled this research. Others at the University of Sydney who have generously offered their time on this include Alun Pope, who fought through streams of pricing data to construct the statistical analysis in Chapter 6; and Martijn Konings, whose support and advice was indispensable. Finally, my thanks to James Culham for very kindly applying his intellect in very useful critique.

In Pakistan, I have received generous support from many people. First and foremost, Maqsood Jan from Peshawar University made very important contributions to this project. I acknowledge his excellent research support, without which this project could be nothing like what it has become. I am also thankful to Asad Farooq and Haris Gazdar for their multifaceted support. The various contributions of Haider Naqvi, Dr Sultan Janjhi, Mohammad Arshad Khan from Ranrraa Development Trust, Qadir Lala and family, Maleeha Naqvi and Sadaf Aziz and family are all gratefully acknowledged.

I am thankful to all my interviewees, but especially to Ali Choudhary and Mushtaq Gaadi, who have continued to share research and answer my many follow-up questions.

Much thanks to Ray Pridmore for exquisite attention to detail, to Andy Scerri for his academic mentoring throughout, and to Giles and Crina, who have both supported this project in many and varied important ways.

Introduction

The financial inclusion agenda calls for the redress of limited access to financial services, notably amongst the poor. From its humble origins in experimental microcredit in Bangladesh, financial inclusion has become a core component of the development work of governments and non-governmental organisations (NGOs) across the developing world. Driven by key philanthropic and private sector interests alongside the United Nations (UN), the International Monetary Fund (IMF) and the World Bank,[1] the financial inclusion agenda now encapsulates not only microcredit, but also access to microdeposit and microinsurance facilities. This suite of financial tools is designed not only to mitigate the kinds of new risks that have been generated in developing economies as a result of economic and financial liberalisation since the 1980s, but to 'enable' and 'empower' the world's three billion poor. Celebrated as the 'key to ending global poverty'[2] and a 'revolution for the unbanked',[3] financial inclusion has become the darling of international development policy.

Financial inclusion's potential as a poverty alleviation tool is premised on its capacities to empower poor households to harness risk. Where the state has wound down welfare policies, and deregulated money and prices through its repeal of subsidies, import tariffs, fixed exchange rates, and fixed interest rates, financial inclusion promises to insulate households against shocks and open up new opportunities for household investment in human capital and entrepreneurship. By enhancing household risk tolerance through access to credit and savings facilities, financial inclusion seeks to spark bottom-up growth at the same time as it offers a safety net. Financial inclusion thus answers to the needs of both social policy and economic policy, marking out money – the basic unit of credit and savings – as the panacea for the new risks faced by households in globalised markets. Yet by engaging access to credit and savings as the tool with which households can attain financial stability amidst the instabilities that are characteristic of open markets, the financial inclusion agenda makes implicit assumptions about the money that constitutes those savings and credit facilities.

In fact, money is not uncontroversial. Rather, the Keynesian tradition, along with the sociological thought on which it draws, marks out money as contested terrain. Indeed, the viability of fiat money demands an unthinking trust in money – a trust long nurtured by central banks in order to ensure the economy-wide acceptability of money at a stable price. Yet where recent developments in money and finance throw up a series of new challenges to money, the precariousness of that trust in money is revealed. Although these challenges remain largely under the radar of public policy discourse, cracks in the veneer of monetary incontrovertibility are increasingly visible.[4] Most obviously with regards to very public uncertainties surrounding quantitative easing, money faces new ambiguities in globalised markets that increasingly detach it from its Keynesian roots and into new unknowns and contestations.

Yet, in many ways, the challenges to money that are posed by globalisation hit peripheral economies hardest. In a country such as Pakistan, the assault on money posed by globalisation may, in fact, be linked to both the persistent failure of the economy to become fully monetised and the slow pace of financial inclusion. This suggests that what is missing in conventional analysis of the monetary environment is a consideration of the changing nature of money itself. Although cast outside of the analytical frame by the persistence of Keynesian assumptions about money's safety and stability in conventional thinking, the rapid change in the monetary environment, provoked by the globalisation of markets, demands new thinking about the viability of local state money as the tool with which to reconstruct household financial stability.

This book analyses the impacts of globalisation on a developing economy's money[5] in the context of the push for financial inclusion. The analysis continues in the Keynesian tradition's recognition of money as a social object, whilst deliberately overcoming the assumptions and disciplinary allegiances that have hindered the development of Keynesian thinking around the tremendous monetary change of which we are now in the midst. By exploring the contradictions that arise between open markets and financial inclusion, the book demonstrates how the changing nature of money, although obscured in both popular and academic settings, is key to understanding the development context.

Globalisation and the Frontiers of Money

Central bank efforts to reassure the public about the reliability of money and finance hint at the contested nature of money. Through intensive public relations efforts, central banks seek to maintain the purchasing power of money in the eyes of the public. These efforts develop a narrative around economic performance that establishes norms and expectations about money and the economy, which are backed by constant reassurance that the central bank is in control.[6] From the

Fed's 'decisive and timely' action as the financial crisis broke (Bernanke 2008) and Draghi's 'whatever it takes' guarantee over the Euro in 2012 (Draghi 2012), to the more mundane promises of a 'positive outlook' and of the central bank's alertness to 'risks to medium-term targets', central banks are essentially promising action to secure money and finance. Yet behind this very contrived discourse is a great deal of uncertainty. As Claudio Borio (2011) observes, central banking has entered into 'unchartered waters' since 2008. Yet the dilemmas posed by the financial crisis have only highlighted concerns about money that had been underlying money management for decades. In fact, the capacity to concurrently control the domestic and international value of money has increasingly slipped out of the control of national central banks as the globalisation of finance has proceeded apace. Although debates about exchange rate regimes grapple with these concerns, they represent but the tip of the iceberg.

Indeed, money and monetary management are rapidly evolving aspects of globalisation. The plight of money, however, has not enjoyed the same focus as has the globalisation of goods markets, either in popular discourse, in politics or in academia.[7] As national economies reverse the market protection of the post-war era, globalisation has been vigorously debated, celebrated and contested across the disciplines of the social sciences. Yet the dramatic changes in money that have accompanied globalisation have not attracted comparable attention, even though money itself has been transformed by degrees unimaginable in the 1960s and monetary theory has been torn up and rewritten more than once over the same period.[8]

One aspect of this change is the diversification of money instruments beyond conventional 'state money'; that is, money produced by the state and the state-regulated banking system – cash, bank deposits and bank credit (and, at a more abstract level, central bank reserves and Treasury bills).[9] This definition of money may have been fitting in the Keynesian era, but it has become increasingly unsuitable as money and finance have globalised and diversified. In the United States, much like in the other advanced economies, the state historically maintained tight controls over money and access to foreign currency and markets. Under this regime of monetary control, the banking system had been the overwhelmingly dominant site of finance for households and businesses.[10] Liberalisation and innovation since the 1980s, however, have dramatically changed the financial landscape.[11] Contemporary conditions offer access to foreign money and foreign markets unimaginable under the controls of the Keynesian years, and financial innovation has produced a plethora of instruments that offer an array of money functions. We have even seen the emergence of cryptographic currencies, defined to be explicitly outside the mandate of state authorities, of which bitcoin is merely the first iteration. Their popularity is growing, and they are increasingly receiving legal recognition as money.

These kinds of innovations have displaced the functional monopoly of simple bank-based deposit and credit facilities typical of money practices in decades past. In this rapid evolution of money and finance, an array of instruments compete with state money in their 'moneyness' because they too are highly liquid stores of wealth. However, they are not produced within the orbit of state money. These 'money-like' assets simply could not have existed without the technological developments and deregulated markets that have followed the collapse of the Bretton Woods system of fixed exchange rates in the early 1970s.[12] As a result, financial innovation is demanding multiple revisions to the formal definition of exactly what counts as money and what does not in the monetary aggregate statistics produced by central banks.[13] This poses an increasingly complex money environment that challenges the role of state money in finance and the central bank's control of finance through control of state money.[14]

Another aspect of this change relates more directly to the predicament of monetary management in the post-Bretton Woods era: without a fixed exchange rate that is backed (even indirectly) by gold, maintaining the value of money and finance becomes a concern of much more abstract dimensions of 'confidence'.[15] Stability in money then depends on people buying and selling (and demanding wages) at nominal prices that are consistent over time. No longer pegged to and redeemable for a set amount of gold, the value of national currency must be deemed by markets to be rational, legitimate and 'true' in order for it to maintain stability. For the economy as a whole, no longer anchored to gold through the value of national currency, stability relies on the central bank's ability to persuade markets that its money – and, increasingly, other 'near-money' claims on the economy – is sound.[16]

These issues came to a head in the wake of the recent financial crisis, in which unprecedented policy responses revealed the limits of conventional policy both in governing a stock of money instruments that now extend far beyond cash and basic bank deposits, and in supporting confidence in this new and complex world of money. The description of these policies as 'unconventional monetary policy', which was taken up by the Federal Reserve at the time, does not do justice to the radical nature of the Fed's actions. In fact, quantitative easing, itself extremely risky, uncertain and controversial,[17] was resorted to where traditional monetary policy had become redundant. Amidst desperate efforts to restore confidence in the value of money through the promise of central bank authority, the crisis response included the radical appearance of effectively negative interest rates on government debt and massive Fed purchases of mortgage backed securities (themselves derivative products produced by private markets). In these policy actions we see money stretched to its outer limits: negative interest rates turn traditional principles of monetary governance upside down whilst the money instrument itself becomes markedly ambiguous as privately issued monies are drawn into the very core of the central bank's state money management practices.[18] As radical policy experimentation grapples with the problem of establishing some kind of control over unprecedented monetary conditions, we find money having slipped away from its traditional boundaries within state money, into the fog that surrounds burgeoning global financial markets.

Yet these new frontiers of money can also be found in the everyday economies of open developing countries: where the core of state money is compromised by the uncertain relationship between the state and money; where 'shallow' financial systems and 'weak fundamentals' meet global markets. In open developing economies, for example, the capacity for the central bank to control money by controlling the price of the money that is issued through the banking system may be inhibited by low levels of banking amongst the population. That is, the traditional role of banks as the site of credit and savings – the primary home of money in the economy – is not weakened by financial innovation pushing money into the unchartered waters of exotic money-like products produced by the non-bank financial sector. Rather, traditional banking is challenged by limited engagement amongst local populations with even basic banking products. This, in turn, undermines the credibility of central bank efforts to control money and prices in the economy, which is exacerbated by the vulnerability to global shocks that comes with open markets. At the same time, instability in the state, the economy and in money itself undermines confidence in state money and the commitment to local currency amongst local populations, a commitment which forms the core of the viability of state money. With the credibility of money threatened by dollarisation[19] and capital flight, and undermined by instability and uncertain monetary policy transmission, the state's efforts to support the social trust in money that is necessary for it to function as legal tender are all the more important.

This study examines money in Pakistan, a 'frontier economy' in the investment world, but also a frontier of money, where conventional notions of money are stretched to their outer limits. In Pakistan, the liberalisation of money and markets has been initiated amidst global markets awash with liquidity. This has weakened the state's grasp over both money and the economy as a whole. In these conditions, the combination of informality in the domestic economy and exposure to skittish global markets demands that the state's efforts to 'anchor expectations' be vigorously and creatively applied.

In Pakistan, national currency management is shaped by global markets, and the link between the state and money – which lies at the core of conventional money theory – is uncertain. Here, we are at a frontier of the legitimation of value demanded by money in the post-gold era and at the limits of the traditional Keynesian monetary system. Alert to the social embedding of money that is characteristic of Keynesian thinking while explicitly seeking to overcome the assumptions and disciplinary allegiances that, it is argued, have hindered the development of Keynesian thought on money under global markets, this book explores the tremendous monetary change in which we currently find ourselves by examining the impacts of globalisation on a frontier economy's money. To this end, the book explores the terrain of risk, of which the financial inclusion agenda is at once a symptom and the prescribed remedy. It argues that this fundamental contradiction has ultimately turned the financial inclusion agenda back on itself, positing a new set of gains that can be reaped from financial inclusion as its credentials for poverty alleviation come under increasing strain. At issue is the central bank's urgent task of normalising money amidst the increasingly problematic instabilities and ambiguities of open markets.

Open Market Money and the Frontier Context

The term 'frontier economy', was coined by the International Finance Corporation[20] and subsequently sustained in investment circles and the financial press as a category or class of investments, for example, in indexed products in 'frontier bonds' and 'frontier share markets' available at the retail level, or foreign direct investment opportunities in 'frontier markets' available to transnational corporations. The term refers to small economies ('price takers' in the language of economics) that are 'investible' and show promise as future engines of growth for the global economy.[21] By definition open to the global economy, frontier economies are thus constituted by their formal institutional frameworks, which are outwardly oriented and committed to liberal market principles. This is in spite of the fact that existing institutional capacity is considered less mature than that of the emerging market economies.[22] Hence, frontier markets ideally have open current and capital accounts,[23] which in turn implies market pricing and a market-based monetary policy, as well as large-scale privatisation programmes that are either completed or underway.

As the 'next generation' of emerging economies, the frontier economy concept is forward-looking, denoting strong potential both for the returns on investment for foreign investors, as well as strong potential for the development of market institutions towards the more 'advanced' norms of emerging economies. Hence, while frontier markets exhibit high growth and 'investibility' for foreign market actors, they are also more unstable than the emerging market economies and retain many of the characteristics more commonly associated with less-developed economies. Frontier markets, for example, tend to have limited formal financial markets and smaller percentages of individuals and businesses that deposit in and borrow from the formal banking sector. In frontier markets, informality is more common and state control over the economy, through both taxation and spending, is weaker. Frontier economies also tend to be burdened by large debt servicing costs and significant military spending,[24] which are a drag on government finances and drain international reserves. Against this backdrop, portfolio and foreign inflows, as well as bilateral and multilateral aid and concessional lending, play an important but precarious role in funding the external deficit that is contracted through a liberalised current and capital account.

In these conditions, the maintenance of open markets poses huge complications to the central bank's task of securing stability in money and thus in the economy as a whole. Frontier economies are particularly vulnerable to fickle capital flows, which can raise and dump the value of money and other financial claims on the economy with little warning.[25] Moreover, in frontier economies, the institutional configurations that underpin the economy can perform poorly in insulating the economy from those shocks, not least with regard to the central bank's stabilisation tools.[26]

Pakistan is demonstrative of this interaction of exposure to shocks on the one hand, and of the weakness of the institutional mechanisms that are designed to dampen those shocks, on the other. In Pakistan, the national currency and the economy that it underpins both displayed marked instability during the transition in macroeconomic and monetary governance to open market principles that began in earnest in the 1990s. This instability persists in the post-reform period, posing persistent challenge to the central bank, the State Bank of Pakistan (SBP). Since the rupee's float in 2000, recurring issues of meeting external payments, limiting speculative panic, and controlling inflation in the economy continue to test both the central bank's commitment to open market principles and its capacity to provide a reliable national money that can provide a baseline level of stability.

For ordinary people, the key challenge posed by the new, open economy is volatility, both in terms of unrelenting low-frequency price instability as well as in larger-scale inflationary shocks. At issue is the interaction between money and prices under a floating currency, on the one hand, and open markets, on the other. With the transition to open market principles, the money which denominates prices is set to float, embedding money's instability in wider pricing patterns. At the same time, prices themselves are set to float through the wind-down of price supports, both direct and indirect, on the kinds of commodities that make up the bulk of the consumer basket amongst ordinary, mostly poor people. Indeed, Pakistan had been a low-inflation economy until liberalisation[27] and had for many decades maintained both fixed exchange rates and fixed pricing on key prices in the economy. In the new economy, however, a new baseline of volatility in everyday prices has become entrenched as money and prices have been liberalised.

For the central bank, the challenge has been to remain on the path to inflation targeting, which policy makers see as the best way to limit distortions in monetary management and maintain openness to global markets. Indeed, inflation targeting is a model of monetary policy practice that is designed for open market conditions. Championed by the IMF in developing economies, and dominant across the developing world and the advanced economies alike, inflation targeting demands predictable, technocratic engagement with the economy within very narrow and clearly defined parameters of central bank policy action.[28] Most importantly, inflation targeting central banks should aim to limit their engagement in the economy to manipulating the short-term interest rate, and to limit the focus of monetary policy to the inflation target, thereby leaving markets for all but the short-term interest rate to operate freely on market principles. By sticking to the 'one tool, one target' rule, inflation targeting seeks to build up the confidence of market actors in the central bank's unswerving and apolitical commitment to maintaining liberalised markets and controlling inflation[29] through distinct and entirely foreseeable means.

Yet the bumpy ride of liberalisation has posed a string of challenges to which the appeal of creeping back into more direct monetary control measures has been particularly strong. This has been the case both where markets fail to equilibrate and where shocks generated in global markets destabilise local markets. The struggle of maintaining a liberal regulatory framework over money during the last two decades has been characterised, for example, by the temptation to restrain 'hot flows' of international capital; to impose limits on interest rates and the exchange rate at which the market engages with the public; to limit certain current account transactions; or to meddle in price setting for key commodity prices. All of these temptations vastly exceed the commitment to open markets and the 'one tool, one target' policy approach that constitutes inflation targeting. In each of these cases, pressures on the liberal regulatory regime have imposed very real costs on stability, which has in some but not all instances been sacrificed by the central bank to the commitment to inflation targeting. This, in turn, has exposed a tough set of trade-offs between what policymakers see as the short-term stability gains of regulatory intervention and the long-term gains of building up confidence in the central bank's commitment to minimal and predictable intervention in open markets through inflation targeting.[30]

These conditions suggest important pressures on money that are only exacerbated by the wider political and economic context. In Pakistan, the state itself has faced huge political pressures with the forced resignation of four consecutive governments in the 1990s, nuclear tests and international sanctions followed by a military coup and dictatorship that lasted right up to 2008. Civilian–military relations remain strained, and the state continues to fall short in the reliable provision of basic services such as education, sanitation and health care, amidst the persistence of very concerning social indicators with respect to nutrition, infant mortality and literacy. The threat of terrorism continues to pose huge costs to the social and economic fabric of the country while corruption, embedded in offices high to low, undermines state legitimacy. Quite aside from the problem of economic and monetary volatility, these conditions undermine the state's backing of money, which lies at the heart of money theory. In Pakistan, estimates of high rates of dollarisation and capital flight reflect a weak commitment to national currency that demonstrates the soft spot of state money in a typical frontier economy context: both the state and money lack credibility and the tripartite system of monetary production and governance between the central bank, the government and the banking sector is somewhat removed from the everyday economy. In Pakistan, we are at a frontier of money, where inexorable pressures can be detected on the core relationships that hold state money together.

Reconfiguring Household Financial Stability through Financial Inclusion

Pakistan's economy transitioned into the new, market-oriented regime of economic and monetary governance in the 1990s. With this, economic growth contracted, inflation appeared for the first time since the oil shocks of the 1970s and the number of people living in poverty more than doubled. By 1999, almost 33 per cent of the population was classified as poor (ADB 2000: 1). With the hard-hitting impacts of adjustment bearing down on households, household financial stability was reconfigured. No longer stabilised through the state's insulation of the national economy – through its subsidies, set prices and welfare state policies – from the vagaries of global markets, households were brought into the fold of financial reform as objects of financial inclusion. In an emerging consensus at the central bank, this approach sought to reconstruct the financial stability of households by including this most basic microeconomic unit in the broader reorientation of the economy around market-based finance. More specifically, the financial inclusion agenda sought to expand the new market-based principles of engagement between the commercial sector and the banking sector to households and the self-employed.[31]

For the central bank, in partnership with the government, a ground-breaking approach was taken that established financial stability as a core pillar of policy.

This approach promised to drive macroeconomic growth forward through bottom-up economic expansion whilst offering households the risk mitigation tools that they need in the new, market-based economic environment. As economic policy, access to finance was envisioned as a means to bolster risk tolerance and thereby spur productivity gains. Financial inclusion sought to allow households to invest in human capital and to offer new product choices to allow smallholders and the self-employed the opportunity to overcome risk minimisation behaviours that are blamed for hampering the uptake of new technology. As social policy, financial inclusion was seen as a key safety net measure insofar as it could give households the tools that they need to manage risks, such as risks to physical health as well as the risks associated with economic downturns that had increased the scale of poverty so severely during the 1990s.

In the two decades since the late 1990s, the support of the government and central bank for financial inclusion in Pakistan has gone from strength to strength, even though uptake of formal financial engagement amongst Pakistani households has been far less impressive.[32] By the mid-2000s, the financial inclusion agenda had become prominent in the global arena – amongst aid agencies, philanthropists and multilateral organisations, including the UN, the IMF and the World Bank.[33] These developments at the global level supported the consolidation of financial inclusion policy within both the government and non-government sectors in Pakistan, in addition to the central bank, which consolidated its own position as a pioneer and leader of financial inclusion initiatives amongst developing economy central banks.

Yet at the same time as financial inclusion offers access to state money as the tool with which to stabilise and ultimately strengthen the engagement of households in economic activity, the economy itself exhibits a series of warning signs about the usefulness of liberalised state money. At issue are the assumptions about the safety and stability of money that are inherent in the financial inclusion agenda. In contrast to the defining characterisation of state money as the safe asset in Keynesian theory, liberalisation has imposed new pressures on state money that undermine its reliability. These pressures imply that state money may not be as robust an instrument as it is commonly assumed to be. Yet state money is nonetheless the tool that is offered by the financial inclusion agenda to households to combat new risks in the new economy.

By ignoring how an increasingly unreliable state money may be compromised in its role as a risk mitigation tool with which to salvage household financial stability, the financial inclusion agenda undermines its own viability. In these conditions, financial inclusion might become more useful to the central bank in shoring up monetary governability than to poor households in stabilising their access to subsistence.

Financial Inclusion and Frontier Money

New pressures on state money in Pakistan are reflected both in the diminishing capacity of the central bank to control money and in the apparently waning commitment of ordinary people to rely on state money for everyday money needs. On the one hand, the grip of the central bank over the economy has weakened dramatically with deregulation, implying weak central bank control over money. It is increasingly recognised that in the new economy, inflation is in large part generated in global markets and thus lies beyond the scope of the central bank's toolkit.[34] At the same time, the domestic economy itself has become increasingly opaque to central bank surveillance, further detracting from the capacity of the state to control money and thus stabilise prices and the economy at large. Informality has spread across the economy in the wake of liberalisation, including an informal market in money that has fiercely outgrown the state's regulatory capacity.

On the other hand, deposit statistics show resistance to the huge efforts of the state to enhance the use of bank accounts for savings amongst ordinary people. Rather than responding to proliferating state initiatives aimed at growing deposits by bringing cash into the banking system, currency in circulation remains remarkably high against slow deposit growth: currency in circulation almost doubled between 2011 and 2015 while deposits failed to push higher than the levels they had been in the very early years of the 2000s.[35] At the same time, non-monetised transactions persist in an otherwise modernising economy. For example, in-kind payments for rural labour have been converted into daily-wage rates denominated and paid in wheat amidst the large-scale shift from sharecropping to daily wages in the rural economy. In a worst-case reading, these indicators suggest that open market pressure on the rupee has driven the inability of the central bank to stabilise money in the new economy and, on the demand side, has led to the failure of economic actors in the everyday economy to embrace the liberalised rupee.

The difficulties faced by the central bank in securing control over the rupee in open market conditions is, in fact, reflected in the evolving framing of financial inclusion in central bank discourse. From the tool of growth and the safety net proposed in the early years of the financial inclusion policy agenda,[36] financial inclusion is increasingly seen by Pakistan's central bank as a tool with which to support the 'normalisation' of money so as to adapt the money environment to the governance tools of regular, open-market monetary policy norms. That is, financial inclusion is increasingly seen as a tool to encourage formalisation of the informal economy and enhance monetary policy transmission[37] – both key milestones on the road from unstable and uncontrollable money to the conventional money of inflation targeting modelling: state money that maintains territorial sovereignty and can be harnessed as a policy tool for economic management. This development in the discourse of financial inclusion emanating from the central bank implies recognition of both informality as a problem of monetary management, and of the weakness of conventional policy tools in securing control over the economy by controlling the rupee.

Indeed, if the liberalised rupee is not working so well for the central bank, it probably is not working so well either for ordinary, generally poor people. This proposition opens up questions about the possibility of contestation of state money amongst the local population. If the liberalised rupee is, in fact, neither governable by the state nor trusted by the population, then what might contestation look like and what does it mean for the push for financial inclusion in Pakistan? We know that hyperinflation disrupts the use of money, undermining its unit of account function by instilling instability in the prices that it denominates and eroding its store of value functions with constant depreciation against goods and services in the economy. But might a more modest but persistent instability, combined with a lack of the kind of credibility in the state that underpins trust in money, generate similar but less severe concerns amongst money users? In a frontier economy that is vulnerable to shocks, might money come to be seen as having more in common with other risky assets in the economy than with the unique risk-free asset it is purported to be by theory? And then, is it possible that ordinary people might engage with money more as yet another risky asset than as money proper?

The key overarching question then becomes: is the central bank misinterpreting the stability needs of households by maintaining outdated assumptions about the money that it issues in the economy? Might it be that state money is, in fact, not the risk-free asset purported by theory, a theory which itself was founded in the Keynesian years of fixed exchange rates and bounded national economies? That is, have the forces of globalisation transformed money, pushing it away from its conventional theoretical form and undermining its ability to function as a tool of risk mitigation? Might money have, in fact, become a subject of risk and object of risk management rather than a tool of stabilisation in its everyday use? And could changing money use that reflects a new riskiness in money constitute a form of monetary contestation, in contrast to the unquestioned reliance on state money as the universal equivalent? If we open up money to the possibility of contestation, the money environment might look quite different to that which is assumed in central bank reports and policy documents.

At issue is the fact that the financial inclusion agenda depends on the reliability of money but fails to address the possibility of monetary change that might undermine that reliability. By assuming the incontrovertibility of state money, the possibility that households' exposure to state money may be a problem in itself is cast outside of the analysis of financial stability altogether. Yet increasingly visible fault lines are appearing in the money environment, both at the global level and, in somewhat more mundane ways, in the day-to-day management of money in the frontier economy context. The challenges posed to the reliability of money by globalisation both at the heights of global finance and amongst small, open economies contradict the role of money as the solution to household financial stability concerns that are the promise of financial inclusion. This poses an intriguing predicament at the intersection of money, globalisation and economic development.

Risk and the Rupee

The examination of money undertaken in this study looks into market processes to explore how new money instruments are generated, not by the state's decree but by the traditional money functions that are exercised in transactions in markets for liquid instruments. This approach essentially explores potential money objects as various combinations of risk and liquidity profiles which can be applied to money functions. This perspective emphasises new risk attached to state money whilst firmly embedding state money in the global context. The result is a portfolio-wide view of the everyday experience of monetary risk by ordinary people – households and small businesses – that hinges on the changing nature of state money that is driven by new exposure to global markets through liberalisation. This analysis is grounded in a context of new risk linked to the globalisation of markets and a focus on the financial agency of economic actors in the everyday economy in relation to the rupee *as a contested form of money*. In this way, the study questions and seeks to extend the boundaries of established approaches to understanding how ordinary, generally poor people engage finance.

As a result, where the central bank identifies a deficit in banking sector engagement amongst the public that should be addressed by expanding financial inclusion to all segments of the population, this study instead posits new and substantive risk carried in state money itself, and the unbanked as amongst those at the forefront of financial innovation. That is, a conventional reading would identify the use of alternative instruments (such as commodities) for key money functions as a form of barter and thus evidence of the glaring need for financial inclusion. Conversely, this study considers such strategies instead as themselves representing financial innovation as ordinary people negotiate a new order of risk in the monetary environment. Rather than reflecting demand for better access to the rupee as money, such strategies are recast as risk mitigation strategies that draw on innovative applications of non-state money instruments in complex financial strategies that attend to new rupee-related risk. In this context, state money is a crucially important locus of risk in the everyday economy. This carries important implications for the capacity of financial inclusion to enhance risk tolerance amongst households, suggesting that financial inclusion may, in fact, be of more benefit to the central bank's efforts to gain policy control over the liberalised rupee than of benefit to the poor.

Outline

By employing a perspective attuned to monetary change, this study paints a distinct picture of money and finance in an open, low-income economy, quite in contrast to the conventional analysis offered by Pakistan's central bank and the financial inclusion literature more generally. The analysis shows how the stability demanded of credible money in Pakistan is undermined by liberalisation and how this has transformed the monetary environment. For the central bank, state money has become increasingly ungovernable. For ordinary people, state money has become a site of new risk rather than a risk management tool. As a result, the monetary environment in Pakistan has become both complicated and ambiguous, and is actively contested. The Keynesian mores of conventional money theory, however, obscure monetary change and the challenges that it poses to conventional conceptions of money. Ultimately, these pressures imply that financial inclusion may be playing out in Pakistan less in the interests of the poor and more in the interests of shoring up rupee governability. This argument is developed over eight chapters.

The first two chapters introduce the global context. Structured around the basic tenets of Keynesian monetary theory, these chapters engage the question of globalisation and monetary change in terms of money's safety and stability and its consequent role in finance: as the safe asset and thus the cornerstone of risk and liquidity. Explored in terms of money at the heights of global finance in Chapter 1, the focus is shifted to frontier economies in Chapter 2.

Chapter 2 maps out key features of the frontier monetary environment, counter positioning this mapping to the conventional reading of monetary policy transmission in developing countries. This chapter explores the links between monetary instability, economic instability and the production of trust in money, in order to set out an analytical space in which the potential for monetary contestation – the inverse of trust in money – can be considered.

Chapter 3 carries out a historical analysis of monetary developments in Pakistan, from independence through to the present. In line with the analytical frame developed in Chapter 2, the emphasis is on how volatility and opacity have become defining features of the monetary environment under liberalisation: from the new threat of inflation and new commodity market dynamics, to the huge growth of informality in money and markets, and the persistently low rates of formal banking sector engagement that become a key policy issue after 2012.

Chapter 4 carries the question of globalisation and money to the level of the household. The chapter sets out how finance theory links the broader theoretical analysis of money in Pakistan to everyday money transactions, that is, how risk is borne as a cost to households in balance sheet terms and how finance theory offers a useful guide to identifying risk mitigation behaviour amongst households. The chapter concludes by summarising the theoretical foundations laid out in Chapters 1 to 4.

Chapter 5 systematically describes the findings from fieldwork and secondary sources, which identify a series of alternative money instruments and strategies in use amongst ordinary people in households and bazaars across Pakistan. These strategies and instruments constitute potential acts of contestation of state money. Indicative rather than conclusive, these findings nonetheless imply aberration from the rule of safe, reliable and uncontested state money that lies at the heart of the central bank's policy and analysis by uncovering a raft of new money strategies: tools and behaviours with which people exercise money functions and manage rupee-related risk in the everyday economy.

Chapter 6 weaves the findings about household money practices that are laid out in Chapter 5 into the broader framework that was set out in Chapters 1 to 4. By drawing these threads together, the chapter shows how liberalisation has generated growing ambiguity and uncertainty in state money. More specifically, state money's distinctness as the safe asset has been eroded by liberalisation, in response to which other liquid markets have evolved to service demand for highly liquid money instruments. This demand, the chapter concludes, reflects complex and innovative financial practices amongst ordinary, generally poor people as they navigate a new environment of risk and liquidity in the new, post-liberalisation economy.

In Chapter 7, the study takes these conclusions back to the literature, demonstrating how theoretical conceptions of money in economic theory tend to impose a static view of money that is not well equipped to incorporate the new pressures placed on money by globalisation. The chapter argues that in Pakistan, money derives its authority not so much from the fiscal capacity of the state or the breadth of the banking system (as it does for state theories of money) but from its capacity to act as the 'monetary invariant'. Here the anchoring function of money takes precedence over the unit of account function in a monetary environment marked by the pressures of globalisation and consequently characterised by fragmentation and ambiguity. This reading of money challenges state theories of money with the evidence of commodity monies operating in Pakistan's new economy. This predicament turns the framing of commodity monies in the literature on its head by positing these monetary forms as not vestiges of a bygone era but as outcomes of financial innovation in the everyday economy, by which risk and liquidity are negotiated by ordinary people in new strategies that essentially hedge an unreliable state money.

Finally, Chapter 8 turns to the implications of this predicament for the central bank, drawing the argument developed across the previous seven chapters to the question of financial inclusion. The chapter demonstrates the substance of monetary contestation – so often alluded to but rarely identified in concrete terms – in the failure of monetary policy transmission and declining bank deposits. It shows how the fractured credibility of the rupee is not only of interest to sociologists and money theorists but is a real and live policy problem for the state. In this light, financial inclusion is posed as increasingly functioning as a solution to the problem of money rather than a solution to poverty.

Conclusion: Financial Inclusion for Whom?

This book shows how the financial inclusion agenda offers money as a social and economic policy solution that can combat new risks and instabilities that have arisen in the wake of the liberalisation of money and markets, even though state money has come to function less as a risk mitigation tool than as a new burden of risk. It argues that the opening of the Pakistani economy to global markets has enacted this transformation in the rupee. A risky rupee undermines the usefulness of financial inclusion as a risk management tool for poor households even as it pushes households to generate new risk management strategies to protect themselves from new monetary risk. The book shows how informal financial innovation that responds to new rupee risk equates to everyday acts of monetary contestation.

For the central bank, the new riskiness of the rupee reflects its inability to grasp policy control over the liberalised rupee and thereby stabilise money and the economy more generally. Yet the contestation of the rupee by households in response to that new riskiness further exacerbates the central bank's inability to effectively govern the rupee under open markets. This predicament is not entirely lost on the central bank. Rather, the central bank implicitly recognizes the failure of financial inclusion to provide financial stability to households in the new economy insofar as it pushes the financial inclusion agenda forward, not so much to support household risk management but to normalize state money. Of impaired use to poverty alleviation, financial inclusion has instead become part of the central bank's toolkit for bringing money back under the control of policymakers.

This book thus builds concrete links between everyday economic engagement at the level of the household and central bank policy choices, which themselves are firmly cast within the global frame. As such, this book contributes to important emerging debates about how poor people engage money and finance, and sets this micro-scale analysis in a comprehensive framework that scales right up to the heights of global finance. This construction generates a set of meaningful links between the abstraction of 'globalisation' and the empirically grounded experience of everyday economic engagement in the periphery.

The book also contributes to the academic literature. By rooting money's credibility in the wider economic setting, the book carries key Post-Keynesian themes of interdependence between monetary, financial and economic spheres through its analysis.[38] Yet by engaging the question of 'frontier money', the analysis finds itself amidst an important gap in Post-Keynesian research. At the same time, the book contributes to Post-Keynesian theory by exploring substantive and empirically grounded monetary contestation, which is otherwise commonly implied but little explored in the Post-Keynesian literature. Monetary contestation is the inverse of trust in money – a trust that is a core tenet of Post-Keynesian thinking. Yet what that contestation looks like in practice is, with a few exceptions,[39] rarely explored.

In exploring the puzzle of why financial inclusion is progressing so slowly in Pakistan, the analysis beats a path that arrives at the tension between a donor-driven agenda to reduce poverty by supporting access to finance amongst poor households, on the one hand, and the central bank's imperative of normalising money in order to exert some kind of control over the rupee in an economy open to global markets, on the other. Along the way, we find a complexity in the post-liberalisation monetary environment that belies conventional statistics. With money and markets exposed to global flows, state money bears a new riskiness that poses fundamental challenge to conventional notions of money. In these conditions, we find ordinary, generally poor households at the forefront of global liquidity, prompting the substantive contestation of money as households juggle new monetary risk with informal strategies of financial innovation that hedge a newly risky rupee. Here we find the central bank grappling to conform to the norms of open market monetary policy despite the radical instability of the rupee that is generated by open market conditions and its consequent rejection, in significant ways, by the local population. It is here that the financial inclusion agenda is found propelled as a means to attend to the problem of open market money rather than to, as intended, the problem of poverty under open markets.

Notes

1. Gabor and Brooks (2017) describe this coalition, which is driving the financial inclusion agenda in global development policy, as the fintech-philanthropy-development complex.

2. This quote is taken from the blog piece by Mathew Driver, 'Why financial inclusion is key to ending global poverty', which was published on the World Economic Forum website on 20 April 2015. See https://www.weforum.org/agenda/2015/04/why-financial-inclusion-is-key-to-ending-global-poverty/ (accessed 1 September 2019).

3. This quote is taken from a presentation by financial entrepreneur Nadeem Hussain at a conference on information and communication technology (ICT) in Islamabad on 18 May 2016, available at https://shamrockcommunicationsblog.wordpress.com/tag/conferences/ (accessed 1 September 2019).

4. Benjamin Braun (2016) illustrates this proposition particularly nicely. Amidst a wider literature on social studies of finance and central banking, Braun considers how central bank efforts to garner trust in money amongst the general public have been challenged by the global financial crisis. Braun shows how growing scepticism on the part of the public has forced the Bank of England, for example, to debunk the 'folk theory of money' that it has long nurtured in favour of a more realistic, but less popularly appealing, depiction of how money is created in its 2014 *Quarterly Bulletin* (Bank of England 2014).

5. For convenience, this study uses the conventional terms 'developing economies' and 'advanced economies'. As discussed throughout this book, however, this terminology implies a linear path of economic development that is not analytically helpful. Nevertheless, for the sake of convenience, this study persists with these terms.

6. The literature on social studies of finance and central banking explores how central banks not only manage expectations but also construct trust in money and the central bank's authority over money through careful discourse with markets and with the public. Key contributions to this literature include Braun (2016), Callon (2007), Hall (2009), Holmes (2014), MacKenzie (2006) and Aglietta (2002).

7. For example, key textbooks on globalisation, such as Frank Lechner and John Boli's *Globalization Reader* (2015) and Jan Aart Scholte's *Globalization: A Critical Introduction* (2017), touch only very lightly on finance and include no substantive discussion on money. This focus on the globalisation of goods markets to the exclusion of the globalization of finance finds a parallel in policy discourse and formal economic modelling. As argued by Claudio Borio (2014), this is reflected in the fact that the current account remains the focus of conventional economic analysis at the cost of consideration of the capital account.

8. For example, money supply targeting, once dominant, was discredited and abandoned in the 1980s (see Chapter 7); the recent financial crisis demanded major rethinking of the 'one tool, one target' premise of inflation targeting (see, for example,

Brookings Institute 2011), and the Bank of England recently officially discredited previously dominant notions of exogenous money in favour of endogenous money (Bank of England 2014; see also Braun 2016).

9. More specifically, the term 'state money' is used to refer to money which is produced under conditions defined by the central bank (for example, prudential regulation including capital requirements) and priced through central bank–led trade with commercial banks (interest rate setting through open market operations) in money produced by the government (treasury bills). This is cash, bank credit and deposits, central bank reserves and, by extension, treasury bills.

10. See Krippner (2011) for a useful description of finance and central banking in the United States prior to deregulation.

11. Malz (2015) provides a very accessible history of the development of financial risk since the collapse of Bretton Woods and the elaborate financial innovation that has accompanied it. For an analysis of changes in the banking sector, see Cetorelli (2014).

12. For an analysis of the separation of money's value from the price of gold that arose through the collapse of Bretton Woods and the deregulation, financial instability and innovation that followed as a consequence, see Helleiner (1994).

13. Lim and Sriram (2003) explore the formal definition of money, which guides the collation of monetary aggregates (M1, M2, M3, and so on) and document the transformation of the contents of these monetary categories. These 'M categories' are discussed in Chapter 7.

14. This set of issues is most commonly addressed in terms of so-called shadow banking, by which the basic function of conventional banking (accepting short-term and liquid deposits on one side of the balance sheet and issuing long-term and illiquid credit on the other, known as 'maturity transformation') is effectively reproduced outside of the central bank oversight that exists for the banking system.

15. Amidst the wider social studies of finance and central banking literature, the problem of confidence as a post-gold concern is discussed by Hall (2009), Holmes (2014) and Aglietta (2002).

16. Again, within the wider social studies of finance and central banking literature, Braun (2016) and Holmes (2014) offer interesting accounts of central bank efforts to cultivate trust in money amongst the public.

17. The media hosted much controversy about quantitative easing (Cashman et al. 2016), which included academic economists (see, for example, Meltzer 2011; J. B. Taylor 2011) as well as more sensationalist commentary (see, for example, Halligan, 2009). Within academia, major concerns about quantitative easing include those around the generation of new bubbles and global spillovers (see, for example, Palley 2011; Chen, Mancini-Griffoli and Sahay 2014; BIS 2014b).

18. Bryan, Rafferty and Jefferis (2015) and Bryan, Raffety and Tinel (2016) emphasise the radical nature of the entrance of mortgage backed securities onto the books of the

Fed. For Bryan, Rafferty, Jefferis and Tinel, this predicament signals fundamental shifts in the evolution of monetary policy as it adapts to financial change, a part of which entails the dramatic repositioning of the household as an anchor for finance through the securitisation of household payments.

19. Dollarisation refers to the use of foreign currency in addition to or to replace local currency. The term does not only refer to use of the dollar – the use of the euro or the Saudi dirham, for example, could also be referred to as dollarisation. In Pakistan these currencies are common, but the dollar is dominant.

20. The International Finance Corporation is the private-sector arm of the World Bank Group. It offers investment, advisory and asset-management services to encourage private-sector development in developing countries.

21. There is no strict definition of frontier economies, although openness to global markets is generally denoted by the term. Frontier indexes for bonds and for equities have proliferated in the last decade amidst booming global financial markets and, more recently, have become an attractive investment in the low interest rate environment. The IMF has produced a particularly useful volume on frontier economies (Schipke 2015). See also Alleyne and Mecagni (2014) and Credit Suisse (2016). Pakistan is commonly considered a frontier market and has featured on the MSCI and Standard and Poor's frontier equity indexes, as well as JP Morgan's Next Generation Markets Index for bonds and Credit Suisse's FM10 index.

22. Such as Malaysia, Brazil and Turkey. Emerging economies are open, high-growth economies that are widely considered as moving towards the kind of market institutions familiar to the advanced economies.

23. Under an open current and capital account, there are no (or few) restrictions (such as capital controls, import licensing schemes or limits on foreign share ownership) on the movement in and out of the economy of goods and finance . A central aspect of an open current and capital account is the free exchange of local currency at market rates. Note that the IMF redefined balance of payments categories in 1993. What had been known as the capital account is now for the most part captured by the new term, the financial account. This book, however, uses the old terminology of the capital account and capital account openness.

24. In Pakistan, for example, two-thirds of the Federal Budget is allocated to debt servicing and military spending (S. Rana 2019).

25. Two very conventional studies on volatility associated with capital flows are Bluedorn, Duttagapta, Guarjardo and Topalova (2013) and Pagliari and Hannan (2017). A broader perspective is offered by Akyuz (2015).

26. For discussion on the stabilization capacity of central banks through monetary policy, see Mishra and Montiel's extensive review of the literature on the efficacy of monetary policy in low-income countries, if not frontier economies, from 2012.

27. See Hasan et al. (1995), Zaidi (2005: 293) and Hamid, Nabi and Nasim (1990: 17).

28. The IMF's *Finance and Development* magazine offers a very accessible description on inflation targeting (Jahan 2017).

29. Of the different measures of inflation, inflation targeting specifically targets inflation in the consumer price index (CPI), rather than, for example, asset price inflation. Within consumer prices, moreover, inflation targeting endeavours to separate 'transitory' price shocks, such as those deriving from commonly volatile food and fuel prices (accounted for as 'headline inflation'), from underlying inflationary trends caused by an excess of demand over supply ('core inflation'). For inflation targeting central banks, core inflation is the proper focus of policy.

30. The policy dilemmas that cast short-term stabilization against long-term commitment to the kind of market-led equilibration that is sought through inflation targeting include the following: in mid-2008, international portfolio outflows were limited and an interest rate floor was imposed on deposit accounts. Limits on the exchange rate have been informally applied to so-called kerb market dealers (see Chapter 3) in 2001 and 2004 through the SBP's threats of regulatory action, that is, 'moral suasion'. The SBP has toyed with the idea of limiting luxury imports through the imposition of limitations on the current account (see, for example, SBP 2017) and intervening in commodity prices, but has not acted on these in the interests of maintaining open markets and limiting central bank intervention in the economy to inflation targeting (M. A. Choudhury, interviewed by the author, Karachi, 20 May 2016).

31. A useful discussion of the emergence of financial inclusion in Pakistan is offered by Staschen (2014). A particularly good primary source, which addresses the ADB funded Microfinance Sector Development Program, is ADB (2000). This document includes a Development Policy Letter from Pakistan's Finance Minister to the ADB, which explains Pakistan's microfinance strategy (Ministry of Finance 2000). See also Oxford Policy Management (2006) and Khalid and Nadeem (2017).

32. This proposition is the central concern of a recent blog post by CGAP, a key actor in the financial inclusion landscape in Pakistan, entitled 'Pakistan Enigma: Why Is Financial Inclusion Happening So Slowly?' (Rasmussen 2018). The same concern is raised in the Financial Inclusion Strategy which was released by the Ministry of Finance and the SBP in 2015.

33. Gabor and Brooks (2017) provide an interesting account of the rise of the financial inclusion agenda in international development policy.

34. See the discussion of studies on inflation in Pakistan in Chapter 3.

35. See Settle (2018) for detailed discussion of deposit statistics in Pakistan. Deposit statistics are presented in the World Bank's Global Finance Development Database (bank deposits as percentage of gross domestic product [GDP]), available at www.databank.worldbank.org (World Bank 2014b). Currency in circulation statistics are available in the SBP's *Handbook of Statistics of Pakistan Economy* 2015 (SBP 2015c).

36. See, for example, Asian Development Bank (2000), Ministry of Finance (2000), Staschen (2014) and Akhtar (2007).

37. See, for example, SBP (2015d) and Dar (2015).

38. See, for example, Dow (2017) on the interconnectivity between monetary, financial and economic spheres in Post-Keynesian thinking as it applies to monetary policy.

39. These exceptions include Weber (2016) and Braun (2016), whose work discusses contestation in terms of the inflationary scares, bank runs and dollarisation, including into bitcoin.

1

The Changing Nature of Money in a Changing International Monetary System

The extraordinary events associated with the global financial crisis of 2007–08 reflect rapid changes in money, banking and finance. Exotic financial instruments, 'too big to fail' banks and hasty deregulation feature heavily in debates ensuing from the crisis. Yet behind these somewhat spectacular concerns lie persistent but increasingly visible challenges to how we understand money and the central banking frameworks that attempt to govern money. This chapter introduces the global markets that are the backdrop of shifting currents in domestic money, by exploring the changing relationship between the state and money at the heights of global finance. In this, we find the transformation of money as burgeoning financial markets push at the bounds of central bank control over money, undermining the theoretical structures through which money and finance are understood and governed. Here we see money less in terms of its philosophical connotations and more in its application in financial markets; a perspective which is carried throughout the book's analysis. This exploration of money at the heights of global markets thereby sets the stage for later analysis by exploring the global context in which frontier money is borne through a perspective on money which is both grounded in finance theory and which addresses the increasingly strained relationship between the state and money.

The chapter opens by identifying the crucial role that state money plays in the financial architecture, as a benchmark for risk and liquidity. These benchmarking functions are intimately linked to notions of money as they are expressed in monetary and finance theory – for example, in asset pricing theory, endogenous and exogenous theories of money creation, and theories of monetary policy transmission – and (as we will see in later chapters) are implicit in central bank discourse and development policy. These depictions of state money demonstrate the uniqueness of money in conventional thinking, a uniqueness that, as Keynes explores in his description of money in the *General Theory* (1936), is tied to the state's sponsorship and control over money in the economy.

Framed in financial terms of risk and liquidity and cast against Keynes' 1930s description of money, the chapter considers how the forces of globalisation have impacted this uniqueness of state money. This analysis explores money as increasingly fluid and ambiguous, and introduces the new challenges to policy and to theory that this predicament generates. More specifically, the chapter address the Keynesian characterisation of state money as safe, stable and produced under the supervision of the central bank, consequently posing volatility, the weakening of the state guarantee over money and the production of money outside of the central bank system as key facets of monetary change. The chapter thus develops a perspective on money and monetary change that provides the foundations for the development of a contrast between conventional notions of how money behaves, which are rooted in Keynesian thinking, and the radical monetary change in which frontier money is borne – change which is becoming increasingly difficult to ignore.

State Money: The Cornerstone of Risk and Liquidity in the Financial System

In modern monetary and economic theory, money is synonymous with state money[1] and state money is understood not as one particular *type* of money amongst others but as the *exclusive* definition of money. The idea of money as exclusively state money is implicitly based on the idea that the state provides and oversees the unit of account, and similarly that the stability and integrity of the unit of account is a core function of state monetary policy. Money as state money provides the foundational unit of monetary theory, which guides monetary policy and is implicit in macroeconomic theory. This is despite the fact that, as will be discussed in later chapters, on closer inspection the exact definitional boundaries of state money are problematic.

Money is defined more precisely by reference to cash, with cash itself a product of state minting. The significance of cash is that it is the most liquid form of money: it can be converted into anything else – goods and services or other asset forms – quickly and without further cost. As is shown in later analysis, liquidity is a central defining attribute under any conception of money. Moreover, 'state cash' (notes and coins) is generally defined as legal tender: within the legal constituency of the state, people are required to accept it as payment. No other form of money can be legally imposed as a means of payment. Indeed, for the early twentieth century state money theorists, the requirement of using state money as the exclusive means of paying taxation was the distinctive status of state-issued money.[2] This body of theory is returned to in Chapter 7.

The liquid and legal nature of 'state cash' carries over into economics and finance theory, where state money has a special role amongst other assets. In central banking practice, state money in its 'narrow' form provides the building blocks for a theoretical schema of 'broad monies' by establishing a baseline unit of measure. This schema delineates various types of money into different monetary aggregates (M0, M1, M2, and so on), which are designed to provide central banks with key information about liquidity in the economy, not least in application to efforts to control inflation. Narrow money (M0 and M1) refers primarily to transactional balances and relates predominantly to money's medium of exchange function: M0 includes currency in circulation and central bank reserves and M1 includes these plus demand deposits held in central bank–supervised commercial banks. Broad money (M2, M3, and so on) refers primarily to liquid stores of wealth that draw more on the store of value function of money, and include forms of money such as savings deposits and term (or time) deposits in commercial banks, money market mutual fund shares, short-dated commercial paper, savings bonds, and so on.[3]

Thus, state money is not restricted to cash, and economists identify assets less liquid than cash, but still highly liquid, as recognisable as money in a hierarchy of monetary categories. This money hierarchy of liquidity[4] posits narrow money that is issued directly by the state at the top of the metaphorical pyramid, followed by progressively less liquid securities (that are produced at progressively further distance from state control) in M1, M2 and M3 (or even M4 and M5, in some jurisdictions).

Already we can note a premise here that becomes critical in our later analysis: that, as the concept of money extends beyond cash, it is the banking system that is positioned next to the state as the custodians and creators of money. We will in later chapters have reason to question whether banks are the only or even the privileged custodians of the most liquid 'near money' assets, and hence whether the ways in which M2 and M3 are characterised are useful methods of framing liquidity in relation to money.

In any case, the baseline provided by state money is not just as a liquid unit of account and means of exchange. It is also a base from which risk can be measured. Because state money in the form of cash is guaranteed by the state with no possibility of default, it is framed in financial analysis as risk-free. It thereby generates no rate of return (rate of interest). Other forms of money and 'near money' are framed as having less liquidity and thereby more risk than cash (they are less transferable into another money type and less a means of exchange). In return, these less liquid forms of money and financial assets normally achieve a rate of return above zero (a positive rate of interest) but they carry risks related to their rate of return (interest rate movements) and risks of default. Thus demand deposits, which are counted as narrow money, offer the lowest rate of return after cash because they are not as risk-free and liquid as cash, but remain within the orbit of the state's guarantee. Specifically, banks have access to the central bank's lender of last resort facility, which is a key defence against potential default. They are also made safer by being subject to central bank supervision and deposit insurance that is administered by the central bank.

Alternatively, broad money instruments, such as a term deposit in a commercial bank, a share in a mutual fund or commercial paper with a three-month maturity, promise a higher return. For term deposits in commercial banks, this return is derived from the loss of liquidity, rather than from higher risk. For broad money issued outside of the supervised banking sector, aside from attracting a return derived from the loss of liquidity, a higher return is justified by the higher risk given that non-bank financial institutions (such as money market mutual funds, let alone corporations) are neither subject to central bank supervision and deposit insurance nor have access to lender of last resort facilities. This relationship demonstrates the connection of money to financial risk generally, whereby narrow money holds the privileged position of being considered risk-free and thereby functions as a baseline measure.

This relationship applies not just to cash and money held in bank accounts but to other sorts of government-issued assets too. Just as cash carries no risk of default, government bonds, which are conventionally denominated in local currency, too are considered risk-free.[5] This is because, in marked contrast to the issue of bonds by corporations or the issue of bonds denominated in foreign currency (so-called Eurobonds), the issuing government of locally denominated bonds can effectively print money or tax its population if it is threatened by the possibility of default. This capacity to conjure up the money required to repay debt effectively overcomes default risk. Hence – amongst AAA rated advanced economies at least – the interest rate at which markets price government bonds is considered to reflect the benchmark 'risk-free interest rate'. This rate reflects the return on (il)liquidity without risk, thus setting a floor upon which a risk premium is built onto corporate bonds and other assets. This offers a direct parallel to the way narrow money is understood as a risk-free asset that provides a baseline for positive interest rates built into broad 'near monies'. The interest rate on a three-month government bond, for example, provides the risk-free rate for a three-month security: the profit that the market deems sufficient for lending at term (for the loss of liquidity over a three-month period) with no risk. The difference between the interest rate on a three-month government bond and a three-month corporate bond reflects the risk premium attached to the corporate issuer.

The risk-free nature of state money is reflected in conventional theories of money demand[6] and is central to liquidity preference theory (Keynes 1936) and portfolio theory (Markowitz 1952, 1959; Tobin 1958), discussed further in Chapter 4. In these theories, narrow money is understood as essentially risk-free, analogous to the risk-free nature of government bonds which feeds into asset pricing theory as the risk-free interest rate. Cash and government bonds thereby play the special role of providing safe assets to risk-averse investors. This is most simply expressed in Keynes' liquidity preference theory: under heightened uncertainty, investors increase their liquidity preference, sacrificing a higher return for the safety and liquidity of cash (Keynes 1936).[7]

It follows that government bonds of states with a lower credit rating than AAA provide the same conceptual basis, placing a floor on risk premiums of all other securities and providing the safe asset for risk-averse investors *within the local economy*.[8] Regardless of a state's credit rating, the risk-free benchmark in each local economy is derived from the supremacy of the state in defining the terms of financial exchange and the ability of the state to print its own money and thereby remain free of default risk within the local economy. That is, a firm based in an economy the sovereign bonds of which may be CCC rated carry that CCC rating as the baseline risk-free measure. The difference between the interest rate on sovereign and corporate bonds of firms in such an economy reflects the risk premium attached to the corporate issuer over and above the 'risk free' sovereign rate in exactly the same way as in an economy in which the bonds are AAA rated. As in any other economy, narrow money thereby provides a benchmark as the safest asset within the financial system while government bonds provide the benchmark risk parameter for pricing risk in other assets inside the economy.

As a corollary, in conventional theory, with state money presumed 'safe', the delineation between the various M-categories (M1, M2, M3, and so on) establishes a relationship that pegs the expansion of narrow money to that of broad money. This puts the state's direct control of narrow money at the centre of the whole monetary system, and it is a premise that crosses standard debates in the macroeconomics of money – from older neoclassical theory, which remains the mainstay of undergraduate textbooks, to more recent developments in New Keynesian and Post-Keynesian schools of thought, which have in part adapted and in part replaced neoclassical thinking to become, respectively, dominant in policymaking circles and the dominant critique of policy.[9]

In neoclassical theory, for example, the relationship between narrow and broad money is understood in terms of a 'money multiplier'. By this reading, the central bank can choose to (exogenously) change the amount of central bank reserves (M0) in the system. As banks are issued with a higher number of reserves, they can expand their lending proportionally in a process known as fractional reserve banking. With the issue of new bank credit, M1 expands, an expansion that ripples out across the wider reaches of broad money as that new credit works its way through the economy (M2, M3, and so on). Hence, neoclassical theory proposes that the value of money (inflation) can be controlled by controlling narrow money, which equates to indirect control over broad money and thus control over liquidity in the economy (Friedman and Schwartz 1963). Although this monetary policy practice, known as money supply targeting, is considered a policy experiment that failed in the 1980s, the 'money multiplier' remains the textbook model of monetary expansion[10] and has remained an important part of central bank discourse.[11] This neoclassical interpretation of the relationship between narrow and broad money is reflected in the continuing importance of monetary aggregates in monetary analysis, including in IMF stabilisation programmes in developing countries.[12]

Post-Keynesians as well as New Keynesians, on the other hand, reject the money multiplier, arguing that broad money expands not because the central bank choses to (exogenously) expand narrow money, but because banks (endogenously) choose to expand credit. Known as endogenous money theory (in contrast to exogenous money theory), this reading proposes that central bank reserves do not function as a binding constraint on credit expansion but instead are provided as a matter of course by the central bank to the banking system. Banks are thus not constrained by reserves but by profit-making opportunities in the economy for which entrepreneurs might seek new loans, and by the risk appetite of banks in choosing to lend. Post-Keynesian theory[13] thereby posits reverse causation in the relationship between narrow money and broad money to the 'money multiplier' story of neoclassical economics.

Either way, however, we see narrow and broad money understood to be structurally linked to state monetary authorities, expressing state money's role as the cornerstone of broader money assets and the benchmark of risk and liquidity. That is, be it through exogenous or endogenous money, money supply is understood to pivot on narrow money yet reach into broad money, both of which are located within banks and the wider financial system and are thus under the control of the central bank through its regulatory practices. This conventional perception of intimate linkages between narrow and broad money is reflected in the theory of monetary policy transmission. Monetary policy manipulates short-term interest rates on bank reserves (M0), and arbitrage across the maturity spectrum carries the interest rate on reserves into the interest rate on bank money (M1) and on to the kinds of assets that make up broad money. Changes in the interest rate on narrow money are thus understood to affect households and firms based on the change in prices across the spectrum of narrow and broad money, including the cost of bank borrowing, the change in the return on savings deposits and the change in the value of financial assets.

Keynes' Definition of Money: The Stable Yardstick

As the rest of this chapter will show, the role of state money as the cornerstone asset is a distinctly twentieth-century financial formation that is vulnerable to the kinds of changing conditions of money and finance that we have seen over recent decades. A sense of this kind of change can be gleaned by setting up a comparison between Keynes' description of money in chapter 17 of the *General Theory* and money as we know in its present iterations. This benchmark is nominated not because Keynes' is either the original or even the most complete theory of money. Rather, the pervasive influence of post-war Keynesianism in economic policy made it 'performative':[14] the advanced economies initiated enough of a Keynesian agenda to make a Keynesian approach to money the practical reality of monetary theory and policy. As such, Keynes' notion of money is intimately linked to the tools that central banks have developed to control money and the broader economy.

Keynes draws out the key features of money in chapter 17 by examining 'wherein the peculiarity of (state) money lies as distinct from other assets' (1936: 222). For Keynes, this distinction between the capacity for state money to function as money and the capacity of other assets to function as money lay in state money's uniquely stable nature. This stability is rooted in the unique relationship between the state and money by which state money is a product not of the market, but of the state. As the rest of the chapter shows, however, the basic premise of state money's inherent stability, and thus uniqueness amongst other assets, can no longer be assumed. Herein we find important aspects of contemporary monetary change that shape monetary conditions in global markets.

In order to explore why state money 'rules the roost' (ibid.: 223) amidst other assets, Keynes conceptualises state money vis-à-vis various commodities in terms of 'own interest rates': 'for every durable commodity we have a rate of interest in terms of itself, a wheat rate of interest, a copper rate of interest', and so on (ibid.: 222). For Keynes, state money carries 'the significant' interest rate (ibid.: 236) because of its unique attributes of exceptionally high liquidity and exceptionally low carrying costs, which feed into state money's exceptional stability. This self-reinforcing interaction between stability and liquidity and the imperviousness of these features to changing conditions in the broader economy was, for Keynes, at the heart of state money's unique capacity to function as money.

At the heart of this proposition is the fact that the value of state money – its interest rate and exchange rate – was designated by policy rather than by the interaction of private production and market demand. Hence, since state money cannot be produced by the market (in Keynes' words, 'labour cannot be turned on at will by entrepreneurs to produce money in increasing quantities' [ibid.: 230]), its marginal return can be expected not to drop over time in the way that the marginal return on other commodities could (for example, where high profits attract increasing supply which, in turn, eventually drives returns down). These unique characteristics denote a stability and thus safety in state money that is a defining feature of money. This safety posits state money as a reliable default asset to which capital could return after being retired out of production, in the same way that it made state money ideally suited as a safe wage unit and day-to-day saving instrument. That is, state money could offer a safer asset in which to store funds in the case of the liquidation of an asset or of wages exceeding consumption, because state money promised to safely preserve value while maintaining liquidity, even in the event of a sharp downturn in economic conditions.

Moreover, as Keynes explains, stability and liquidity are mutually reinforcing attributes which support the anchoring function of money. Keynes uses the key role of wage denomination in state money to interrogate this relationship, linking wage denomination to the denomination of debt. Keynes states that 'the convenience of holding assets [that is, wages] in the same standard as that in which future liabilities [debt] may fall and in a standard in terms of which the future cost of living is expected to be relatively stable, is obvious' (ibid.: 236). That is, by denominating wages in the same unit that denominates debt, price risk on the value of that debt is reduced: if the unit of account in which wages are denominated depreciates, it will not affect capacity to pay off debt, which too will depreciate proportionally. In the same way, by denominating wages in the same unit that denominates living costs more generally, the benefit of stability in future living costs is accrued. Here we see the anchoring function in state money, insofar as the usefulness of state money is reinforced by its ability to change in step with the value of other key prices in the economy. Moreover, the denomination of wages in state money, Keynes notes, in turn, enhances liquidity in state money by entrenching its dominance as the money object circulating in the economy. However, the stabilising role of state money carries yet further. Keynes argues that the inherently greater stability of state money as opposed to other commodities for wage denomination enhances stability in wages themselves; in turn, the stability in the value of output (which is essential for supporting investment in the economy) is itself rooted in the 'stickiness' of wages.

All in all, Keynes emphasises how state money's inherent stability, which is derived from the state's administration of state money and drives its superior attributes of liquidity, anchors the economy at the same time as it reinforces state money's uniqueness as money in the economy.

> Thus we see that the various characteristics, which combine to make the money rate of interest significant, interact with one another in a cumulative fashion. The fact that [state] money has low elasticities of production and substitution and low carrying costs tends to raise the expectation that money wages will be relatively stable; and this expectation enhances money's liquidity premium. (Ibid.: 238)

Hence, Keynes writes that

> if a commodity can be found to satisfy these conditions then assuredly it might be set up as a rival to [state] money. Thus it is not logically impossible that there should be a commodity in terms of which the value of output is expected to be more stable than in terms of money. But it does not seem probable that any commodity exists. (Ibid.: 238)

Keynes' explanation of why state money, and not some other commodity, was uniquely equipped to act as money thus revolves around its stability and safety as a product of the state rather than the market, which enhanced its liquidity and facilitated its role as an anchor and stable yardstick measure for the wider economy. These characteristics are echoed in the operational definition of money offered by monetary aggregates, by which assets are defined as money if they have a stable enough value (which itself reflects high liquidity) and they move in step with various macroeconomic growth indicators across the wider economy (which essentially indicates an anchoring role). Moreover, as discussed further in Chapter 7, these are the central themes of money theory, which are repeated throughout an expansive literature: commodity theories root commodity money in its liquidity (Menger 1892), chartalist theory harnesses money to the state (Knapp 1924 [1905]; Lerner 1947; Bell 2001; Wray 2012) and the central character of money as a 'stable pole' in contrast to fluctuations amongst other goods remains a central theme in the literature on the sociology of money (Simmel 1990 [1900]; Dodd 1994; Ingham 2004). It is these characteristics – of stability, of liquidity and of state backing – that have protected state money as the privileged form of money in the economy, thereby facilitating the cornerstone role of state money as benchmark for liquidity and risk, as discussed earlier.

Yet state money has changed in crucial ways since Keynes wrote the *General Theory*, not least as a result of the departure from fixed exchange rates. As the rest of the chapter shows, changes in the international monetary system have undermined these key attributes that had been described by Keynes as unique to state money and upon which the cornerstone role of state money is premised. The huge growth in international flows following the repeal of capital controls is one important aspect of this change.

The Stable Yardstick Measure after Bretton Woods

By the mid-twentieth century, floating exchange rates had long been out of fashion amongst economists. Floating rates were associated with the trade protectionism and monetary instability that had, as Ragnar Nurkse had argued in an influential study published in 1937, been driven by damaging and unnecessary speculation. Floating exchange rates were not entertained in mainstream debates about the monetary system until after the publication of Milton Friedman's seminal paper 'The Case for Flexible Exchange Rates' in 1953 (Krugman 1989; Irwin 2017). Reclaiming speculation from the rebuke of those such as Nurkse, Friedman proposed that arbitrage would maintain stability at equilibrium rates, thereby smoothly adjusting the external account balance to reflect changes in a country's fundamental economic position. In the event, when the gold peg was abandoned and currencies were floated in the early 1970s, exchange rate instability proved to be much greater than had been expected. The post–Bretton Woods system was rapidly characterised by erratically shifting exchange rates, often with little relation to 'fundamentals'.

These fundamentally new conditions of money de-anchored from gold pose an instability in money that is in sharp contrast to the state money described by Keynes in chapter 17 of the *General Theory*. Constant change in the value of money in part reflects formidable growth in global financial markets. This suggests that state money has found itself atop an ever-growing pyramid of liquid 'near money' assets as the post–Bretton Woods era has progressed. Certainly the huge and much more complex nature of today's financial markets strikes a radical contrast to the controlled flows and narrow array of instruments of mid-century finance.

The blossoming of eurocurrency markets, which effectively offer 'offshore' access to money at 'unofficial' exchange and interest rates, was but one complication to money in the post–Bretton Woods years.[15] More generally, financial deregulation on the part of the state and innovation on the part of private markets created new financial instruments, expanded leverage and allowed for much greater movement of finance across borders. These changes took place amidst a more general deregulation of the key currency economies, under which growing cross border flows interacted with the wind-down of state-sponsored protective measures such as capital controls, fixed exchange rates, stable interest rates and commodity price stabilisation schemes, all of which fed into a new order of instability. More specifically, however, innovative strategies such as securitisation combined with low interest rates to generate sharply growing global liquidity after the mid-1990s as credit and money expanded.[16]

All this equates to an environment of constant flux. In these conditions, financial management strategies amongst corporations, the financial sector and state institutions themselves have become extremely complex, demanding constant balance sheet adjustments as hedging and liquidity requirements respond to constantly changing conditions.[17] Any large movement in financial markets (not least those undertaken in regular central banking activities) thus prompts a cascade of rebalancing transactions that generate expanding flows.[18]

These growing flows are expressed in fluctuations in monetary indicators not least because, where they involve currency exchange, they impact exchange value by generating supply and demand pressures on currency values. The growth of foreign exchange transactions from US$3 trillion per day in 2007 to US$5 trillion per day in 2016[19] (BIS 2016) gives some indication of the growing scale of cross-border flows.

These conditions disrupt Keynes' notion of state money acting as a stable yardstick measure, which hinges on the interest rate being subject not to the volatility of market pricing but to price setting by the state. Although in the post–Bretton Woods system the central bank effectively sets the short-term interest rate, this fact alone no longer guarantees stability in the price of state money. Rather, the exchange value of state money has become a key locus of monetary instability, not only in times of crisis but also in terms of everyday volatility.[20] No longer more stable than other commodities in the economy, state money now oscillates by the millisecond.

Yet the expansion of financial flows – and complexity within those flows – poses a more complex set of questions for the capacity of state money to maintain the monetary attributes that Keynes had considered definitional to money. These are explored in the next section, in terms of the state guarantee and the production of money by the state. At the heights of global finance, we see a more complex monetary environment, which, as we will set out in the next chapter, shares a number of characteristics with the frontier context.

The State Guarantee and the Production of Money outside the Central Bank

The notion of stability in money is complex. Beyond one-dimensional and quantifiable exchange rate or interest rate stability, the relationship between the state and money constitutes the state guarantee that vests state money with another kind of stability. This stability allows state money to function as the benchmark safe asset, which entails a distinct stabilising role for the whole gamut of 'near monies'. This section shows how the changing relationship between the state and money compounds new conditions of monetary volatility in generating subtle but fundamental pressures that push money away from its twentieth-century Keynesian expression. The changing nature of money creation is a case in point.

Empirical literature demonstrates that the huge growth of credit in the United States since the 1980s has moved away from its traditional relationship of proportionality to central bank reserves and broad money indicators.[21] The bulk of credit creation is now located in non–bank financial institutions that lie outside of central bank control. This represents a departure from textbook descriptions that are based on the simpler intermediation processes of Keynes' era. With credit creation occurring outside of central bank control, central banks are no longer able to impose binding reserve requirements and much money creation occurs outside of the infrastructure of the state guarantee to depository institutions, a state guarantee constructed through deposit insurance, lender of last resort access to the central bank's discount window and central bank supervision.[22] As Nicola Cetorelli writes, 'a much more complex, assembly-line system, with a multiplicity of entity types' has replaced the traditional money creation system whereby 'commercial banks as central brokers provide[d] all the services needed for the intermediation of funds' (2014: 1).

At the same time, commercial banks themselves have undergone 'significant transformation … from being focused commercial bank entities [to] become[ing] instead progressively very complex bank holding companies, with control over dozens and dozens of … subsidiaries, with depository institutions, in many instances, constituting only a small fraction of their entire organizational count' (ibid.: 4). These changes posit a much-weakened link between the state and money (via the supervised banking system), which ultimately undermines state money as the cornerstone of the financial system through its credible state guarantee. That is, the mechanisms of the state guarantee, for example, through lender of last resort facilities and deposit insurance, are being left behind by the shift out of traditional banking. This marks a key shift into new monetary territory.

Moreover, there are no easy answers to this problem. The state guarantee of implicit and explicit insurance of financial systems may well have encouraged the massive expansion of leverage that has contributed to the growth of money instruments in the global economy. Indeed, this assumed promise of state backing, not just for the supervised banking sector but the financial system as a whole, was realised in the global financial crisis. After witnessing the market chaos following the collapse of Lehman Brothers, the Fed effectively bailed out not just non-bank financial institutions but the whole mortgage backed securities (MBS) market, by committing to massive purchases of these 'distressed' assets. Yet this came at significant cost. Quite apart from the slew of popular upheaval that registers discontent over the state's expanded bailout – from 'Occupy Wall Street' to the phenomenon of Donald Trump's presidency – there were and continue to be significant operational consequences.

One such consequence relates to the question of how central banks can balance systemic stability with the fiscal costs implied by extending the central bank guarantee beyond the regular banking sector to the kinds of instruments that are captured by the term 'shadow money'.[23] Moreover, given that such a guarantee implies a moral hazard that can exacerbate financial institutions' risk taking behaviour,[24] a more basic question arises: do central banks even have the capacity to back financial institutions that operate outside of the central bank system? The push for macroprudential regulation after the global financial crisis takes a step towards reconfiguring regulatory oversight but this too raises fundamental challenges. How, for example, can a central bank balance government oversight with central bank independence and a commitment to the liberal financial order? Can nationally oriented regulation address global markets? And how can shadow banking be included in the macroprudential framework?

Open questions around the changing nature of the state guarantee over money have been extended even to the reliability of the state's foundational money instrument, the treasury bill (T-bill). This has traditionally been the 'bedrock' of global finance – safe and stable. T-bills have traditionally constituted core holdings around which institutional investors such as sovereign wealth funds and pension funds build their portfolios and have been the money instrument by which the central bank undertakes monetary policy. T-bills have provided an ideal asset with which the whole gamut of financial actors hedge risk. Regulators, however, are concerned that current conditions associated with financial innovation and the globalisation of finance have fundamentally altered the market.[25] Algorithmic trading is blamed in part for the disruption (Leong 2015). In any case, T-bill markets have witnessed unprecedented volatility events in recent years. That volatility combines with low and even negative yields to undermine the cornerstone role of T-bills as the quintessential safe and stable asset next to central bank reserves themselves. As a result, institutional investors are shifting away from traditional holdings of T-bills and are negotiating new strategies for balancing liquidity, safety and return by replacing their T-bill holdings with alternative assets, such as corporate bonds, commodities and infrastructure.[26] As well as marking an important underlying tendency in the role of state money as financial cornerstone, these changes necessarily mark a shift in institutional investment towards greater risk taking as the safety characteristics of institutional investors' primary safe asset holdings are eroded.[27]

At the same time, questions around the changing relationship between the state and money turn onto the state itself as a locus of fractured safety. Bailouts and other crisis-related policies in the wake of the recent financial crisis imposed huge demands on state finances, causing, in turn, a spate of sovereign ratings downgrades across advanced economies. These downgrades explicitly express perceptions of decreasing safety in the state guarantee over money. Most immediately, this large-scale downgrading of advanced economies has diminished the stock of safe assets in global markets. This predicament raises its own issues for maintaining monetary policy credibility, for limiting borrowing costs for the private and public sector, and for supporting a beneficial distribution of risk within an economy. It simultaneously pushes the global financial system into a new normal of greater instability.[28] At issue for this study, however, is the inability of the credibility of the traditional state guarantee to endure in the face of a financial system so complex.

In broad terms, the inability of state money to function as backstop for the wider economy and financial system in the wake of the recent global financial crisis attests to change in money vis-à-vis the broader economy. Specifically, the extraordinary actions taken by the Fed in response to the recent global financial crisis suggest that traditional monetary policy practice (manipulating the interest rate on state money) has not provided a potent enough tool for stabilising the economy. Instead, by purchasing MBS and doing so from financial institutions that lie outside of the supervised banking system, the Fed has been forced to effectively expand its guardianship to private sector 'near-monies'. Abandoning the traditional 'T-Bills only' policy, MBS are being transferred onto the Fed's books as if they were state money. While the Fed's implicit and explicit backstopping of the non-bank sector has quietly become a norm of monetary policy,[29] the entrance of MBS into the Fed's balance sheet in the role traditionally occupied by T-bills casts fundamental new questions about the changing nature of state money as money.[30] In simple terms, it implies that state money, in certain circumstances at least, no longer 'rules the roost' (Keynes 1936: 223).

Conclusion: Qualitative Change in Money

This analysis has shown how the degeneration of state money, both with regard to its stability and its safety as a product of the state, has superseded its twentieth-century Keynesian expression. That is, new complexity in money and finance strikes a contrast to Keynes' insistence on the safety and stability of state money, itself premised on the production and regulation of state money by the central bank. For Keynes, the state sponsorship of money was seen to facilitate a virtuous cycle of stability and liquidity, which anchored the economy and satisfied an optimal yield, carrying cost and liquidity in state money that, in turn, protected the primacy of state money in functioning as money in the economy. However, as financial markets have evolved, not only has state money shed key attributes that Keynes had pinpointed as definitional, but a proliferation of liquid assets has intruded into state money's domains of store of value, standard of deferred payment and means of exchange. This predicament undermines state money's exclusivity as money and reveals how much money has outgrown the narrow bounds of its Keynesian origins.

This picture complements assessments of the quantitative dimensions of financial innovation. As financial markets grow and new liquid stores of wealth are developed, the quantity and make up of money shifts as notes, coins and simple bank deposits become smaller and smaller components of the overall money supply. With such a proliferation of 'near monies', central banks are left in control of an asset (state money) that commands less and less power over the broader economy as state money comes to sit atop an ever-larger pyramid of liquid assets. That loss of influence results from the state money component of broad money becoming proportionally smaller in relation to the 'near money' constituents that circulate in the economy but which are produced outside of the central bank money system.

By revisiting Keynes' description of state money, however, we are reminded that although these quantitative concerns do raise certain challenges to central banking, there are more qualitative and complicated aspects of greater salience. For example, in terms of money itself, what are we to make of the Fed's MBS purchases? Essentially, an asset that is conventionally considered to be non-money is assuming a key role of traditional state money in the central bank's support mechanisms for financial stability. By taking MBS onto the books of the Fed in order to stabilise the financial system, MBS are being treated as if they are a kind of money. The demarcation around money thereby becomes ambiguous. The line between state money and broader monies blurs as the state's monetary policy transactions shift in part to monies that sit well below state money in the hierarchy of liquidity. This suggests that monetary conditions have altered radically and that the challenges facing money and central banking lie deeper than one-dimensional concerns over the central bank's direct control over a shrinking proportion of aggregate money and near-money instruments. At issue is the subtle but persistent change in money at the heights of global finance by which money has slipped away from Keynesian convention, disrupting state money's cornerstone role in wider financial markets and opening up new questions around money's governance.

Indeed, the kinds of new near-monies that are increasingly encroaching on the traditional territory of state money are not limited to so-called shadow bank money. The rise of electronic money and the growing prominence of digital currencies pose a further qualitative challenge to state money.[31] A recent instance is the rise of digital currencies such as 'bitcoin', which is now being recognised by some key central banks as a form of 'money'.[32] Bitcoin is essentially challenging central banks and society at large to reconsider conventional depictions of what money is. The critical issue in the digital money debate is bitcoin's disconnection from the role of the state as the issuer, the regulator, and ultimately the definer of currency. Can there be globally traded money disconnected from the state's own money?

Digital currencies offer a technologically advanced challenge to the conventional definitions of money with reference to the state, just as algorithmic trading challenges the safety of T-bills, financial innovation challenges central bank control over money creation and rapid capital flows facilitated by computer technology challenge the stability of state money. These kinds of challenges reflect how technological change is a crucial aspect of the changing global context within which central banks attempt to control their national monetary environment. The question explored in the following chapters is whether challenges to state money come only at the frontiers of computer and satellite technology, or whether they are about the way in which social relations adapt locally to volatility in high finance, in which the innovation is not so much in computer algorithms as in social innovation and adaptation. As the rest of this book shows, this should be a matter of pressing concern to the financial inclusion agenda.

Notes

1. Recall from the introduction the definition of state money used throughout this study: loosely, money that is produced by the state and the central bank–regulated banking system; so, cash and bank credit/deposits. More specifically, state money is money which is produced under conditions defined by the central bank (prudential regulation including capital requirements) and priced through central bank–led trade with commercial banks (interest rate setting through open market operations) in money produced by the government (treasury bills). That is, cash, bank credit and deposits, central bank reserves and, by extension, treasury bills. See Chapter 7 for an in-depth discussion of state money theory.

2. See, for example, Knapp (1924 [1905])

3. Lim and Sriram (2003) provide a useful discussion of the history of the M categories and their contents.

4. Following Minsky, Mehrling (2012) poses this as a 'natural hierarchy of money' in which each layer of the pyramid is defined by the degree to which different monies carry credibility as a promise to pay. More credible money is easier to sell and thus more liquid.

5. As will be addressed later in this chapter, the state's provision of safe assets is extremely important to financial markets but has come under considerable strain. See Damodaran (2010), IMF (2012) and BIS (2013).

6. Demand for money is a key variable in selecting appropriate monetary policy actions, which is calculated, in part, based on comparisons with other assets in terms of risk and return. A useful review of the money demand literature is undertaken by Sriram (2001).

7. The rationale here is that, under heightened uncertainty, investors place more value on flexibility. Hence, rather than maintaining illiquid holdings, a spike in uncertainty will prompt a shift out of assets that are difficult to liquidate and into assets that can easily be liquidated, that is, bank deposits.

8. See, for example, Storchak (2013) for a very interesting discussion of sovereign risk and risk-free assets at the Bank for International Settlements.

9. That is, New Keynesian thinking and its monetary offshoot, known as 'the New Consensus', add some key aspects of Keynes' thinking to the neoclassical framework and provide the theoretical backing for inflation targeting, which remains dominant in central banking policy (see Arestis and Sawyer 2002 for a critical analysis of the New Consensus). Post-Keynesianism, alternatively, is generally regarded as truer to the critique of neoclassical economics that Keynes' offered. It provides a more progressive and, in some iterations, quite radical policy agenda which has remained for the most part outside of policy power. Post-Keynesianism has, however, developed into an important critique for policy.

10. See, for example, popular textbooks, Mankiw (2008) and Mishkin (2010).

11. Braun (2016) offers a particularly interesting reading in arguing that the money multiplier is part of the 'folk theory of money' that is nurtured by central banks in order to build trust amongst the public in the central bank's control over money.

12. See Lim and Sriram (2003) for a discussion of the continuing importance of monetary aggregates. This is reflected in Bernanke (2006) and, specifically for low-income countries, in the IMF's discussion of evolving monetary policy frameworks (IMF 2015) and studies such as that by Berg, Portillo and Unsal (2010).

13. The commitment to endogenous money, however, varies considerably between these two schools of thought. A thorough analysis is undertaken by Arestis and Sawyer (2006).

14. See MacKenzie (2006), Callon (2007) and Holmes (2013) on performativity, discussed further in Chapter 2.

15. Two particularly interesting accounts of the challenges posed to monetary governance in the post–Bretton Woods years are provided by Helleiner (1994) and Krippner (2011). See also Eichengreen (2011).

16. For quantification of global liquidity, see, for example, Schularick and Taylor (2012) and Brana, Djigbenou and Prat (2012).

17. An accessible discussion of the tools with which finance hedges risk is provided by Malz (2015).

18. Michell and Toporowski (2014) offer a useful description of these dynamics.

19. This figure is roughly equal to a third of the entire annual GDP of the European Union. See Schaefer, Ross and Strauss (2013).

20. One interesting example of the substantive problem of everyday exchange rate instability is provided by Hericourt and Poncet (2015), who examine data on Chinese export firms to draw out how monetary instability in destination economies affects exporters decisions.

21. For example, Bennett and Peristiani (2002) provide a very accessible examination of the evolution of bank reserves away from their traditional role as a binding constraint

on credit expansion. Schularick and Taylor (2012) show how money and credit aggregates have decoupled, reflecting increasing leverage in the financial sector.

22. This set of issues is most commonly addressed in terms of so-called shadow banking, by which the basic function of conventional banking (accepting short-term and liquid deposits on one side of the balance sheet and issuing long-term and illiquid credit on the other, known as 'maturity transformation') is effectively reproduced outside of the state guarantee that exists for the banking system. Emphasising the important function of state backing for the banking system, Strahan (2008) describes how the rise of capital market funding more generally, and shadow banking specifically, has undermined the traditional orientation of the banking sector, attached to which is the 'safe haven' status of bank deposits that is a function of the state guarantee over the banking sector. The implications of this shift away from traditional banking for central bank control over the financial system are discussed by Singh and Stella (2012), who address the problem of central bank control over liquidity as bank reserves lose their relevance in a system of credit that has shifted outside of the banking system. Moe (2014) takes up this problem in terms of the shift from the traditional guarantee over the banking system through the availability of *lender of last resort* funding to individual institutions within the banking system, to implicitly guaranteeing whole markets by becoming the *market maker of last resort*. This shift was evident in the Fed's effective bailing out of the mortgage backed securities (MBS) market during the global financial crisis and is necessary if the state is to maintain a state guarantee over credit under current conditions. Another interesting contribution comes from Ricks (2012), who explicitly engages the monetary nature of shadow money.

23. Shadow money refers to the liabilities issued by 'shadow banks', a term which refers to a set of financial institutions (often components of regular banks) that have a similar role to traditional banks in the financial system but are not regulated as banks. Shadow banks effectively offer maturity transformation (like traditional banks do, taking in shorter-term deposits to fund the issue of longer-term loans) but do not use traditional retail deposits to undertake this intermediation. Shadow banks include investment banks, money market funds and certain hedge funds as well as certain divisions of traditional banks, which effectively issue short-term stores of value (shadow money), for example, in the issue of 'repos' funded by collateral, or MBS funded by short-term commercial paper. See Ricks (2012) for a clear discussion of shadow money or, for a brief overview, see Gabor and Vestergaard's discussion at https://www.ineteconomics.org/perspectives/blog/towards-a-theory-of-shadow-money (accessed 1 September 2019) and the IMF's description at http://www.imf.org/external/pubs/ft/fandd/2013/06/basics.htm (accessed 1 September 2019).

24. That is, a central bank guarantee over the wider financial system may function as a perverse incentive for financial institutions to take on excessive risk, knowing that they will likely be bailed out by the state. See Moe (2014) for an interesting discussion on this predicament.

25. See, for example, Alloway and McKenzie (2014) in the *Financial Times* or, for a much more thorough assessment, BIS (2014a).

26. See, for example, Park (2013).

27. As raised, for example, in IMF (2012).

28. This is a key issue in post-crisis finance. For conventional views on the decline of safe assets, see IMF (2012), BIS (2013) and Golec and Parotti (2017). One particularly interesting take on these developments is offered by Bryan, Rafferty and Tinel (2016).

29. In the wake of the global financial crisis, the Fed shifted to a corridor system. As Roc Armenter and Benjamin Lester (2016) show, this entails implicit subsidies to shadow and other non-bank institutions insofar as they became eligible counterparties to the Fed in overnight reverse repurchase transactions (that set the upper bound on the interest rate) and are able to indirectly benefit from overnight interest on reserves held at the Fed (that set the lower bound on interest rates). Through these mechanisms, the Fed has extended some degree of support to the non-bank sector.

30. This argument is taken up by Bryan, Rafferty and Jefferis (2015) and Bryan, Rafferty and Tinel (2016).

31. For an interesting discussion, see Weber (2016).

32. See, for example, ECB (2012).

2

Money at the Frontier

Emerging economies in Asia have seen capital flows boom. Between the early 1980s and the mid-2000s, capital flows to emerging economies like Thailand and Malaysia grew by a multiple of 10.[1] Yet as the regulatory environment and the financial architecture that it constructs have opened up to the global economy, frontier markets have also seen huge growth in flows.[2] In Pakistan, for example, capital inflows have shot up by a multiple of 20 over those same years. However, this huge growth in flows has been accompanied by an increasing instability in those same flows. Starting to rise after 1988, capital flows to Pakistan became extremely volatile after 2000.[3] Shifting rapidly from negative territory to spikes of US$8 and US$10 billion, capital flows have cut a figure of sharp peaks and troughs in the new millennium. This is typical of capital flows to frontier economies, which after 2010 not only exceeded those to emerging economies in GDP terms but were also accompanied by a marked rise in volatility (Rodrik 2015). These sorts of data are indicative of a dramatic 'opening up' of developing and frontier economies to a global financial economy, as well as of a distinct instability accompanying those flows.

Key to this predicament is the mode of monetary governance in the frontier context. By definition open to global markets and constituted by less 'mature' institutions than their emerging cousins,[4] formal monetary management in frontier economies tends to track the inflation targeting norm set by the advanced economies with a regulatory regime sometimes called 'inflation targeting lite'.[5] Frontier markets have thus moved away – as reflected in their 'investability' – from previously dominant norms of the protected markets and direct monetary policy tools of earlier decades (such as setting exchange rates and prices), towards open markets and the indirect tools of market-driven monetary policy (that is, attempting to control inflation by setting the short-term interest rate).[6] Yet the replication of advanced economy monetary policy is challenged by the complexity of the institutional context, both formal and informal, which is implied by the 'frontier' label.

This chapter interrogates this distinct monetary disposition. Training the focus on the monetary context specific to frontier economies – which are low-income economies yet are open to global flows – the chapter carries the analysis of the three interlocking Keynesian markers of money raised in Chapter 1 over to state money in the frontier context, thus considering state money's stability, safety and the monopoly production of money by the central bank in open, low-income economies. But first, the chapter maps out the monetary space through an analytical framework that emphasises the interconnections between the monetary and economic spheres and highlights the potential for monetary contestation, by which social trust in money may become threatened.

The chapter opens by setting out the historical specificity of money as we know it in the advanced economies. Drawing on the international political economy (IPE) literature, the chapter casts conventional notions of modern money not as a natural culmination of the forces of modernity but as the result of a concerted policy project bound to historical circumstance that is specific to the advanced economies. This proposition demands the re-examination of state money in developing economies, where divergent histories of monetary and broader civic development suggest that assumptions attached to conventional notions of money and monetary governability may not apply.

The chapter goes on to map out key features of the frontier monetary environment, counter positioning this mapping to the conventional reading of weak monetary policy transmission in developing economies, which typically blames shallow financial markets, uncompetitive banking sectors and exchange rate intervention for dysfunctional policy transmission. To the contrary, this chapter argues that contestability in money analytically precedes these 'usual suspects' of transmission dysfunction, implying that conventional analysis relies on mistaken assumptions about money. This premise orients the analysis of frontier monetary conditions around how trust in money is generated (rather than around the depth of financial markets, the conditions of banking sector competitiveness or the degree of departure from the equilibrium exchange rate) through a framework that is sustained across the length of the book.

Grounding itself in Philip Mirowski's conception of money as the 'working fiction of the monetary invariant' (Mirowski 1991: 580), the analysis considers state money at the frontier in terms of Keynes' definitional attributes of money (introduced in Chapter 1) but embeds those attributes more specifically in wider economic processes. This perspective joins instability to unknowability, exploring how ambiguity and volatility in the broader economic environment feeds into uncertainty in money. The critical contribution of this analysis is to consider how uncertainty relates to the production of trust in money, both as a policy practice and as a process generated amongst ordinary people through everyday social and economic exchange.

The chapter contends that in open, low income economies the instability that is generated by liberalisation is exacerbated by local conditions, such as economic informality and the commodity market dynamics of open, developing economies.

The chapter argues that deep-seated uncertainty can thereby be generated in the economy and that this uncertainty, in turn, can detract from everyday trust in money. The chapter thus delineates the space in which money operates in the frontier context and the space in which later chapters examine money use and money's contestation as it interacts with the push for financial inclusion.

The Historical Specificity of Monetary Sovereignty

The assumption that 'functional' money and reliable governance over that money is a natural culmination of the forces of modernity is challenged by the IPE literature on monetary sovereignty and territorial currencies. The key contributions by those such as Emily Gilbert, Eric Helleiner, Benjamin Cohen and David Woodruff, forcefully argue that money as we know it in its advanced economy forms is the result of explicit nation-building policies that pertain to specific historical conditions. Only as a result of 'painstaking and deliberate state policy' (Zelizer 1994: 205) have these economies been able to consolidate state control over money. David Woodruff, for example, sees monopoly over the definition and creation of money as the critical expression of the state's capacity to achieve 'dominion over the monetary sphere' (Woodruff 1999: 209). For Emily Gilbert and Eric Helleiner, this is a question of establishing a 'distinct currency that is both homogenous and exclusive within [its] territorial boundaries' (Gilbert and Helleiner 1999: 1). This scholarship implicitly marks out a contrast between advanced and developing countries by elaborating upon the historical specificity of money in the advanced economies. This suggests that in frontier economies, money itself (and, as a corollary, the policy challenges of managing that money under open markets) may well be distinct from conventional notions of money and money's governance that are derived from observations of money in the advanced economies.

The historical analysis that has been developed in this literature emphasises the heterogeneous and unstable nature of money prior to the nineteenth century in what are now the advanced economies. In western Europe, for example, the poor predominantly used second order currency such as copper and bronze coins and low-denomination tokens that were often privately issued. These could not be easily converted into official money, which was used by wealthier segments of society and which itself had been developed in large part in response to the fiscal demands of war. Foreign currencies circulated irrespective of national boundaries and 'exchange rates' between different forms of money were unclear and unstable. Even official money itself was not homogenous, with degraded coins and notes circulating alongside better quality, newly minted money. Money was thus heterogeneous and monetary spaces were deterritorialised (Cohen 1998).

From this perspective, monetary sovereignty and the consolidation of money's governability is premised on the state's administrative capacity to enforce the exclusivity of legal tender, which was 'the culmination of a process of organised coercion and political negotiation similar to those that resulted in the other powers defining the modern nation-state' (Woodruff 1999: 3). Rather than a natural policy development, monetary consolidation was thus a hard fought for power in the push to forge the nation state and, with it, a territorialised market and money to enjoin a newly forged national identity. This process involved the construction of institutional structures such as nation-wide policing systems, the spread of national networks of post offices and state regulated banks and railway stations, as well as military conscription and the consolidation of the taxation system. A territorial conception of money thus only took hold in the nineteenth century, and consolidation of the monetary system along national lines in the United States, Japan and much of Western Europe was only completed in the decades leading up to the First World War.

Early policy efforts aimed at building a single, central bank–administered national currency took a further step in the twentieth century with the rise of Keynesianism. Keynesian macroeconomic management expanded the policy apparatus, in the process subsuming monetary policy into the core of government policy. More than a tool for supporting the unification of the national market and bolstering national identity, or for augmenting public revenue through seigniorage, the function of national currency as a tool for macroeconomic management came to the fore. Under Keynesian policy, monetary management became a key part of an overall nationally oriented demand management strategy in which the economy was governed as a discreet economic unit, protected from the global economy through capital controls and trade policy. Developments in national aggregated accounting schemes, such as the balance of payments format and the 'M-category' monetary aggregates, reflect what was – at least notionally – a discreet and cohesive national economic unit in which money could become a key policy tool for economic management.[7]

This trajectory implies a linear developmental path of intensifying state control over money from the early years of national currency consolidation through the Keynesian era: from a tool integral to the construction of the nation state, to a policy tool for managing macroeconomic performance within the hardened economic boundaries of the nation state. Yet, as Gilbert and Helleiner write, 'national currencies ... are not the natural apex of monetary development, but a fragile, historically specific construction' (1999: 18). In fact, as this literature demonstrates, the homogenous and exclusive nature of territorial currencies has never been as totalising as is often assumed (ibid.: 2). Moreover, the forces of globalisation are posing new challenges to the national orientation of territorial currencies, much of which relates to the use of rival foreign currency within the boundaries of the nation state.[8] By this reading, globalisation has generated a new order of currency competition, which disrupts monetary governance within the notionally exclusive realm of the nation state amidst a wider realignment of international currency blocks and monetary unions. In Benjamin Cohen's words, this suggests an 'outdated myth of One Nation/One Money' (1998: 92), which persists in scholarship and popular thinking alike despite the many ways in which monetary relations have pushed beyond the bounds of the nation-state to become internationalised in the post–Bretton Woods era.

This recognition of the fragility of sovereign money implies that not only might monetary governance become contested but that money itself is contested terrain. By positing fragility in sovereign money, this body of literature opens up the possibility of contestation in money. It also sets up the context for enquiry into money and monetary governance in the developing world. If money in the advanced economies is a unique product of the national history in each of those countries, then frontier money warrants examination in terms of its own historical and institutional context. Indeed, if the monetary space can be fragmented[9] and if the homogeneity and exclusivity of territorial currency can be undermined, then we are faced with a picture of money in stark contrast to the conventional notions of money that are derived from Keynesian thinking and reflected in the policy literature.

The Failure of Monetary Policy Transmission in Low-Income Countries

Scholarship on the historical specificity of monetary sovereignty, therefore, contradicts assumptions that monetary evolution naturally culminates in uncontested 'territorial currency' in developing economies, which may have been subject to alternative historical trajectories. This is especially so with regard to the experience of colonisation, which constructed national institutions of monetary and economic governance in line with distinct principles of service to the colonial power.[10] By emphasising the role of history in shaping present-day monetary institutions and the possibility of fragmentation in money and monetary governance, the IPE literature offers a contrast to the conventional notions of money that are implicit in the mainstream policy literature. A sense of this contrast can be gleaned from the expansive literature review of the empirical evidence of monetary policy transmission in low-income countries, which was undertaken at the IMF in 2012. This review casts significant doubt on the efficacy of monetary policy. Its authors, Prachi Mishra and Peter Montiel, conclude, 'It is very hard to come away from this review of the evidence with much confidence in the strength of monetary policy transmission in low-income countries.'[11] Yet it is in Mishra and Montiel's interpretation of which factors are driving the weakness of monetary policy transmission that the assumed incontrovertibility of money becomes evident in Mishra and Montiel's assessment. Here the contrast between a conventional economic reading and the IPE literature's reading of a potentially fractured money that is subject to incomplete governance comes into relief.

The IMF review takes a static view of monetary conditions and thereby leaves aside the examination of how globalisation has generated monetary change over time. It does, however, identify a clear disconnect between state money and the economy at large. In particular, the review identifies the overwhelming failure of the empirical literature to demonstrate functional monetary policy transmission – that is, to produce statistically significant results that demonstrate a causal link between the cost of state money set by monetary policy, inflation and expansion (or contraction) in the economy at large. The bank lending channel is expected to be the most effective monetary policy transmission channel in low-income countries.[12] Yet the review finds that whilst in some regions central banks appear unable to influence commercial bank interest rate setting behaviour, in other regions, central bank policy rate changes do carry through to bank rates, but these then fail to carry through to aggregate demand. The review blames these failures of monetary policy on the usual suspects: shallow markets, non-competitive banking sectors and exchange rate intervention. According to this reasoning, these features distort the price of money, thereby pushing the monetary system off kilter by generating the wrong monetary signals and incentives. Instead of prompting the investment, saving and consumption decisions that would bring the economy back to a safe, low-inflation growth rate, the economy remains unresponsive to monetary policy signalling, which is drowned out by distortions in the economy. These features, according to one of the authors of the review, reflect 'dysfunctionality' in low-income economies (Mishra 2016).

But could it not be that the theory itself is dysfunctional? Is it not theory that has failed to explain money and monetary control in low-income countries, rather than money and economic processes somehow becoming delinquent from what is expected of them? Reflecting on the historical specificity of money and its governance in the advanced economies, is it not that traditional monetary policy transmission entails assumptions about the nature of money and its sovereignty that is ill fitting to the developing economy context?

Wherever dysfunctionality is posited, however, Mishra and Montiel's conclusion that 'the stabilisation challenge in developing countries is acute indeed' (Mishra and Montiel 2012: 25) sparks no controversy. Whatever its drivers, instability is a very real problem for policymakers and local populations alike. The following section poses a perspective by which instability is not only a result of failed monetary policy but is a significant contributing factor to the failure of monetary policy to command control over the economy. Acknowledging the potential for monetary fragmentation, the discussion develops a framework for analysing the monetary environment in open, low-income economies. Crucially, this framework does not assume the kind of monetary incontrovertibility implicit in conventional economic analysis, such as Mishra and Montiel's study, and encapsulated in the idea of the 'myth of One Nation/One Money' (Cohen 1998). By contrast, the framework developed in this chapter maps out the dynamics by which money may become contested.

By considering trust in money in terms of the economy-wide instability and uncertainty that liberalisation exacerbates, this analytical framework suggests that trust in money (and its potential deficit) is based on the wider institutional context in which money is embedded. It is contended that instability generates uncertainty, which erodes trust in money and opens money up to contestation. This premise is explored in the rest of the chapter in terms of the economic conditions in which money is embedded in low-income and frontier economies, thus offering an alternative reading of why monetary policy performs so poorly. By this reading, contestability in money analytically precedes the shallow markets, uncompetitive banking sectors and exchange rate intervention that are the focus of conventional analysis. That is, a more productive approach may be to analyse the contestability in money that invariably precedes and contributes to – indeed, largely causes – the standard suite of monetary deficiencies in low-income economies.

Money, Trust and Complex Instability

For Mishra and Montiel (2012), competitive financial markets and freely floating exchange rates are crucial preconditions for functional monetary policy transmission. This proposition is implicitly contested by IPE scholars in the literature on territorial currencies. It is also explicitly contested in the sociological literature, where the argument is made that money and monetary governance can only be effective if there is adequate trust in money. For much of this literature, trust in money is intimately linked to trust in the state.[13] From an anthropological perspective, alternatively, money is derived more from the acknowledgement of private debt between social actors than the history of state coinage,[14] although these two positions are not mutually exclusive. In either case, the contrast to mainstream economics stands insofar as the assumed immutability of money in conventional economic theory is challenged by questions around how trust in money is realised. This section thus delves more deeply into the premise of potentially incomplete monetary sovereignty and the mythical nature of the 'One

Nation/One Money' assumption by undertaking a more focused analysis of the sociological grounding of fractured monetary sovereignty. In setting out an alternative framework to that of conventional economics, a framework which considers social trust in money and its potential for contestation, the discussion herein draws on a varied set of views from within the broader social sciences literature on the economy, money and central banking.

To begin with, a useful approach to monetary contestation can be found in the literature on the social studies of money and central banking. Addressing money in the advanced economies, this literature carries the focus on trust into a detailed examination of how central banks cultivate perceptions amongst markets as well as ordinary people about money, monetary theory and central banking. At issue is not only the legitimation of money and of the central bank's authority over money in society at large, but more specifically the way that markets are persuaded to maintain belief in the specific value of currency that prevails (for example, of the Australian dollar to the US dollar at today's exchange rate, or the value of the Australian dollar in terms of what it can buy on the market today and what it can be expected to buy in a week or a month). From this perspective, market perceptions about the capacity of the central bank to control money are intimately linked to perceptions that the value of money is 'correct': the central bank must be perceived by markets as being effective in keeping the future value of money at the 'right' level in order for businesses to set prices and workers to demand wages in line with a stable and reliable inflationary trend. In other words, central banks must be deemed to be in control for the challenges of monetary governance to remain contained. More broadly, central banks must speak 'to the people ... not only to manage expectations, but to inspire trust, both in the monetary authority and in money itself' (Braun 2016: 3).

In common with the IPE literature, the premise of potential monetary contestability sets this literature apart from the approach to money and monetary policy undertaken in mainstream economics, such as the study by Mishra and Montiel. Rather than taking trust in money as a given, this strand of research on money and central banking posits the cultivation of trust in money as an active field of policy that is crucial to money's governability. Although the emphasis lies more in how trust in money is maintained rather than in what happens if that trust fails, the social studies of money and central banking literature nonetheless demonstrates that where these efforts *do* fail, money may become contested in substantive ways. Less oriented towards the IPE literature's focus on the use of foreign exchange within the national jurisdiction, this literature instead focuses on how monetary contestation is expressed in inflation scares and bank runs as well as in outright 'exit' from national currency's monetary networks into alternative monies, such as bitcoin.[15]

Yet in a frontier economy, central bank discourse – that is, 'speaking to the people' – is not very influential over the wider social discourse. This is one of the features of the frontier context that could be ascribed to the 'immature institutions' that are definitional of frontier economies. Given these conditions, this study takes from this literature the precarious nature of social trust in money but looks elsewhere for the key drivers that generate that social trust in money that is crucial to containing the threat of rejection of local currency as legal tender. At this point, we thus turn towards the material experience of money use. Specifically, a more empirically based notion of how the monetary legitimacy that is bestowed upon money by everyday economic actors affords money its governability can be derived from Mirowski's description of money as the 'working fiction of the monetary invariant' (1991: 580).

The monetary invariant refers to the stability and predictability of value across time – be it actual or perceived – that is so central to Keynes' definition of money. From this perspective, money crucially must be stable enough in order to be accepted across society as a reliable measure of value that can provide stable pricing patterns 'as if a value invariant exists' (Mirowski 1991: 580), that is, regardless of the reality of fluctuation in prices inherent to a system that is denominated in a money which is itself in fluctuation. At issue here is the perception of monetary stability as that which underpins trust in money, quite aside from the central bank's success or failure in garnering public confidence in money through more abstract means. It follows that where instability in money and prices undermines perceptions that local currency is functioning as a stable measure (as the monetary invariant), economic actors may reject the legal tender status of local currency and 'explore options for exit' (Weber 2016: 25).

This more mundane foundation of trust in money provides the basis for an understanding of monetary legitimation that is based primarily on the stability of money. However, in the provision of the monetary invariant, monetary stability cannot be separated from broader system-wide predictability in the economy. That is, stability in money is intimately linked to stability in prices across the economy so that instability in money is a problem for the economy as a whole just as instability in the economy is a problem for money. This position echoes Keynes' views on money. As described by Keynes in chapter 17 of the *General Theory*, basic reliability in the value of money permits 'sticky' wages, which permit some degree of certainty around the future value of output, which, in turn, permits investment. That is, stable money links into stability in other indicators, notably wages, and thereby supports the system of investment and production, drawing stability in wages into the network of monetary indicators. Thus Mirowski's notion of money as the 'working fiction of the monetary invariant' can be extrapolated upon to conceive of monetary trust as rooted in stability, not only in money, but in the networks of prices and other economic indicators that express money's function as a(n) (un)stable measure.

Support for this notion of trust in money being embedded in the stability of the wider economy can be drawn from other parts of the social studies of money and central banking literature, notably from the 'performativity' literature.[16] According to this literature, conventional variables, metrics and calculations that are drawn on in monetary and economic analysis do not reflect the state of money and the economy (in the way that a camera reflects reality) but shape economic and monetary outcomes by generating stability and predictability in money and the economy (as an engine that drives reality [MacKenzie 2006]). From metrics like the yield curve, to calculations such as the output gap, and right across central bank discourse, calculative frameworks do not observe monetary phenomena but construct norms for economic behaviour to follow (and thus 'perform' certain outcomes).[17]

Monetary policy is, of course, based on such a reliable structure of indicators and relationships. Here expectations can, according to inflation targeting theory at least, be harnessed. That is, economic agents themselves perform the stabilisation of prices by setting and demanding prices that internalise what the central bank tells them is the inflationary environment. Thus, the central bank calls on a series of statistical indicators as well as its own epistemic authority in announcing its forecast of future inflation. Where central bank policy is credible, a central bank inflation forecast of stable low inflation will prompt low increases in wage demands and low increases in prices set by businesses. Households too will factor in stable and low future inflation into their own future-orientated consumption and savings decisions. If the central bank's policy rate changes, it demands and enacts reliability in the chain of cause and effect that is constituted by the behaviour of economic agents and ultimately realises the central bank's inflation target.[18]

Although the emphasis in this literature is on the performativity of the policy edifice, for present purposes we take from this the notion of money and monetary governability thus embedded in a web of economic indicators and economic relationships. By this reading, trust in money depends not only on an exchange rate and interest rate that are deemed 'correct', but rather on a whole web of metrics, calculations and causal relationships that construct a sense of reliability and stability in the monetary environment in general and in the 'monetary invariant' in particular. In the frontier context, these calculative frameworks are not constructed out of the stuff of central bank discourse, as they are in the advanced economies – for example, the different indicators that are drawn on to justify the central bank's assessment of the inflation outlook, like house prices, or business investment or the unemployment rate. With central bank discourse remote to the vast bulk of the economy and its economic actors, these metrics will be different in the frontier context and will consequently anchor expectations of the future value of money and indeed trust in state money itself in different and probably less robust ways than the edifice of central banking in the advanced economies.

G. L. S Shackle (1972) offers a useful reading of how economic uncertainty is experienced and transmitted, which augments the sense of money and monetary trust embedded in the perceived stability of the wider economic environment. Exploring the mental processes that drive economic behaviour (which he refers to as 'epistemics'), Shackle considers how the inner workings of the imagination fill in the gaps in economic information. Described by Alan Coddington (1975) as 'knowledge surrogates' that accompany 'knowledge deficits', conjecture, expectation and adaptation here join 'scarcely recognised suggestions', inferences and principles of interpretation to fill out our understanding of everyday economic circumstances and guide our economic behaviour (Shackle 1972: 112). By this reading, trust in money is couched in the everyday experience of the economy through continuous and eclectic economic feedback in a much more complex and unquantifiable way than is offered by standard theory as 'expectations'. Shackle thus emphasises the deep social grounding and subtle transmission of economic confidence (or the lack of it), accentuating the social embedding of economic phenomena and the vulnerability of confidence in money and the economy to contagion from disparate shocks originating across the social and economic realm.

These perspectives are drawn together in this analysis to offer a reading of monetary legitimacy that rests primarily in monetary stability, but is indelibly couched in the (in)stability and (un)certainty of the wider economy, its metrics and statistical outputs, and in everyday discourse amongst ordinary people about the economy and money's performance. This reading suggests that formal monetary indicators are but part of the story of money and monetary trust.

From this perspective, the discussion that follows seeks to explore how changes in global markets and finance are putting increasing stress on the regularity and predictability of economic processes that, it is argued, undermine state money in less-developed and frontier economies. Oriented around issues of economic uncertainty, the discussion explores the institutional environment in which money operates. It does this by examining instability and opacity in the indicators and relationships in which 'the monetary invariant' is embedded. This discussion suggests that money and monetary policy cannot be properly assessed without engaging with the broader economic context, and that monetary contestation which is driven by uncertainty poses a real threat to state money and its governability.

Uncertainty in the Context of Less-Developed Economies

The 1997 Asian financial crisis rapidly reversed the forward momentum of financial liberalisation, which had been gathering steam across emerging and less-developed economies since the early 1990s.[19] The crisis demonstrated the huge costs that unrestricted capital flows could foist upon currencies and their respective economies by crashing exchange rates, throwing debt markets into turmoil and generating massive increases in poverty and unemployment across the region. In the wake of the crisis, an invigorated research agenda developed new and more rigorous approaches to understanding the dynamics of open markets for finance, developing concepts like herding, contagion and the so-called sudden stops[20] in order to address the reckless snowballing of financial flows that was observed during the crisis.

Yet it is the humdrum everyday of open financial markets that attracts far less attention. By 2000, the deregulation of capital flows in emerging and less-developed countries resumed, with capital accounts across developing and emerging markets ratcheting to ever greater degrees of openness through the early and mid-2000s. Under open financial markets, the threat of crisis is a key concern for monetary governance. But other less quantifiable but nonetheless persistent threats to the monetary environment persist.

Guided by the framing of money developed in the first part of this chapter, the discussion here is predicated on state money not as the supreme macroeconomic tool of mid-century Keynesian thinking nor the One Nation/One Money that continues to be mythologised by more recent theory. Rather, it contends that state money is dependent on social trust. By this reading trust in money is grounded in perceptions of stability and is vulnerable to uncertainty. The rest of the chapter seeks to explore the everyday monetary environment in which money functions in the frontier context by developing a sense of the instabilities and uncertainties that might be fostered by open market dynamics. First addressing uncertainty, the chapter goes on to consider how the stability, safety and monopoly creation of money by the central bank (which lies at the heart of Keynesian notions of money) might fare in the frontier context. This discussion begins with commodity market dynamics, which have become a key locus of change in the monetary environment as frontier economies have opened up to global markets.

The importance of commodity markets to open, low-income economies is reflected in conventional statistics. Both the balance of payments and the consumer basket in developing countries tend to be more concentrated in primary commodities, representing important economic exposure to global markets which themselves tend to be particularly, and increasingly, volatile.[21] Generated in part by growing financial investment in commodity markets since the mid-2000s, commodity markets have come to express volatility in pricing patterns familiar to asset markets.[22] This poses important hurdles for the 'stability challenge' in low-income economies (Mishra and Montiel 2012: 25).

On the one hand, sudden changes in global commodity prices can cascade through domestic macroeconomic and monetary indicators and threaten self-reinforcing spirals of currency depreciation under persistent if not dramatic speculative pressure. Price volatility can produce erratic swings in the balance of payments that carries into the exchange value of national currency as price effects carry through the typically large portions of the external account that are based in primary commodities in low-income economies.[23] Pressure on the exchange rate can, in turn, generate valuation effects on reserve coverage[24] and can directly impact reserve levels in conditions where payments for certain commodities are made on the central bank's books.[25] Reserve levels are a particularly sensitive indicator because they are often central to credit ratings agencies' sovereign ratings and are commonly linked to speculative pressure.[26]

On the other hand, recent concerns over food price inflation have prompted a series of studies that show how shocks specifically in food commodity prices carry inflation into the broader economy.[27] These suggest a role for key food prices in anchoring pricing patterns in the broader economy – not an anchor that necessarily stabilises broader prices but an anchor to which broader prices are linked in a discernible pattern. This anchor is impacted by instability in global markets and in those circumstances food commodities carry volatility from global markets into economy-wide inflation trends.

In summary, increasing exposure to global commodity markets that comes with economic liberalisation generates greater volatility in national currency itself, greater volatility in economy-wide inflation, and greater volatility in a series of key macroeconomic indicators, such as the balance of payments position and the reserve coverage ratio.

Moreover, the problem of instability driven by open markets is complicated by informality, which is typically pervasive in low-income countries and pertains to external flows as well as domestic production, trade and finance. Most directly, the informal economy acts as a 'shock absorber' for the formal economy because it is less inhibited by regulation and formal contracts and can make sudden cuts to production or adjust wages and final prices in order to push shocks, for example, in the price of inputs, onto workers and consumers. This is reflected in the greater price and wage flexibility in developing countries.[28] Informality also enhances opportunities for capital flight, dollarisation and other financial responses that the state might limit within the formal domain in order to contain shocks. Through these channels, informality can thus amplify commodity price shocks that are derived from global markets.

Yet informality also plays into instability and uncertainty in less direct ways. For example, informality obscures statistical indicators, which casts opacity over the statistical representations of money and the broader statistical indicators in which money is embedded. Such opacity feeds into a sense of uncertainty and hampers the real and perceived capacity of the central bank to control inflation. The low penetration of the banking sector that is typical of low-income countries is a case in point. The World Bank's Global Findex survey finds that in some developing countries less than 5 per cent of savers report using formal financial institutions. Similarly, the use of formal financial institutions for borrowing is commonly below 10 per cent of all borrowers (Demigurc-Kunt and Klapper 2012: 33–38). This suggests that credit and savings are overwhelmingly located outside of banking sector statistics. In these conditions, informal market exchange and interest rates may play more important roles in the economy than official rates. This suggests that these kinds of undocumented transactions at once distort the reliability of key monetary indicators and frustrate statistical representations of stocks and flows of money, undermining the reliability of knowledge about the economy's functioning and its variation over time.

At the same time, the kinds of macroeconomic data that conventionally predicate shifts in market sentiment are plagued by ambiguity: the unemployment rate does not necessarily reflect conditions for workers or business in an environment of informality and extreme casualisation of labour, and GDP figures may account for only a minority of economic activity amidst the dominance of informal production and exchange. Other examples further demonstrate the ambiguity of statistical indicators in the frontier context: a surplus in the current account may indicate a combination of exchange rate effects and price changes in key commodities rather than the intrinsic improvement in productivity implied by conventional analysis, while an increase in imports may indicate not more imported goods on the market but a surge in capital flight, such as through trade misinvoicing or *hawala* transactions.[29] This statistical uncertainty builds on instabilities generated by open markets, undermining confidence amongst economic agents about the state's capacity to assess economic conditions and pursue stabilisation policy.

Indeed, for monetary governance, and inflation targeting in particular, this kind of instability and opacity is a key issue. Inflation targeting is predicated on the credibility of the central bank's interest rate target, which, in turn, is based on the central bank's inflation forecast. In order to construct that forecast, the central bank draws on a diverse set of economic information. Crucially, the central bank must decipher if prevailing inflation is being driven by strong demand in the economy as a whole or if individual price shocks (such as volatile food and fuel prices) are ratcheting up the inflation index. In the language of inflation targeting, this is a question of whether prevailing inflation is in fact 'core' inflation or 'headline' inflation. For inflation targeting central banks, core inflation is the proper object of monetary policy and will (theoretically at least) be responsive to an interest rate change, as higher interest rates bring demand down and ease 'overheating' in the economy. Headline inflation, however, is seen rather as 'statistical noise' – an appendage rather than a structural component of the economy. Hence, monetary policy need not attend to headline inflation: easing back on demand will not help inflation when price rises are generated by, for example, a higher oil price which feeds through the myriad of prices on products that rely on oil as an input.

Yet if information about the economy is opaque and instability is driven concurrently by multiple sources, the central bank's capacity to decipher 'transitory' headline inflation shocks from 'core' overheating will be undermined. And with this, the credibility of central bank policy will be undermined. Here conventional statistical indicators that should guide credible policy, and thus undergird stable and entrenched expectations amongst the public, are in fact unknowable.

Moreover, even within the logic of conventional economics, the problem of instability and opacity runs deeper than central bank credibility. At the heart of inflation targeting (and market economics more broadly) is the notion that prices act as signals to markets that indicate to entrepreneurs where unfulfilled demand can be serviced. The problem of inflation is thus a problem of the scrambling of information by which higher prices may not demonstrate scarcity (which can be profitably attended to by increasing production) but may instead pertain to some kind of unknown exogenous shock, be it a commodity price shock or wrongly calculated monetary stimulus (by which an increase in production would simply create oversupply).[30] In conditions of multiple shocks and opaque economic information, firms thus cannot know if inflation is being driven by the 'wrong' interest rate having been implemented by the central bank, or by a commodity price shock or by demand actually calling for more production. By this reading, opacity and instability is thus a problem for efficient allocation in the economy more generally, as well as a problem for the central bank in deciphering the right monetary policy stance.

Yet a conventional reading of the problem of inflation still does not do justice to the depth and complexity of volatility and uncertainty in open, low-income economies, where we find volatility in money and markets that is both mutually reinforcing and exacerbated by informality. This level of complexity renders the distinction between price instability driven by 'scarcity' and price instability driven by 'monetary shocks' significantly less relevant. At issue is more than one dimensional monetary instability but instead the persistence of constant shocks to value that reverberate throughout the economy. In these conditions, the sequence of cause and effect that is understood to generate efficient resource allocation by inflation targeting central banks, cannot be expected to hold.

Proposed here is a reading of instability and uncertainty that strikes a contrast to conventional analysis by focusing on money itself. At issue is the proposition that volatility and opacity in the full gamut of economic indicators – from exchange rates, interest rates and prices, to the economic relationships that underpin monetary management and production processes – ultimately undermine the stable yardstick measure of value that is linked to the definition of money. More specifically, confidence in money's value is anchored in the web of calculative frameworks, metrics and indicators that ground social trust in money, although this set of indicators will differ in a frontier context where conventional discursive tools of certainty and central bank control are more remote to everyday economic discourse. Regardless of central bank discourse, where instability is persistently experienced in day-to-day exchange, economic unpredictability becomes a conscious part of economic life. Here Mirowski's 'working fiction of the monetary invariant' no longer holds. Rather, a deep-seated economic uncertainty disrupts state money. As is explored with regard to the Pakistani rupee in the rest of the book, money is thereby exposed to contestation that undermines its governability and challenges its usefulness as a tool of economic development.

This kind of unpredictability recalls the anchoring issues that are scattered across the literature on financial globalisation. The wholesale shift of world markets to greater tenors of risk as safe assets become not only more scarce but more risky is one example of these concerns, an example which was raised in Chapter 1.[31] Another example pertains to concerns about the decreasing ability of LIBOR to provide a benchmark for common risk.[32] This hints at the degradation of traditional anchors as money and finance undertakes structural change that undermines the possibility of constructing the kind of all-round benchmark that LIBOR has traditionally represented. A further example can be seen in the crisis facing the credibility of credit ratings in the aftermath of the recent financial crisis. In recent years, bond spreads and default rates implied by market pricing of some AAA rated securities have diverged significantly from credit agencies' ratings (IMF 2012).[33] In all of these examples, the universally accepted reliability of risk calculation frameworks is apparently under strain. This predicament ultimately weakens the role of state money as the anchor of the economy, not only in the narrow terms of the capacity of state money to function as a nominal anchor but in the broader terms of the structures of calculation and predictability in which state money is embedded. These examples of anchoring issues are drawn from the heights of the global economy. Yet they offer a parallel with the predicament of less-developed countries, where uncertainty crystallises in the lack of an effective anchor that can ground the economy in some kind of benchmark of safety.

The Keynesian Benchmark and Money in the Frontier Context

The sorts of conditions outlined in this chapter as characteristic of frontier economies do not bode well for the Keynesian benchmark applied in Chapter 1, which was oriented around stability, safety and the production of money under the control of the central bank. In fact, the Keynesian benchmark casts money in open, low-income economies as barely recognisable – not in a literal sense, but in the terms proposed by Keynes in chapter 17 of the *General Theory*. For many low-income economies, state money is undermined by volatility and the threat of sovereign default, whilst the growth of foreign exchange in local circulation presents a constant threat to the dominance of local state money. In each case, these circumstances are exacerbated by the open market dynamics that increasingly characterise developing economies. These conditions pose a stark contrast to Keynes' definition of money, undermining state money's role as the stable yardstick and safe asset under the monopoly production of the central bank. This final section of the chapter briefly reviews state money in light of the frontier conditions set out above. This review of state money is taken up in the terms of the Keynesian benchmark that was applied to money at the heights of global finance, as related in Chapter 1.

Stability in Money

At the most basic level, the liberalisation of markets has generated volatility in exchange rates because of the greater and more volatile supply and demand pressures on domestic currency that arise from convertibility of the currency through an open capital and current account. The huge growth in gross capital flows as well as trade as a percentage of GDP reflects the equally huge growth of these pressures on domestic currency over the last two decades.[34] Yet as open economies increase the share of imports and exports in their domestic economic activities, there is also greater scope for unstable prices in global markets to transfer into the domestic economy.

   Data showing huge growth in capital flows is loosely indicative of pressures imposed on the currency through the capital account. Moreover, the volatility of capital flows to developing economies, and especially frontier economies, has sharply increased as capital flows have risen. Yet as net figures, available data on capital flows obfuscate the flows in and out of the capital account that cancel each other out in net terms, but generate real pressures on the economy on a day-to-day basis. Be it the sudden stops and sharp reversals in flows characteristic of financial crisis or the persistent volatility of global markets in normal times, these flows drive exchange rate changes that then generate valuation effects across the external sector.[35]

On the current account side, developing economies, and especially frontier economies, tend to be 'price takers'[36] and yet have much greater exposure to world markets because, in relative terms, their exports and imports make up much larger proportions of GDP as compared to the advanced economies. Additionally, they tend to have much greater concentration in both the consumer basket and the balance of payments, especially in primary commodities.[37] As discussed earlier, all of these factors feed into the vulnerability of local money and markets to price shocks in global commodity markets. That terms of trade volatility is nearly twice as high in low-income countries as compared to the rest of the world (IMF and World Bank 2011) reflects the hugely important role of commodity markets in transmitting instability from global markets into the domestic economy. In developing countries, price shocks to key commodities in global markets tend to carry more strongly into local pricing patterns, have longer lasting effects and be more frequent.[38] At the same time, exchange rate instability tends to feed more quickly into domestic prices.[39] These characteristics may help to explain why prices tend to be more volatile in developing countries.[40]

These kinds of stylised facts suggest entrenched volatility in state money, as well as entrenched volatility in prices, which, whether rooted in exchange rate dynamics or supply shocks, are experienced as instability in state money. This kind of entrenched instability contrasts sharply with the stability in state money that is described by Keynes.

State Money as the Safe Asset

Just as contemporary conditions in developing economies detract from the notion of money as the stable yardstick, so too do they detract from the credibility of the state guarantee over money and the financial system as a whole. Increasing pressure on state money as the safe asset contrasts with the premise of the tight relationship between the state and money described by Keynes. Specifically, in recent years markets have expressed perceptions of risk in excess of the theoretical designation of state money as the cornerstone asset in the domestic economy. Wenxin Du and Jesse Schreger (2016a, 2016b), for example, find that developing countries have in recent years come to pay a significant credit spread over the risk-free rate on sovereign debt denominated in local currency.[41] These findings reflect an excess of perceived default risk that disrupts the underlying logic of the risk-free status of sovereign debt, by which states need never default on sovereign debt denominated in local currency because the state can effectively print its own money.

The same can be seen where the floor on interest rates implied by the risk-free status of sovereign debt is violated. Since the late 1990s, corporate debt in developing countries increasingly receives a lower interest rate from markets, and better credit rating from credit rating agencies than the risk-free rate carried by local sovereign bonds (Borensztein, Cowan and Valenzuela 2013; Grandes 2016).[42] Here again, market mechanisms defy the risk-free status of sovereign debt, implying an order of sovereign risk in developing countries out of step with the basic principles of finance theory as they had developed up until the 1990s.

Moreover, credit ratings issued by ratings agencies tend to be more volatile in low-income countries. Alex Bergen (2013) finds that countries with a rating of A, AA or AAA have almost a 95 per cent chance of maintaining their rating over a year, while those with a CA rating have only something like a 25 per cent chance (ibid.: 16). This implies that in frontier economies, even when a relatively high credit rating is achieved, there is little confidence that it will not soon reverse. In such circumstances, the state guarantee appears both weak and volatile.

The Production of Money outside of the Central Bank

At the same time, alternatives to local state money are prominent in formal and informal dollarisation in developing countries, which undermines the monopoly position of local state money as money in the local economy.[43] The convertibility of the current and capital accounts that is central to the liberalisation process has facilitated the greater availability of foreign currency holdings. This occurs as foreign cash exchange is legalised, banks are permitted to offer foreign exchange accounts, and foreign markets are more easily accessed, both through the legal and illegal transfer of capital abroad.[44] Although formal dollarisation can by definition be accounted for in national statistics, informal dollarisation and illegal capital flight cannot be quantified. Research by Ruth Judson (2012) at the Federal Reserve suggests that US dollar bills circulating outside the US more than tripled between 1995 and 2011, climbing from some US$150 billion to more than half a trillion dollars by 2011. These figures offer some degree of quantification to at least one form of money that conspicuously circulates outside of local central bank monetary provision in developing economies.

Conclusion: An Analytical Framework for Money in the Frontier Context

It is not only shallow financial markets, poor competitiveness in the banking sector, and exchange rate intervention that must bear the blame for weak monetary policy transmission in open, low-income economies. Contrary to such conventional analysis, proposed here is a primary order of monetary contestation rooted in uncertainty, which precedes the 'distortions' conventionally associated with weak monetary policy transmission. Indeed, the delinquency of money suggested by findings across the empirical literature on monetary policy transmission does not offer a useful explanation of the problems of monetary governance that prevail in open, low-income economies. Rather, the 'dysfunctionality' in money that conventional analysis proposes demands better theorisation of money at the periphery.

This chapter has sought to engage complexity and uncertainty in low-income and frontier economies in order to develop a deeper contextualisation of the challenges posed to money by liberalisation. By drawing on a series of insights from across the social sciences literature on economy, money and central banking, the chapter has set out an analytical framework that looks beyond conventional approaches to the monetary environment and its attendant 'stabilisation challenge'. This framework poses money as intimately embedded in the broader monetary environment, its uncontested functioning contingent on perceptions of stability. Yet stability itself, as the second part of the chapter has shown, is fiercely challenged by open market dynamics. This instability feeds into uncertainty, which is nurtured not only through erratic shifts in macro and monetary indicators but in the possibilities of informality in money and markets. This frustrates statistical representations of money and the economy, undermining the reliability of knowledge about the economy for the public and the state alike. Far from the One Nation/One Money ideal and its consequent one-dimensional concerns about instability such as those entailed in the inflation targeting policy framework, the broader monetary context in which trust in money is grounded in open, low-income economies is more likely to be characterised by instability and ambiguity.

The chapter thus opens up the space for contestation: if money relies on trust and that trust is undermined, money may, in fact, be actively contested. What that contestation looks like and what that means for the central bank and its financial inclusion agenda is explored in later chapters. Before that, however, the following chapter turns to an analysis of the monetary environment specific to Pakistan. Following the broad themes of instability and opacity in the economy that have been set out herein as key contours of the frontier money environment, Chapter 3 takes a macroeconomic and monetary perspective on the rupee since partition. It is not until Chapter 6, however, that the meaning of instability and opacity in Pakistan's new economy that is explored in the following chapter is applied to an assessment of the rupee.

Notes

1. Capital flows refer to all liabilities on the financial account in current US dollars. Statistics quoted here are from IMF Balance of Payments data available at http://data. imf.org. As discussed later in this chapter, these kinds of statistics are conventional but, as net figures, do not adequately reflect financial integration.

2. For a quantitative measure of increasing capital account openness, see Ito and Chinn (2019). See also Jahan and Wang (2016). On the growth of flows, see IMF (2015).

3. Pakistan's balance of payments is graphed over time on Figures 6.1 and 6.2 (p. 154).

4. As mentioned in the introductory chapter, the definition of 'frontier economies' varies. Openness to global markets is most often a key criterion, which reflects the derivation of the term in the investment community. Frontier markets are 'investable' and have formal institutional structures that pertain to the market and its governance that are considered 'less developed' than those of the 'emerging economies', such as Brazil, Russia and Turkey. By some but not all definitions, frontier economies are low-income or less-developed economies. See, for example, Schipke (2015), Credit Suisse (2016) and Alleyne and Mecagni (2014).

5. On 'inflation targeting lite', see Stone (2003). On the applicability of 'inflation targeting lite' to Pakistan in particular, see Moinuddin (2009).

6. See Hove, Mama and Tchuna (2015) and IMF (2015).

7. On the Keynesian nature of these indicators and the challenges posed by global integration, see, for example, Dabrowski (2006) and, for an earlier evaluation, Radice (1984).

8. Notably, in Helleiner (2005), Cohen (1998) and Helleiner (1998).

9. Woodruff's study of money in Russia (1999), for example, identifies the erosion of monetary sovereignty in the wake of the collapse of the Soviet Union. Woodruff identifies failure in state policy to enact the kind of state-building that was necessary for the state to command control over money in the decade after the transition. The fragmentation in the monetary environment that ensued included economic actors' shift out of the rouble and into a complex network of barter transactions.

10. For example, see Bagchi on the colonial origins of the Indian banking system (1987, 1997).

11. Mishra and Montiel (2012: 24) go on: 'We failed to uncover any instances in which more than one careful study confirmed results for the effects of monetary shocks on aggregate demand that are similar to the consensus effects in the United States and other advanced countries.' Mishra and Montiel write that although methodological shortcomings in the literature contribute to these findings, 'facts on the ground' are likely an important part of the story.

12. By the bank lending channel, a change in interest rates affects the availability and cost of credit, which, in turn, feeds into aggregate demand. This is the most direct of monetary policy transmission channels in contrast, for example, to the asset channel or exchange rate channel, which engage more complex financial processes.

13. For example, although the link between trust and the state is central to the work of Ingham and the chartalist school more generally (see Chapter 7), this relationship is also key for contributions to money theory from sociologists such as Simmel (1990 [1900]) and Dodd (1994).

14. For example, Hart (2009).

15. See, for example, Braun (2016) and Weber (2016).

16. See MacKenzie (2006), Callon (2007) and Holmes (2013).

17. On the yield curve, see Christophers (2017); on the output gap, see Heimberger and Kapeller (2017); on central bank discourse, see Holmes (2014) and Hall (2009).

18. Comprehensive analysis of the performativity of monetary policy is provided by Holmes (2013)

19. See Ito and Chinn (2019).

20. For a literature review on contagion, see Pericoli and Sbaracia (2003); on herding, see Devenow and Welch (1996) and Chari and Kehoe (2004); on sudden stops, see Calvo (1998).

21. For a good all-rounder on commodity price volatility in developing countries, see (UNCTAD 2012b).

22. See Cheng and Xiong (2014) for a review of the economics literature on the impact of financial investment on commodity prices, including consideration of recently arising volatility in commodity prices, as well as cross-commodity correlations and correlations of commodity prices with prices in other asset classes.

23. Two useful sources on this issue are Gokram and Singh (2011) and Akyuz (2015). See also UNDP (2011).

24. For extensive discussion on valuation effects on reserves arising from exchange rate changes, see Lane and Milesi-Ferretti (2005).

25. This is not uncommon in developing countries where foreign exchange markets are 'thin'. In Pakistan, for example, the central bank has paid for oil imports on behalf of the private sector for certain periods. This allows the central bank to slowly accrue enough hard currency rather than have the private sector make large dollar purchases in single transactions, which can shock the market and feed speculative pressure. See SBP (2005: 135, 2005b: 135, 2007: 147).

26. For example, see Khalid (2014: 5).

27. This literature has blossomed after the 'world food price crisis' that first peaked in 2007. See Loening, Durevall and Birru (2009), Walsh (2011), Adam et al. (2012) and Anand and Cashin (2016).

28. A high degree of wage flexibility linked to large informal markets is designated a defining feature of developing economy conditions in Agenor and Montiel's advanced undergraduate text Development Macroeconomics (2008). These dynamics are explored in greater detail in the Pakistani context by Choudhary, Naeem, et al. (2011) and Choudhary, Mahmood, et al. (2013).

29. These examples are both drawn from the case of Pakistan, discussed in the following chapter. *Hawala* is an informal money transfer system, traditional to South Asia. See El-Qorchi, Maibo and Wilson (2003) and Thompson (2011).

30. Conventional wisdom suggests, for example, that if the central bank calculates that the economy is not running at full capacity, it can drop the interest rate in an effort to stimulate growth. But if it miscalculated the output gap and the economy was, after all, at full capacity, then that stimulation will generate inflation. By this reading, firms may be

unsure if they should invest in new capacity because inflation signals that there is strong demand across the economy, or if they should maintain current levels of output because the inflation is simply a monetary phenomenon of 'too much money chasing too few goods'.

31. See, for example, IMF (2012), BIS (2013a) and Golec and Perotti (2017).

32. LIBOR (the London Inter-Bank Offered Rate) functions as a global risk-free rate, which provides a benchmark from which interest rates on financial instruments are calculated in global markets. For concerns raised at the Bank for International Settlements (BIS) about the increasing weakness of LIBOR, see Nakaso (2013). Bryan and Rafferty (2016) consider the implications of changes in the reliability of LIBOR in terms of the anchoring problems in global financial markets.

33. See, for example, IMF (2012).

34. See, for example, IMF (2015) and Schipke (2015).

35. On sudden stops, see Calvo (1998). On the determination of exchange rates by capital flows rather than the conventional forces of the current account, see, for example, Singh (2009) and UNCTAD (2012b).

36. That is, frontier markets do not operate at a large enough scale to influence prices on global markets.

37. See Gokarn and Singh (2011) and UNDP (2011).

38. See Walsh (2011) and Anand and Cashin (2016).

39. See Agenor and Montiel (2008).

40. See, for example, Choudhary, Faheem, et al. (2016).

41. Du and Schreger explain that this has arisen in the context of changing debt dynamics in developing countries over the last decade or so. Developing country sovereigns have increased issue of local currency debt but corporations in developing countries have continued to issue large amounts of dollar denominated debt. This has raised the default risk on sovereign local currency debt (which theory has traditionally posited as risk-free because a sovereign can print its own money to pay back its own debt and 'inflate away' the debt) because of the damage that depreciation could inflict on highly dollar-indebted corporate sectors. Rather than depreciate national currency by inflating away the debt, sovereigns are more likely to actually default on local currency debt so as to protect the balance sheets of national dollar-indebted corporations.

42. As Borensztein, Cowan and Velenzuela (2013) show, corporate debt only ever received a higher credit rating than the sovereign rating after 1997. Although the local sovereign rating continues to have a strong influence over corporate ratings, 'the sovereign ceiling' has increasingly been pierced in the years since 1997.

43. Discussed at length in the IPE literature, see Cohen (1998, 2000), Helleiner (2005) and Bowles (2008).

44. See Kar (2010) on how open markets facilitate the expansion of illegal capital flows.

3

The Transformation of Monetary Governance in Pakistan

Money and monetary governance in Pakistan have radically transformed since partition. Through four distinct periods – the pre-liberalisation era that lasted up to the late 1980s, the years of liberalisation through the 1990s, the boom years of the early to mid-2000s, and the post-liberalisation period from 2008 onwards – the economy has shifted from a developmental state into an economy open to global markets. This radical restructuring of the economy has redefined the rupee.

Guided by the analytical framework outlined in Chapter 2, this chapter undertakes a brief history of the rupee that emphasises the development of instabilities and opacities under the liberalisation of money and markets. The chapter tracks the twists and turns of SBP policy to show how the hostile conditions surrounding the rupee in the 1990s – including the new inflationary dynamics of liberalised markets and the seemingly unmanageable threat to rupee stability in the lead-up and aftermath of its float in 2000 – were only relieved when the War on Terror prompted a repositioning of the economy in global markets. With abundant inflows and stable commodity prices in global markets, the SBP was able to accommodate the new patterns of payments that arose with liberalisation while protecting the rupee's value.

Yet beneath the benign macroeconomic conditions, two key issues remained unaddressed. One was informality, which was growing across the economy, and its monetary transactions, presenting an increasingly menacing threat to the capacity of the state to implement policy. The other was the liberalisation of key commodity prices, a process which the state appeared ultimately unwilling to carry out in respect of certain key prices. This led to a series of last-minute policy U-turns on the state's commitments to multilateral donors to let prices float.

Building on the analysis proffered in Chapter 2, this chapter presents these issues as issues of money and monetary management. Not only is informality a hindrance to monetary policy forecasting and transmission, but key commodity prices, such as those for wheat and electricity, are crucial to the stability of the monetary environment because they function as anchor prices. While never clearly spelled out as problems of economic governance, let alone as monetary issues, this chapter shows how the actions of the state with regard to both informality and commodity prices reveal their importance in maintaining stability in money and the economy at large.

These issues became all the more pressing after the 2008 crisis. With inflation surpassing anything seen in the 1990s, declining banking sector engagement amongst the public and growing informality in money and in markets, the SBP faced a formidable challenge in its efforts to maintain control over the economy by enforcing known bounds to markets and money. This chapter provides a backdrop for the argument developed in the rest of the book, that these challenges were not merely about secondary impacts of depreciation or inflation on the economy but were rather more fundamental. As later chapters propose, these challenges to SBP management imply a deeper contestation of the rupee's integrity and the role of state money in the economy, a contestation that casts doubt on the capacity of the rupee to serve the stabilisation role of financial inclusion within development policy.

The chapter thus explores the mechanics by which liberalisation disrupts 'the working fiction of the monetary invariant' by generating new instability and uncertainty over money and monetary governance by way of persistent volatility and growing informality. Chapters 6, 7 and 8 refer back to the events recounted in this chapter, set out here as historical context, in order to interrogate how this empirical predicament ultimately undermines the rupee and its amenability to the financial inclusion agenda.

The chapter thus expands upon the abstract proposition that was developed in Chapter 2 – of globalisation posing significant challenges to state money in frontier economies – by considering the concrete experiences of SBP as the guardian of money in Pakistan under conditions of change in the international monetary system. As such, the chapter explores the particulars of monetary uncertainty and policy disruption, as the book moves from earlier chapters on the increasingly uncertain nature of money under conditions of globalisation in general, to the particulars of what this monetary predicament means to the everyday lives of ordinary people, and finally, to its implications for a development strategy that is staked on state money's capacity to function as a risk management tool.

The State Bank of Pakistan and the Developmental State: From Partition to the 1980s

The State Bank of Pakistan Act, 1956, widened the SBP's functions beyond the core monetary management with which it was mandated at inception in 1948. The new developmental role assigned to the SBP was in line with the 'developmental state' model that sought to guide economic development by forging institutions to promote industrial expansion.[1] Although there were important policy shifts in the years between partition and the early 1990s, an ethos of macroeconomic planning and control carried right through the period. As such, the management of the rupee and of prices remained a central policy tool, even in periods when market mechanisms were given more slack.[2] The combination of control over money and control over pricing in the broader economy supported monetary stability throughout this era, which encompassed stable pricing for food commodities,[3] fixed exchange rates, and low and stable interest rates.[4] Although the central bank certainly faced difficult policy challenges at certain junctures, monetary instability as such was never a key policy issue, and inflation did not become a policy concern until the 1990s.[5]

An important aspect of monetary control throughout these decades was the control of the external sector, both through control over access to foreign exchange and direct and indirect controls over imports and exports. This allowed the central bank to limit supply and demand pressures on the rupee, which supported the use of the exchange rate as a policy lever. Throughout much of these decades, the rupee was maintained at an 'overvalued' rate, which acted as an effective subsidy on industry by reducing the cost of imported inputs.[6] The balance of payments was protected from destabilising import demand with stringent import controls, including direct quantitative limits, a licensing system and high tariffs.[7] During these decades there was no foreign exchange market. Foreign exchange was, in the words of Abbas Mirakhor and Iqbal Zaidi, 'almost a forbidden word' (2004: 10). Any foreign exchange that was earned by expatriate Pakistanis and exporters had to be surrendered to the central bank and could effectively only be purchased by jumping a series of stringent bureaucratic and other hurdles at rates set by the central bank.[8]

Internally, money was controlled through credit allocations to priority sectors and administered interest rates that were for the most part negative in real terms.[9] Real interest rates were kept low in a deliberate effort to restrict the accumulation of financial savings and channel capital directly into industrial investment, whilst at the same time enhancing the affordability of government debt.[10] High reserve requirements imposed on commercial banks guaranteed demand for government debt even at low interest rates and administered interest rates kept rates low for those that had access to formal credit. Established through the 1960s and 1970s, sectorally focused development banks were key to the directed credit programmes and subsidised credit schemes that targeted priority sectors. In the 1970s, the government established the newly expanded National Savings Scheme (NSS), which offered non-bank funding of the government deficit in zero-coupon five- and ten-year bonds that were offered to the public. These offered high and stable returns to savers and deferred deficit funding to the state, becoming an increasingly important part of government debt after the 1980s (Ministry of Finance 2001: 18; SBP 2010a: 41, 2010b: ch. 3).

In terms of prices, monetary stability was supported by a web of direct price controls and a series of support mechanisms, including government bodies engaged in production, sale, import and export in various agricultural commodities.[11] These controls extended right across the economy and included key prices in the consumer basket and on raw materials for industry, such as the wheat price, prices on electricity and fuel, and the price of cotton for the textiles industry. Controls on prices, on the rupee itself and on the external sector more generally, supported stable monetary conditions and a low inflation environment.[12] In the 1960s, inflation was fairly stable, averaging 3.3 per cent. In the 1970s, like in the rest of the world, inflation peaked around the oil shocks but by 1985 had dropped again and stayed around 5 per cent. This was significantly lower than the prevailing inflation amongst Pakistan's South Asian neighbours (Hamid, Nabi and Nasim 1990: 17).

Management of the economy as a discrete macroeconomic unit thereby supported economic growth and monetary stability. The economy's boundaries were controlled through high tariffs and tight controls over foreign exchange, which limited monetary integration with the global economy and maintained both money and key markets as tools of macroeconomic policy through stable and deliberate pricing policies. These conditions supported the rapid industrial expansion and impressive growth rates that were realised in Pakistan during this era, particularly in the 'golden years' of the 1960s. In 1965, for example, Pakistan exported more manufactures than Indonesia, Malaysia, Thailand, the Philippines and Turkey combined. Average annual growth between 1961 and 1990 was reported at an impressive 6 per cent (World Bank 2002: i).

There was much political upheaval over the decades[13] and considerable efforts were made towards free market reform under General Zia's rule in the 1980s. However, little privatisation was actually achieved and the economy did not become more open or more externally oriented.[14] Throughout this period (and including the shift in 1982 to a managed float linked to a basket of Pakistan's key trading partner currencies)[15] the rupee remained a key policy tool on a short leash in the state's control. That is, money continued to be controlled through direct and indirect price controls, quantitative credit allocations and administered interest rates. At the same time, external exposure continued to be controlled through tariffs, import restrictions, tight foreign exchange controls and an exchange rate set at a rate that supported policy priorities. A web of state intervention remained in place in respect of agriculture and electricity which were key to the economy's pricing patterns. Although this macroeconomic regime generated some very serious imbalances in the economy, it nonetheless proved successful in securing monetary stability across the economy.

Liberalising Money and Markets: The 1990s

The Structural Adjustment Program, attached to the large IMF loan in 1988, set the economy on a new, more open track and, in the early 1990s, the reform process began in earnest. Economic management was redirected away from the protection of the macroeconomic unit from global forces and towards integration into the global economy. At the same time, monetary management was reoriented. Just as the economy was remodelled around principles of market competition, so too was money. The pivot of policy around securing Keynesian balance in the economy's external interaction (and thereby securing exchange rate stability) was thus reconstructed around the promise of a floating exchange rate passively equilibrating the external account.[16] At the level of the street, these changes most importantly implied a radical restructuring of the pricing system. Direct and indirect price controls were removed and the policy edifice supporting stability in money itself – that in which prices are denominated – was liberalised.[17] In agriculture, prices rose as liberalisation brought local prices closer into line with global markets.[18] Simultaneously, sharp increases in energy pricing were passed onto households as deregulation in the energy sector gathered steam.[19] For the first time, inflation became a major policy concern.[20]

At the same time, the government sharply cut expenditure (not least in development spending) while slashing public sector employment. Real wages dropped, GDP declined and poverty rose sharply, returning to levels not seen since the1970s.[21] By 1999, almost a third of the population was classified as poor (ADB 2000: 1) and the 1990s had been dubbed 'the lost decade'. Yet both for ordinary people struggling with higher and more volatile prices on subsistence goods and for policymakers struggling to control money and prices, the problem of inflation in the 1990s was but a taste of the challenge of monetary instability yet to come as a result of the introduction of open markets.

Money and Monetary Policy

Formalising the realignment of the central bank's activities around the principles of open markets, a series of changes were made at the legislative level between 1993 and 1997 to establish 'central bank autonomy' and thus lay the groundwork for the shift to inflation targeting.[22] Although the SBP's mandate outlined in the 1956 SBP Act was not changed, the shift to central bank independence implied the reinterpretation of 'price stability' in order to accommodate inflation targeting policy. The focus on price management thus shifted to a narrow measure of core inflation, or 'non-food non-energy' measures, that sought to separate transient 'noise' from underlying inflationary trends. Monetary management thereby became an arms-length exercise focusing on controlling monetary aggregates and manipulating interest rates in pursuit of control over core inflation.[23]

A wide-ranging reorganisation of money and finance was thus rapidly embarked upon. Monetary policy shifted towards market principles with directed credit phased out, interest rate caps abolished and mandated bank holdings of government debt as a liquidity buffer (the liquidity ratio) reduced. In January 1995, the SBP began conducting open market operations, by which the policy rate is released to banks. Rather than the set interest rates and credit allocations of decades past, the banking sector was now tasked with carrying the policy rate into market rates on bank deposits and lending, and thereby with feeding central bank stimulus (or contractionary pressure) into the wider economy. In the banking sector, privatisation began in the early 1990s and quickly gathered steam. The Banks (Nationalization) Act was amended and two of the 'big five' banks were promptly privatised in 1991, in a process that lasted up to 2007 and beyond.[24]

Foreign currency accounts, introduced in 1973 but legal only for expatriate Pakistanis, were made available to all residents, free of taxes and restrictions, in 1991.[25] At the same time, a private market for foreign exchange was phased in with the establishment of Authorised Money Changers, who were permitted restricted trade in foreign exchange cash, although they were not permitted to undertake foreign transfers.[26] The Authorised Money Changers system sought to formalise the still small illegal market of money changers dealing in cash, while the full convertibility of the capital account promised effective formalisation of foreign transfers carried out in the illegal market by offering legal avenues for those flows (IMF 2001: 20). Although implicit foreign exchange price controls were maintained in the early transition years, these were lifted in stages.

Within just a few years, the rupee had become more or less freely convertible, although it remained pegged to a trade-weighted basket of currencies until 2000, when it was set on a 'clean float'. After the float, the central bank committed to limiting foreign exchange market intervention to 'smoothing volatility', rather than seeking outright to control the value of the rupee. As the rest of this chapter shows, this dramatic reorientation of monetary governance set in train a complex set of policy challenges to the SBP's efforts to support the stable anchoring of money and prices in an era of open markets. These challenges reveal how liberalisation has destabilised money and the economy in ways that are not obvious to conventional analysis.

Trade and Investment

On the current account side, the liberalisation of the trade regime was rapidly pushed forward after Pakistan became a member of the World Trade Organisation (WTO) in 1995. Maximum tariffs had been reduced from 425 per cent to 250 per cent between 1988 and 1994 (Nabi 1997: 148), and were cut back to only 25 per cent by 2003, with all quantitative restrictions eliminated (Karim 2014: 6). These changes demanded a shift in the tax regime away from trade and towards a general sales tax (GST). In an effort to entice foreign investment, the reform programme included the abolition of controls on foreign ownership and on income remittances on foreign direct and portfolio investment, along with a series of tax holidays and tariff concessions granted to foreign investors. At the same time, the public-sector enterprise privatisation programme that had begun under General Zia was expanded, with 105 manufacturing units put up for privatisation, most of which had already been sold by 1992 (Zaidi 2005: 342).

Key Commodities

The liberalisation of key sectors, such as agriculture and electricity, were part of the broad sweep by which the barriers that had limited interaction between the domestic and global economy (and thereby permitted targeted pricing policies within the economy) were dismantled. These reforms are important to the analysis presented here because they released controls over key anchor prices, exposing those prices to the vagaries of global markets with implications for pricing patterns right across the economy.

With regard to agriculture, the 1988 Structural Adjustment Program set out to reinvigorate the limited reforms that had been achieved earlier in the 1980s, so as to effectively privatise the sector as a whole and institute market pricing. Ration shops, through which basic subsistence commodities were sold at subsidised prices against ration cards, had already been disbanded in 1987. This marked a significant shift in the government's approach away from subsidised food provision.[27] As the decade progressed, major reductions on subsidies for agricultural inputs were implemented, dropping from nearly 10 per cent of budgetary expenditure in 1980 to 1.5 per cent by the mid-1990s (Chaudhry and Sahibzada 1995). At the same time, government procurement at fixed prices of crops other than wheat and sugarcane were eliminated and the monopoly control of agricultural imports and exports by the state was withdrawn. As such, the complex edifice of policies that had supported agricultural prices, which themselves were key inputs to the manufacturing sector,[28] was in large parts dismantled in the 1990s. Yet even though important aspects of government intervention remained, especially in the major crops and principally in wheat, the system of government intervention had been hugely reduced.[29] At the level of the street, this carried into a jump in agricultural prices, themselves key constituents of the consumer basket, as prices were brought into greater alignment with global markets.[30]

Similar changes were seen in the energy sector. The state had committed to deregulation and thus to bringing prices more into line with global markets, first through its 1988 Private Sector Energy Development Project with the World Bank, and then in its 1992 Strategic Plan for Power Sector Privatisation and the 1994 Power Policy. Along with other lenders, notably the Asian Development Bank (ADB),[31] the vertical integration of the state's provision of power had been unbundled into generation, transmission and distribution corporations, which were set on a path of privatisation. A major step in this process was the introduction of independent power producers (IPPs) to the sector in the mid-1990s. With the introduction of private-sector energy producers to the market, pricing reform was given a new boost and the nominally independent National Energy Price Regulation Authority (NEPRA) was established in 1997. As the state moved towards liberalising prices, it slashed its subsidy on electricity for agriculture and revised electricity prices up,[32] generating a sharp increase in household expenditure on electricity and natural gas between 1994 and 2001.[33]

Yet the celebrated introduction of private sector generation by IPPs soon degenerated into controversy, which essentially pivoted around the problematic implications of instituting market prices for electricity.[34] This controversy flags early signs of the specifically monetary nature of the mounting problems associated with the liberalisation of key commodities.

Problems started when the generous government subsidies paid to the IPPs, which were key to the terms of agreement by which investors sold power to the system, were effectively disputed by the government in the late 1990s. For the government, private power production proved more expensive than planned.[35] Considering it politically unfeasible to further raise consumer tariffs, the government tried to renegotiate lower payments made by the state to private power providers in exchange for the energy that they provided to the grid. These negotiations, however, became increasingly hostile and ultimately failed. In 1998, the government issued 'Notices of Intent to Terminate' to companies representing two-thirds of the private power capacity contracted. These were based on claims of corruption and technical problems, amidst counter claims of coercion and intimidation.

The predicament faced in the energy sector in the 1990s in some ways mirrors the problems which surfaced after 2000 in the agricultural sector and which are discussed later in the chapter. In both cases, the state was ultimately unwilling to expose consumers to market prices, which were both considerably higher than the set prices of the pre-liberalisation era and inherently unstable. The short-term interests of the government in limiting price rises no doubt was central to the state's reversal on the liberalisation of these key prices. Yet the problem that price liberalisation in key commodities posed to the state's control over money and prices was also becoming increasingly clear.

In academic research, work on inflation had remained focused on money supply as the primary driver of inflation right into the 1990s,[36] even though the impact of food commodities on inflation had long been an important consideration in agricultural price setting.[37] Only in the mid-1990s did commodity prices start to be seen as important for domestic inflation. In examining the unprecedented levels of inflation that arose in the early years of liberalisation, the national economics institute, the Pakistan Institute of Development Economics, found that key commodity prices were the most important contributing factors to new inflation in the economy (Naqvi et al. 1994). This position was taken a step further by economist Aynul Hasan and his colleagues, who found that liberalisation had unleashed new inflationary dynamics in the economy. Under these conditions, Hasan and his colleagues suggest, it was not money supply, but wheat and energy prices that primarily drove inflation (Hasan et al. 1995).

Although this work was breaking new ground by focusing on commodity price dynamics under the new open market conditions, it was still captured within a distinctly pre-liberalisation perspective. For these authors, wheat and electricity prices played into inflation because of the one-off shocks constituted by upward revision of government pricing on wheat and electricity. It was only much later that the problem of exposure to global commodity prices was cast both as a problem of multiple exposures and as a problem of volatility in global markets, rather than of one-off revisions in government pricing.[38] As the relationship between global prices and domestic inflation became increasingly pronounced, the exchange rate, which is itself a proxy for exposure to global markets, became an increasingly important feature in studies of inflation.[39] As a result, it was only in the post-liberalisation years that volatility in global markets became broadly accepted as key drivers of inflation and the problems revealed in the 1990s of access to subsistence amongst ordinary Pakistanis could be seen as a real threat to rupee governance.

The Early Years: Stabilising the Rupee under Open Markets

As the economy launched into the twenty-first century, the major challenge facing monetary stability was no longer the problem of inflation. Following the float of the rupee in 2000, the preeminent policy concern rapidly shifted to the need to support some kind of stability in the rupee, entwined with which was the increasingly pressing need to access foreign exchange so as to satisfy potentially large gaps in the current and capital account. By dismantling state control over external transfers, liberalisation opened the way for large and unpredictable shifts in the amount of foreign exchange demanded to undertake current and capital account transfers.

For the rupee, these issues play out in three key dynamics. First, persistent trade deficits drive long-term 'adjustment' in the value of the national currency that pushes its value down over time. Second, short-term shocks to the exchange rate arise in the case of large payments, such as for oil, debt repayments and other 'lumpy' transfers, by which the rupee's value can suddenly dip as the market is flooded with rupees being exchanged for a large amount of dollars.[40] Third, speculation, itself facilitated by the hugely expanded slew of counter-positions made available by liberalisation,[41] can exacerbate these dynamics. Speculation generates both much greater volatility through the course of adjustment and much more spectacular short-term shocks with lower dips and sharper peaks. Be it a short-term shock or a more sustained 'adjustment', depreciation makes foreign payments (for example, on debt or imports) more expensive in local terms, demanding more rupees be sold on the market to access dollars and thereby generating a cumulative effect. This interaction between foreign exchange and domestic currency stability is conventionally located in the formal foreign exchange market. However, the drift towards undocumented currency, which as we will see was in significant ways spurred by the SBP's own policy choices, further complicated this predicament. Ultimately, as undocumented money markets blossomed, the state's capacity to monitor and control money, and specifically national currency, diminished.

In the direct aftermath of the float in July 2000, the exchange rate had embarked upon a path of depreciation, losing value 'at a mind-boggling rate' (Malik 2001). This period was characterised by low foreign exchange reserves and a vulnerable external sector. Indeed, from 'a position of weakness' (SBP 2001a: 158), the state had been forced to sign a Standby Agreement with the IMF in late 2000, in order to avoid a balance of payments crisis and shore up the rupee's value. Through the transition to a floating exchange rate, the IMF forbade the SBP from using direct measures to protect the exchange value of the rupee, forcing the SBP instead to stick to open market policy, thus relying on high interest rates alone to attract stabilisation in the exchange rate market.[42] In its *Annual Report* of 2001, the SBP complained that, contrary to the 'general tendency to advocate floating exchange rate regimes', the price of a free float was proving to be excessive exchange rate volatility, enhanced incentives to dollarise and high interest rates (SBP 2001a: 158).

Here the SBP was dealing with a complex of new issues as it sought to manage the rupee as a floating currency under largely liberalised current and capital account conditions. Indeed, the growing role of speculative pressure in 'playing' the floating exchange rate did not subside. Be it through forex loans, foreign exchange bank accounts in Pakistan or abroad, cash, or holding out on processing import and export receipts, access to the foreign exchange tools that facilitate the assumption of counter positions to the rupee had become accessible on a scale unimaginable under the pre-liberalisation regime. As the decade progressed, the SBP bemoaned spending huge amounts of reserves on stabilising the exchange rate in order to hinder speculative pressure.[43] The bank raised concerns about 'snowballing' dynamics whereby the liberalisation of controls on the current account, for example the reduction of tariffs, created deficits that encouraged panicked selling of the rupee, whilst the rupee depreciation, in turn, made the current account deficit even worse.[44] The problem was compounded by the fact that if the central bank intervened, pressure would be placed on reserves, which could prompt an additional wave of rupee sell-offs.

As we will see, liberalisation magnified the threat of speculative pressure through the interaction of the exchange rate on informal markets, foreign inflows and the current account. This predicament provoked condemnation of the informal money markets in the press, by which the informal markets were blamed for enhancing instability in the exchange rate by generating speculative pressure. Yet it was not until many years later that the threat posed by informality in money and in markets could be seen in more nuanced ways: as a threat to the central bank's capacity to control money and, more broadly, as a driver of uncertainty in the economy. In order to understand how Pakistan's informal money markets came to pose such a threat to the rupee, however, we must go back to 1998, when the push for economic openness sharply reversed amidst international isolation imposed on Pakistan as a result of its nuclear tests.

The SBP's Kerb Purchases

Since 1998, the SBP had been funding balance of payments transfers by purchasing dollars from the so-called kerb market, that is, the informal cash markets that dealt both within a limited mandate of legal foreign exchange cash and, more commonly, in illegal foreign exchange cash and foreign transfers, known as *hawala* or *hundi* transaction.[45] By funding the balance of payments from foreign exchange sources external to the official foreign exchange markets in which the exchange rate was set, the SBP's kerb purchases offered access to hard currency while effectively sheltering the rupee's value from the pressures of the balance of payments transactions.[46] This very controversial foreign exchange programme was strongly opposed by the IMF, in large part because it supported the development of 'multiple currency practices'.[47] This aside, the dollar purchasing programme was clearly generating a dangerous level of growth in the informal money markets.[48] The depth of liquidity in the informal market had already surprised the SBP when it started the kerb purchasing programme.[49] Yet heavy central bank buying from the informal market could, as the SBP argued itself, only be expected to drive greater growth in the market.[50] Indeed, the dollar purchases on the kerb market came to a value of over US$5.5 billion between July 1998 and May 2002 (SBP 2004b).

As the SBP itself made clear, the kerb purchasing programme did not offer a sustainable policy path.[51] Salient to the present analysis is the SBP's prioritisation of the problem of currency instability despite the SBP's own concerns with kerb purchases. In retrospect, kerb purchases were not only unsustainable but generated what grew into a very significant problem for the rupee, a problem that the SBP itself had partly fuelled by its heavy patronage of the market in those early, formative years.

Informal dollar purchases had arisen as a result of the financial constraints imposed after Pakistan's nuclear tests in 1998, when the central bank froze foreign currency accounts (FCAs). FCAs had grown significantly through the 1990s, due to the generous conditions offered by the SBP to deposit holders, and had become an important source of hard currency for balance of payments transfers.[52] Anticipating capital flight in the wake of sanctions imposed on Pakistan in response to nuclear testing, however, the central bank froze FCAs in May 1998. This policy choice was effective in hindering panicked capital flight and thereby staved off an immediate balance of payments crisis.[53] However, the freezing of FCAs produced a hesitancy amongst households and businesses in using FCAs for foreign currency holdings, which persisted for many years. This forced the central bank to look elsewhere to gain access to the hard currency needed to fulfil transfers booked through the balance of payments. With US sanctions in place, Pakistan was denied funding from the international financial institutions, such as the World Bank and IMF. Indeed, Pakistan only narrowly avoided being designated a state sponsor of terrorism by the US State Department after nuclear tests in 1998, the military coup in 1999 and growing evidence of nuclear proliferation in secret deals with North Korea, Libya and Iran.

This predicament pushed the SBP into the kerb market for hard currency purchases, which allowed it to fulfil its balance of payments obligations without putting severe downward pressure on the value of the rupee. Yet, as mentioned, by the SBP's own admission, kerb market purchases were bound only to strengthen the kerb market as a site of illegal money transfers and undocumented foreign exchange cash. Although little recognised at the time,[54] in this way the considerable expansion of the kerb market over the decade came to pose a persistent threat to the rupee and its management in a number of different ways.

The Problem of Kerb Market Expansion

Much of the public discourse around the informal money markets is oriented towards the problem of capital flight as a zero-sum loss to the national economy. Certainly, it is broadly accepted that illegal capital flight through the informal money market occurs at a huge scale.[55] Moreover, although the illegal *hawala* trade traces its history back thousands of years,[56] the liberalisation of money and markets since the 1990s greatly enhanced the ease with which legal and illegal capital flight could be undertaken. Specifically, the netting out of illegal capital flight can be more easily hidden amongst larger flows of ostensibly legal international transfers in the same way that greater international trade flows provide more opportunities for companies to misinvoice trade.[57]

Apparently more pressing for the central bank than illegal capital flight, however, was the pressure placed on the rupee by speculative activity in the kerb market. As demand for the dollar in informal markets rises, the gap between the dollar exchange rate in the formal and informal markets increases, pushing up the so-called kerb premium.[58] This, in turn, prompts remittances to be transmitted through informal kerb dealers rather than formal channels, as overseas workers seek to benefit from the better rates offered in the kerb market on the currency exchange that is entailed in sending wages home to Pakistan. For the SBP, the problem lies in the fact that where remittances follow the better rates offered in informal markets, they are diverted from formal to informal markets. As a consequence, they flow neither through formal exchange markets nor the current account. The absence of those remittances lost from formal markets effectively put downward pressure on the rupee's value and worsen the current account gap. This deficit then causes further pressure on the value of the rupee, adding to depreciation, while making the national accounts (which are a key indicator for currency speculators as much as credit rating agencies) look weaker than they actually are.[59]

At a more abstract level, however, the rise of the informal money markets poses a further set of challenges. One such challenge is the problem for the central bank of a vast yet unknowable pool of liquidity that lies outside of the central bank's framework. Even currency in circulation figures cannot be unambiguously established, given that the Pakistani rupee circulates as the dominant money medium in parts of Afghanistan, which dilutes the amount actually circulating in Pakistan. In the case of foreign exchange, the depth of liquidity in the kerb market that was revealed by its capacity to absorb the billions of dollars' worth of the SBP's own kerb purchases conveyed a sense of the very significant scale of foreign currency circulating in the Pakistani economy in the early years after the float.

The circulation of this undocumented foreign cash undermines the rupee's exclusivity as money in the economy. This is most obviously an issue for the SBP's dependence on monetary aggregates for monetary policy formulation,[60] which lose their precision as an indicator as non-rupee money picks up money roles in place of the rupee. At a greater level of abstraction, the circulation of significant sums of non-rupee money undermines the lynchpin role of the rupee in the economy which promises a conduit for the transmission of monetary policy into the wider economy.

A more immediate concern, however, is that the circulation of foreign exchange imposes an opacity around money, which leaves forecasting and target-setting in a grey zone of uncertainty. Here the punctures imposed by liberalisation on the economy as a discrete economic unit are exacerbated: the finite bounds of the economy, already undermined by convertibility in the current and capital account, become even leakier with unknown sums of money instruments moving into, out of, and around the economy.

This is not just a problem of unaccounted liquidity moving around the economy but is a problem of uncertainty spread across a whole series of economic indicators. The specific nature of *hawala* is of particular concern in this regard. Transacting in illegal outward capital flight, authentic inward remittances and money laundering that exploits the 'no questions asked' policy on inward remittances, *hawala* nets out flows between networks of domestic and foreign dealers. Where dirham may be deposited for remittance transfer by a Pakistan worker with a dealer in the United Arab Emirates (UAE), for example, it must be paid out in rupees to the worker's family by a dealer in Pakistan. The dealer in the UAE and the dealer in Pakistan must then settle their accounts, which can occur through a complex set of transactions, such as by drawing on a combination of import and export misinvoicing with undocumented trade and other misreported transactions, as well as with authentic trade and financial flows.[61] *Hawala* thereby reinforces uncertainty around the veracity of statistics by meshing a whole series of categories of flows together, mixing legitimate flows related to trade and finance with illegitimate flows, underreporting some and over-reporting others, while others are undocumented altogether.

Through all this we see how the kerb purchasing programme answered to the SBP's short-term needs for greater stability in the rupee in the years after the nuclear tests, but also how this effective support for the kerb market created a monster. In the years around the float, the SBP had struggled with meeting its obligations under an open current and capital account without either setting off panic in foreign exchange markets or facing the long-run decline of the rupee's value generated by the hard currency demands of the balance of payments. Yet, as we will see, kerb purchases ultimately undermined the SBP's capacity to administer the rupee as money in the economy. By supporting the growth of informal money markets, kerb purchases implied a whole set of negative impacts on the rupee in terms of its value, its knowability and the transmission of monetary policy more generally. The informal markets thus quickly came to serve as a reflection of the ambiguity of the vastly new parameters of the external sector under liberalisation. Yet it was not until later years in the decade that the complexity of the post-liberalisation monetary environment became clear and, more specifically, the threat to monetary management posed by the informal markets came to light.

Turning Tides: The War on Terror and the Boom Years

The SBP's frustrations in those early years over the failure of the floating rupee to find stability in the open market, however, rapidly reversed. With the War on Terror ratcheting up the international focus on Afghanistan, the hard currency constraint revealed by liberalisation was quickly relieved. For the purposes of this analysis, what these boom years reflect is the near-unabating challenge of managing the monetary system as an open market system, even under extraordinarily good financial conditions. Despite the stellar performance of traditional macroeconomic indicators between 2001 and 2007, the rupee continued to be threatened by speculative pressure and an unstable kerb premium.[62] At the same time, the state proved unwilling to let key prices fluctuate with the market. Although liberalisation ostensibly remained a policy goal, some price controls that had been liberalised in earlier years were effectively re-imposed in the early 2000s, generally at the cost of the cancellation of foreign funded liberalisation programmes. These very expensive policy backflips demonstrated the threat of instability implied by the floating of wheat and electricity prices – an instability that was congruent with the recognition in local academic work of the key role that commodity prices were playing as drivers of inflation in the new economy.

After the 11 September terrorist attacks in 2001, Pakistan was quietly moved off the shortlist of pariah states and was instead designated a 'frontline state' in the War on Terror. As a result, international sanctions were removed, the Paris Club debt was rescheduled and new concessional loans from the IMF and other multilateral financial institutions were made available to support General Musharraf's commitment to 'join hands with the international community' in fighting the scourge of terror (SBP0 2002a: 161). The US and EU offered further grants and concessionary loans. These included periodic 'reimbursements' made by the US to Pakistan for services rendered in the War on Terror (known as Coalition Support Funds), as well as privileged access to US and EU markets for Pakistani exports for the coming years.[63] In addition, Pakistan's external account benefited from a process of reverse capital flight as anxiety heightened amongst the Pakistani diaspora amidst the intensification of surveillance of funds to and from Pakistan in an international effort to curb 'terror funding'. The SBP declared financial year 2001–02 'one of the most positive years in terms of external sector developments' (SBP 2002a: 154). With the hard currency constraint suddenly relieved, the rupee faced improved prospects of stability.

Financial conditions in Pakistan continued to improve over the following years. Pakistan enjoyed good access to international markets, demonstrated in a series of Eurobond[64] and other sovereign debt issuances. Over these years, Pakistan received a series of new debt write-offs, grants and concessional loans while low interest payments from the 2001 rescheduling lasted until around 2007.[65] In addition, foreign direct investment (FDI) and portfolio inflows were booming.[66] These factors served to keep the balance of payments affordable despite mounting current account deficits. The growing trade gap, largely influenced by oil prices and relatively stagnant exports, was perceived as increasingly problematic only in the second half of the decade.[67] What was more important for the IMF and SBP's own assessments through the period between 2001 and 2007 was the vast improvement in reserves and the growing confidence of international markets in the Pakistani economy.[68]

Domestically, conventional monetary indicators were looking up. GDP growth increased every year between 2001 and 2005, reaching 8.4 per cent. This was the second highest rate of growth in the world in 2006. Inflation remained low until 2005 when it peaked for a short period but nevertheless remained below double digits. The real exchange rate was trending in appreciation through these years and was deemed by the IMF as broadly appropriate, even a little undervalued given export growth and the reasonable balance of payments position.[69] In the newly privatised banking sector, deposits and advances were posting unprecedented growth and non-performing loans were at an all-time low. Banking sector assets grew at a rate of 23 per cent per annum between 2002 and 2007,[70] amidst strong profits and healthy capital adequacy indicators. Inflation and the current account gap were seen by the IMF as 'the price of success' (IMF 2005: 5). In early 2006, *Newsweek* declared that 'the proof is in the numbers.... [Pakistan] has become the world's most surprising economic success story' (Moreau 2006).

The optimism generated over these years was not confined to external observers. Within Islamabad society and government alike, much hope was harboured for the policy continuity that a military government could offer in cementing structural change in the economy.[71] Continuity was a salient concern after the political instability of the 1990s, through which the rotating regimes of Nawaz Sharif and Benazir Bhutto repeatedly ended in premature dismissal. This optimism was expressed in the ambitious commitments made by the government to build upon the policy repositioning of the 1990s by strengthening its commitment to consolidate liberalisation in the key areas of agriculture and energy. Yet in respect of the most important commodities, as we will see, the state provided confirmation of its earlier hesitation around imposing market prices[72] by ultimately reneging on its commitment to liberalisation at the point at which market prices would have begun to carry through to the consumer. Of interest to this study is the particularity of energy and wheat prices that was revealed by these repeated policy backflips. Although liberalisation had taken a hold of almost the entire economy, it was electricity and wheat pricing that stood out as the key sticking points for the state, which, in turn, reflects the key role of these prices in the economy as a whole, and not least with respect to monetary conditions.

An Optimistic Reform Agenda in Key Commodities

In 2001, the ADB supported the state's efforts to complete the process of liberalisation in the agriculture sector with a loan that sought to implement a programme of agricultural liberalisation. Much change had been undertaken in the sector since early reforms in the 1980s, but support price programmes in one form or another still covered 70 per cent of Pakistan's cropped land in 2001.[73] The ADB loan that was signed off at the end of 2001 specifically targeted wheat but actually addressed the agricultural sector as a whole.[74] It committed the government to the phasing out of agricultural price supports and subsidies, and to the divestiture of state involvement in the production and sale of agricultural goods. Crucially, this included the complete phase out of all government involvement in the procurement, sale, import and export of wheat over five years. The programme thereby sought to establish the dynamics of market pricing in wheat in the same way that market pricing was being pursued amongst other less important agricultural commodities, through both deregulation and privatisation.

Yet as price supports on wheat were drawn down in 2002 through sharp reductions in state procurement, the wheat price surged and dropped, posing a sudden shift to fierce instability in the most important commodity for consumers in the economy.[75] The state quickly reversed its drawdown of the procurement programme in order to reimpose some stability in the market. This rapid U-turn on wheat reform prompted delay in the second and third tranches of the ADB loan which led to its eventual abandonment. The summary report found that the programme had not achieved even half of its objectives and a number of implemented reforms had been reversed even before the programme's completion. Specifically, wheat, the single most important food commodity in Pakistan and the heart of the original agreement, had 'failed to [be] remove[d] … from state control' (ADB 2010: 3). Recognising the cost burden borne by the poor as a result of rapid liberalisation, the ADB identified 'the failure of the [project] design to tackle the main poverty issue' (ibid.: 2) as a key programme weakness. One of the project's target outcomes had been to reduce rural poverty through greater efficiency in agricultural markets. The summary report, however, acknowledged a considerable rise in rural poverty driven by the higher cost of subsistence commodities to landless, non-agricultural and small landholding households (ibid.: 7, 9).

A similar story unfolded in the case of electricity reform. Already in the 1990s, the government had been subjected to delays of tranched payments and cancellation of entire programmes in relation to a number of energy sector loans. An important hydropower project that had been funded by the World Bank in 1995, for example, had struck major obstacles when the government reneged on its commitment to undertake 'critically needed' increases in consumer prices for electricity in 1997 (World Bank 2004: 19). Much like the ADB's assessment of the agricultural liberalisation programme a decade later, the bank concluded in its appraisal of the project's failure that the political and social implications of the substantial increase in electricity prices that was demanded by the project had not been properly taken into account in the initial project design.[76] The legislation of NEPRA in 1997 promised to resolve the problem of government backflips on electricity pricing policy by securing legitimacy over electricity pricing for consumers as well as the state and investors. That is, as an independent authority, NEPRA set out to act as a fair arbiter of pricing decisions for electricity that could balance the demands of consumers with the cost of production. NEPRA was envisioned as a solution both to the state's rather conflicted contestation of the implementation of its own market pricing policies, and to the kind of conflict between the government and the private sector that was seen in the IPP project. However, NEPRA itself increasingly became the government's adversary in the matter of energy prices.[77] Despite the critical role that the state's unwillingness to pass higher energy prices on to consumers had played in the disaster of the IPP privatisations in the 1990s and the overall 'disappointing' achievements of reform since the mid-1990s (Parish 2006: 14), the government maintained earlier commitments to market pricing in the energy sector in a new round of loans. As reiterated in the Energy Sector Restructuring loan agreement signed with the ADB in late 2000 and the Structural Adjustment Credit II programme signed with the World Bank in 2002, the state promised to push forward with market pricing. Yet, in each case, key reforms proved unsustainable. Some reforms that had been enacted were reversed even before the projected programme completion date, while others were designated as unsustainable in programme reviews a decade later. On both counts, a key issue again was the state's resistance to handing over control over prices to the market.[78] Specifically, the government had resisted tariff reform and put pressure on NEPRA for downward revision on tariffs in 2002. In 2003, the government undermined NEPRA altogether by issuing its own below-cost prices to consumers regardless of the price issued by NEPRA in rates that were frozen by the government right up until 2007. It was therefore unsurprising that the power sector reform component of the Structural Adjustment II loan was deemed unsatisfactory in the World Bank's programme evaluation.[79] With nearly half the initial loan cancelled, the ADB loan was similarly deemed 'less than effective' and discontinued in 2004 (ADB 2014: iv). Whilst upward tariff revisions were undertaken in 2007, the new higher prices still remained below production costs and below the NEPRA tariff.[80]

Persistent Instability despite Good Times

The state's enduring hesitancy to float key prices on the market reflects the importance of these prices for the economy, and indeed for the political settlement. For the state, the issue may well have been viewed as a short-term problem of the political costs associated with one-off price rises as prices 'adjust' to higher global prices. The political cost arises from the consequent increase in the cost of living and the discontent amongst the population that this induces.

From the perspective of this study, however, the issue of key commodity prices takes broader significance. From this perspective, it is a problem of long-term exposure to enduring volatility in global pricing patterns – not a one-off adjustment but a persistent issue of both an increase in the cost of living and increasing volatility in that cost. Moreover, this volatility is not only about the actual costs of wheat and electricity, but about the anchoring role that these prices play in the economy. That is, volatility in the cost of wheat and electricity carries strongly into broader inflationary trends. This was beginning to be recognised in studies of inflation in the 1990s.[81] In those studies, the threat that the liberalisation of key commodity prices poses to the task of controlling inflation through interest rate management becomes apparent. Yet, more than this, in circumstances where money is actively contested, the anchoring role of key commodities constitutes a much more profound threat to the rupee. Keynes' discussion of the nature of money is central to this predicament and is returned to in Chapters 6, 7 and 8.

For present purposes, however, the point is that the generous macroeconomic conditions that prevailed through the boom years cast a distinct salience over the state's conflicted approach to its own liberalisation agenda. With inflation and poverty rates rising sharply in the mid-1990s, the World Bank had recognised that imposing market prices carried social and political costs that ultimately undermined the feasibility of liberalisation.[82] Identifying this as a transfer of risk onto consumers, the World Bank recognised sharply fluctuating commodity prices as a genuine concern for the government. Yet, in stark contrast to the 'lost decade' of the 1990s, the years after 2001 were boom years by any of the conventional macroeconomic measures. This predicament prompts the question: if the state is not willing to unleash market pricing on citizens in prosperous years of economic growth, falling poverty and relatively stable monetary conditions, then when could the right time for liberalisation be?

The exposure of the rupee that is posed by the balance of payments under open market conditions gives rise to the same predicament. Even in those boom years, SBP policy reflected the persistent threat of balance of payment funding to the rupee's value. One concern was the concentration in the trade account amongst a limited number of core exports and imports. This rendered the balance of payments vulnerable to unpredictable price effects in the short term and declining terms of trade in the long term, especially in relation to oil (a key import, the price of which has tended to go up) and textiles (a key export, the price of which has tended to go down). In Pakistan, these effects produce long-term depreciation as well as short-term shocks to currency markets, which, in turn, generate the speculative pressure that is a very persistent and important problem for the SBP. Concerns over speculation had not abated since the rupee's float in 2000.[83] This is reflected in the SBP's decision, in the middle of the boom years, to shift oil payments out of the foreign exchange markets and on to its own books. Although condemned by the IMF, the SBP sought to stymie the speculative attacks that tend to follow a dip in the rupee's value following large oil payments by the private sector. By taking over hard currency payments on the part of private sector oil importers, the SBP could slowly accumulate hard currency rather than allow the private sector to demand large amounts of hard currency in single transactions.[84] Whether or not this move was successful is debatable,[85] but either way these kinds of departures from orthodox policy *even in the best of years* reflect a persistent problem of monetary instability under open markets.

Indeed, the economy's fortunes soon reversed. With this, the problem of monetary instability was amplified by huge proportions. On the surface, the boom's sudden reversal posed speculation as a far greater threat to the SBP, and the liberalisation of prices as a far greater threat to consumers. Yet beneath this lay rather more fundamental problems for the rupee.

A Squandered Boom?

By the end of the decade, the boom years were seen by many as having been hopelessly squandered.[86] By 2005, the preferential treatment of Pakistani exports to the EU had expired. A new agreement in the WTO relating to textiles, together with new anti-dumping measures in the EU, posed an extremely challenging environment for one of Pakistan's major exports. This situation worsened by 2007. The further liberalisation of textiles and other key manufactures at the global level lowered the demand price in global markets and thereby threatened the export sector on a number of fronts.[87] The sustainability of the growth in exports registered since 2001 was thereby cast into doubt. These concerns about the export sector were exacerbated by a persistent concentration of exports within a narrow range of low-value-added products.[88] In fact, the trade gap was later revealed to have been even worse than assumed at the time. Massive over-invoicing of exports linked to the abuse of export promotion schemes was later estimated to have constituted approximately 15 per cent of major exports for 2005 (SBP 2007: 157). Large imports of machinery in the same year, seen at the time as a hopeful sign of a future increase in productivity, were shown to have largely been constituted by consumer products, such as cars and white goods, rather than commercial investment goods.[89] Concerns about the economy's inability to make substantive improvements in productivity throughout these years carried over into criticism of the SBP's low interest rate policy through the period. Critics argued that the boom years had left the economy carrying a heavy burden of non-performing loans after strong growth in consumer lending led to defaults later.[90] Moreover, critics also argued that the speculative lending, which had contributed to the nearly four-fold increase in the Karachi Stock Exchange between 2004 and 2007, had taken place to the detriment of productive business lending, the latter of which had stagnated.[91] FDI, which is conventionally associated with a string of productivity benefits but attracted more attention in Pakistan in terms of the relief it offered to the balance of payments, became subject to similar criticism. Early complaints of 'enclaved investment with few spill overs' (SBP 2003: 157) became stronger over the years. FDI proved unable to reach far beyond the low hanging fruit of newly privatised sectors such as telecommunications, banking and oil and gas, thus generating minimal prospects for productivity gains.[92] Moreover, the drag on the rupee generated by growing outflows of foreign investment income became a persistent concern after 2004.[93] The SBP was by 2007 bemoaning the 'mixed blessing' of FDI and its failure to move into the more productivity-enhancing export sector (SBP 2007: 130).

By this point, delayed payments associated with the 2001 debt rescheduling were starting to come due and the tax-to-GDP ratio had reached a new low. The celebrated Tax Administration Reform Project (TARP), which had been implemented in partnership with the World Bank and other lenders in 2005, was showing signs of weakness.[94] The shift from taxes on trade to a GST, which was core to the reorganisation of the economy on open market principles, had caused a major decline in the tax-to-GDP ratio after the 1990s. Tax reforms undertaken in the early Musharraf years had been defeated by protests, but were redoubled in 2005 with the TARP.[95] Yet with further declines in the tax-to-GDP ratio coming to light in 2007, it became increasingly apparent that tax reform had failed to implement a system that could support the state's finances in the absence of significant trade-related taxes.

By implying a growing informality in the economy, the low tax-to-GDP figures that came out in 2007, in turn, cast doubt over the SBP's efforts to formalise the kerb market in the optimistic years after 2001. With the initiation of the War on Terror, surveillance over foreign transfers had been ramped up. This caused a sharp shock to the informal foreign exchange market, which was expressed in the collapse of kerb premium as the informal market shrank precipitously. Seeing this as an opportune time to eliminate the *hawala* trade altogether,[96] the SBP attempted to legalise the informal market for foreign transfers by opening up the regulatory space to informal operators in 2002.[97] The new policy created a tier for foreign transfers through newly established 'exchange companies' that lay below the banking sector.

The kerb premium remained subdued right through 2002, thus implying minimal activity in the informal market for foreign exchange, but informality in the market remained nonetheless evident. In 2004, the SBP undertook a further push to formalise the sector by opening yet another space for informal dealers to operate as regulated dealers. This regulatory change targeted small informal dealers who could register as 'Category B' exchange companies. The newly established 'Category B' exchange companies required a lower capital base but were limited to cash exchange and were not permitted to undertake transfers.[98] Still, the kerb premium never quite disappeared, rising again in 2005, 2006 and 2007 in informal money markets across the country, which were becoming increasingly active.[99]

All of this put the rupee in poor standing to weather the coming global storm. The boom years had seen no real progress on key issues like informality, both in the economy at large and specifically in informal money markets, and few if any gains on structural economic issues like productivity and the balance of payments. As the global economy plunged into crisis in late 2007 and early 2008, Pakistan's economy entered its own 'home grown' crisis (Ul Haque 2010). With the extraordinary inflows linked to the boom years winding down, the SBP now faced the formidable challenge of managing the rupee under open markets and doing so without the helping hand of generous foreign liquidity. It was in these years that the challenges to the liberalised rupee crystallised as the monetary environment shifted into a new normal of persistent volatility and increasing opacity.

'A Distinct Change of Sentiments'

Although the crisis arising in the United States was seen as largely remote to local conditions,[100] economic conditions rapidly deteriorated in 2008. For ordinary people, rising inflation was the key issue. Inflation had reappeared since mid-2007 but soon far exceeded anything seen in the 1990s, rising to over 25 per cent by the summer of 2008. With food and energy prices soaring on international markets as panicked global investors diversified into international commodity markets,[101] the central bank was faced at once with a sharp growth in the import bill and with food price inflation bloating poverty statistics. These developments caused the rupee to falter, its exchange value declining as its purchasing power dropped precipitously. Reserves plummeted from US$14 billion to just US$3.4 billion between June 2007 and October 2008. The SBP aggressively ratcheted up interest rates and chastised the government for its indiscipline in maintaining subsidies at a growing cost to the state whilst simultaneously sharply increasing its reliance on central bank borrowing[102] to fund the year's gaping deficit.[103] For the SBP, as for the IMF, the monetisation of public deficits was combining with higher commodity prices to produce the high inflation that the economy was suffering under. Yet, in the face of pressure from the SBP and (more importantly) the IMF, the Musharraf government and the Zardari Pakistan People's Party (PPP) government that followed resisted the removal of subsidies, notably on electricity but also on food and fertilizer. The persistence of subsidies exacerbated the fiscal deficit but, some at the SBP argued, were important for putting downward pressure on inflation insofar as subsidies dampened food price rises.[104]

At the same time, the external position had deteriorated sharply. The SBP announced 'a distinct change in sentiments' as the combination of crisis at the global level and increasing perceptions of country risk at home marked an end to the 'congenial international and domestic environment [that] had allowed Pakistan to comfortably finance its large current account deficit through non-debt creating inflows and concessional loans' (SBP 2007: 116).

Expecting a poor reception in international markets themselves rocked by the global financial crisis, the SBP had taken a last-minute decision to cancel its planned Eurobond issue in 2008.[105] Yet the SBP's concerns about the country's standing in the international economy may have been more a nod to souring US relations,[106] which was not helped by political instability amidst the downfall of General Musharraf, the murder of Benazir Bhutto and the spate of bombings on high profile civilian and military targets in Pakistan's major cities which surged in 2008 and 2009. Disquiet about the state's alleged double dealing in the War on Terror was being voiced in the United States with increasing certainty.[107] Amidst this, an incident of US 'friendly fire' killed 11 Pakistani Army personnel in mid-2008, putting further heat on an already strained US–Pakistan relationship.

In light of these problematic external relations and diminishing prospects of foreign investment flows, the record current account gap thus presented a far more alarming picture to the SBP than the growing current account gap had in years passed. Pressure on the balance of payments, and thus on the rupee, worsened.

No longer considered 'the price of success' (IMF 2005: 5), in its 2008 *Annual Report* the SBP had expressed serious concern about the current account deficit being of a deeper, more structural order of problems than the central bank had dealt with in the past.[108] The current account's 'stubborn structural problems' (SBP 2013a: 98) were at least in part rooted in the digression in exports from manufactured to semi-manufactured goods and primary commodities, with terms of trade declining and a steady decline in exports to GDP.[109] The 2011 *Labour Force Survey* found that declining employment in manufacturing was being picked up not by services, conventionally associated with progress along the developmental path, but by agriculture, instead suggesting developmental regression.[110]

With the sudden reversal of the financial fortunes of the Pakistani economy, the central bank was forced back into negotiations with the IMF. Although fraught with conflict, these negotiations resulted in a Standby Agreement of unprecedented proportions in late November 2008. The eventual agreement entailed the shift of all oil-related payments off the SBP's books and a redoubling of efforts on tax reform that would increase documentation of the informal sector. It also required the raising of interest rates and slashing of subsidies, particularly those on electricity and fertilizer, which had put such a huge strain on the fiscal balance at a time of rising oil prices.[111]

In the meantime, the state cobbled together a mix of emergency measures and longer-term policies that sought to shore up the country's finances. A floor on equities sales was rapidly imposed in order to slow portfolio outflows; and a tax amnesty was launched, which offered generous terms of asset legitimation in exchange for a series of relatively small initial payments.[112] Longer-term measures included a legislative package promoting FDI in agriculture, which essentially sought to privatise commons under conditions exceptionally generous to foreign investors;[113] and the Pakistan Remittances Initiative, which sought to incentivise the transmission of remittances through formal channels, and thereby through the current account and the exchange markets in which the rupee is set.[114] A crackdown on the kerb market brought immediate benefit by reducing misinvoiced outflows amongst exchange companies by hundreds of millions of dollars per month.[115]

These redemptive measures, however, were not helped by continuing tension with the United States, which worked against the central bank's efforts to protect the rupee by reassuring markets. In 2009, the SBP complained of 'erratic' Coalition Support Fund reimbursements from the United States (SBP 2009a: 160), which were being withheld in an escalating tit-for-tat conflict between the two ostensible allies. The same year saw the Kerry-Luger Bill[116] passed in the US Congress, signalling that US funds were far from guaranteed as hostilities between the two countries increasingly came to the surface.[117]

As the SBP scrambled through 2008 and 2009 to maintain its payment obligations while limiting the damage on the rupee, commodity price inflation in global markets slowed. Inflation drew back down to around 10 per cent by mid-2009 and after sharp slides in 2008, rupee depreciation settled to a more gradual decline. Yet, although the worst had passed relatively quickly, a set of longer-term challenges to the SBP's management of money were becoming increasingly defined. One such challenge is informality. As the scale of informality, both in money and in markets, became increasingly clear, so too did the obvious nature of monetary governance failure. The object of policy – money and the economy – was clearly slipping out of the grasp of the authorities into an opaque realm beyond the bounds of quantification and control.

The Problem of Rising Informality

Of immediate concern, with the turn of the nation's fortunes, was the faltering World Bank–funded TARP that had been launched in 2005. In 2009, committed funding was finally withdrawn and the project was terminated due to 'unsatisfactory' follow-through on the part of the government (World Bank 2012b). The same year saw the tax-to-GDP ratio hit a new 35-year low at less than 9 per cent of GDP, amongst the lowest in the world (World Bank 2015). The inability of the state to impose a tax regime that could pick up where the liberalisation of trade and trade-related taxes left off posed formidable challenge to the state, not least because, unlike in the early Musharraf years when the first tax reform project had been abandoned, the failure of the post-liberalisation tax regime had by now become entrenched. Although conventional analysis identifies this as a revenue problem, this study emphasises instead the way that the low tax-to-GDP issue plays out as a monetary policy transmission issue and a data issue for monetary policy formulation more generally. The multifaceted challenge that this predicament thus poses to the rupee's governability is addressed here.

To start with, the extraordinarily low tax-to-GDP ratio implies a dominant informal sector, which undermines monetary policy transmission in two distinct ways. First, informality points towards low levels of engagement with the formal banking sector. This, in turn, undermines the 'bank lending channel' that is considered the dominant channel of transmission in developing countries.[118] Second, price flexibility is considerably greater in the informal sector and in developing economies more generally, which disrupts the 'sticky prices' that are key to transmission.[119]

At the same time, informality creates a grey zone in central bank target-setting by undermining the credibility of microeconomic data and its macroeconomic aggregations, such as GDP and the output gap. As prominent economist Zafar Mahmood has argued, if 70 per cent of currency is circulating in the informal sector, then monetary policy is only taking into account in its analysis and target-setting the 30 per cent that is in the formal economy.[120] However, this is more than a problem of informal markets circulating goods and services that are not captured by GDP statistics. As the kerb market crackdown in 2008 showed, the opacity that informality casts over Pakistan's new economy poses fundamental problems to the state's capacity for economic and monetary governance.

The kerb market crackdown of 2008 complemented the increasingly apparent intransigence of the economy to documentation by revealing a series of unsettling snapshots of a very large and complex informal market in money, suggesting formidable capacity to impede central bank knowledge of and control over money. For example, the crackdown revealed that one single exchange company was undertaking hundreds of millions of dollars' worth of illegal transfers on a monthly basis, its documented international transfers representing only about a third of its total transactions.[121] Further, massive smuggling of cash came to light. A figure was put on this some years later by the governor of the SBP, who proposed that US$25 million was being smuggled out of Pakistan's four major airports on a daily basis (*Dawn* 2013). This suggests that the undocumented component of trade amongst exchange companies was much greater than previously realised and could well be far larger than the portion of transactions that are in fact documented.

These kinds of statistics suggest a high and, crucially, unknowable degree of porousness at the economy's external boundaries. Yet it also suggests huge undocumented liquidity within the economy and vast false reporting in statistics. Indeed, the 2008 kerb market crackdown revealed complexity in informal money market flows that further complicates the veracity of balance of payments representations, implying significant data issues right across the gamut of economic and financial statistics. This is exemplified in the arrests in November 2008 of directors of the exchange company Khanani and Kalia International. These arrests coincided with a dramatic drop of some US$200 million – a 30 per cent decline over a month – hitting aggregate bank and exchange company remittance inflows.[122] In the direct aftermath of the arrests, flows through exchange companies from the United States, where Khanani and Kalia International had controlled some 20 per cent of the remittance market, dropped sharply, as did exchange company flows from the UAE. A month later, aggregate flows from exchange companies were largely restored, with the share of remittances from the United Kingdom and, to a lesser extent the UAE, filling the gap that had been left behind from the drop in US remittances. Remittances from the United Kingdom, which had consistently constituted about 10 per cent of exchange company flows, had rapidly shot up to over 60 per cent of those flows.[123] The sudden drop in flows and the rapid restoration and substitution of flows from one locality to another poses an unlikely scenario which suggests considerable misreporting at Khanani and Kalia that is likely replicated across the sector.

Yet the critical issue here is the complex nature of the informal money market, which implies misreporting well beyond the category of remittance flows alone. Indeed, inwards remittances are but one set of flows on the books of informal money dealers. The business of *hawala* usually involves the netting out of a series of flows through a series of channels, as dealers in different locations settle payments between themselves. These channels include illegal capital flight, as well as undocumented cash exchange. This is combined with legal and illegal import and export trading in goods themselves (that is, in kind transactions and smuggling), misinvoicing on trade payments, and legal financial transfers.[124] At the same time, the so-called retail trade in undocumented foreign exchange cash, carried out by the same dealers as those who undertake *hawala*, is a flourishing business right across the country. The cash liquidity of the retail trade, which exchanges rupee cash for dollar and other currency cash, is intimately linked to the *hawala* trade.

The impossibility of being able to know where illegal *hawala* flows are showing up in the state's external accounts (if at all) thus casts a pall of unreliability over the data – from import and export statistics to financial flows, which feed out across the whole range of macro data. By hinting at the scope of fraudulent reporting of remittance flows associated with *hawala* transactions, the 2008 crackdown thus revealed an overwhelming opacity around what was happening both internally and in the economy's external interactions. For monetary policy, this casts a shadow of uncertainty over the statistical inputs that construct monetary policy at the same time as it suggests a considerable (but unknowable) pool of non-rupee money instruments in use inside the economy.

The continuing vibrancy of the informal money markets in Pakistan suggests that the 2008 crackdown ultimately achieved little in terms of taming the market. Indeed, some argue that the informal market has grown so large and that illegal capital flight through *hawala* has become so entrenched amongst elites that the market is now beyond the reach of the law. For Mohammad Hanif Akhai, a former SBP senior official who was directly involved in kerb regulation in the years after the float, the opportunity of stamping out the kerb market was lost in in the years after 2000. Indeed, in 2002 the kerb premium was almost extinguished entirely. However, Akhai argues that the market has grown to such a degree since then that controlling the market is now well beyond the capacities of any state authority, least of the all the SBP.[125]

From this perspective, the 2009 Pakistan Remittances Initiative (PRI) is an innovative (albeit expensive) policy response to the problem of ever-expanding informal money markets. The PRI effectively offers a state-funded subsidy on formal remittances flows,[126] which has hugely boosted the competitiveness of formal remittance services. By making it much cheaper for remittance senders to use formal channels, the PRI has wiped out much of the competitive advantage of *hawala* dealers in the market for conventional remittance flows. The potential for the PRI to be used for money laundering remains a concern and it is broadly recognised that there are still very large portions of remittance flows that remain undocumented. However, the huge growth of remittances seen in recent years is widely attributed to the PRI.

For the SBP, the PRI is targeted primarily at bringing remittances through the current account and thereby strengthening the exchange rate by formalising demand for the rupee that is otherwise lost to informal markets. As such, the PRI aims to shrink informal markets by bringing business into the formal market. Yet the PRI could also strengthen the intermediary role of the banking system – and thereby the transmission of monetary policy – by supporting greater flows of cash into bank deposits. Expanding engagement with the banking sector, moreover, moves the economy towards more comprehensive formalisation, thus pushing back on the problem of opacity in economic and monetary dynamics that are associated with a lack of formality.

Indeed, in the years following the PRI's launch, the predicament of banking sector engagement became a growing concern when the celebrated upward tracking of deposit and lending statistics since 2001 sharply reversed in 2008. By 2011, deposits across the banking sector dropped to a low of 27 per cent of GDP, lower than they had been in 1993. Worse yet, private sector credit dropped from rates of around 28 per cent between 2004 and 2008, to just 18 per cent in 2011. This was well below even the lowest rates in the 1990s.[127] On the surface, declining deposits and credit (known as disintermediation) pose a further challenge to the efficacy of monetary policy given that monetary policy transmission is premised on the impact of interest rate changes on the economy that are carried through deposit and lending rates at banks. However, like entrenched volatility and growing informality, disintermediation in Pakistan may, in fact, point towards more fundamental issues for money in the economy. Disintermediation is, after all, where uncertainty in money comes home to roost.

Disintermediation and the Drop in Deposits

With the initial shock to deposits in 2008, the SBP rapidly implemented a temporary floor on interest rates on savings deposits.[128] The interest rate floor was designed to ensure a guaranteed return on banked savings that could help to counter losses in the real value of deposits arising from inflation. At the same time, the SBP hastily cut back a series of reserve requirements in order to loosen the liquidity strain on banks and incentivise longer-term deposits.[129]

As intermediation deteriorated further, the bank released a series of policies aimed at both drawing customers back into the banking sector as well as expanding banking sector engagement with those previously 'unbanked'. In 2009, the SBP bolstered the branchless banking network (otherwise known as mobile phone banking), itself heavily promoted by the SBP, by channelling government payments through the branchless banking network. These payments, such as compensation to internally displaced people and, later, income support payments through the state's flagship social safety net programme, reached millions of recipients over the ensuing years.[130] Despite this, deposit statistics in general, and the use of 'mobile wallets' more specifically, remained low.[131] Regulatory revisions to branchless banking were issued in 2011 in order to relax regulation and thereby increase the use of mobile phone deposit facilities.[132] These measures were accompanied by a financial literacy programme, launched in 2012, which sought to encourage those 'underbanked' as well as 'unbanked' to engage with the formal banking sector.[133]

Other measures targeted the role of the interest rate in the economy. In 2010, the SBP mandated commercial banks to offer investor portfolio securities (IPS) accounts to customers. These accounts were designed by the SBP for the commercial banking sector and offer investment in government securities through the convenience of a bank account. The IPS account endeavoured to both draw cash back into the banking sector by offering an improved return, while enhancing the knowledge and relevance of the SBP's policy rate amongst the public in order to improve the transmission of the policy rate through the economy.[134]

In 2013, the floor on interest rates on savings deposits was revised, abandoning the promise of the interest rate floor as a temporary measure and pegging the return to the policy rate.[135] On the credit side, the SBP sought to increase private sector credit by issuing a series of programmes that offered subsidised credit to various target sectors of private business. The SBP had offered special financing conditions for machinery upgrades in the agricultural sector in 2009 and in 2010 it issued a Credit Guarantee Scheme, by which the central bank shares the risk of lending to small and rural enterprises with commercial banks.[136] Indeed, the decline in lending to small and medium enterprises (SMEs) had been much greater than the overall decline in credit to the private sector. As credit to the private sector tumbled between 2007 and 2011, credit to SMEs within the shrinking portfolios of private sector credit at banks halved.[137] A Microfinance Strategy was launched in 2011, which focused on improved borrowing.[138] This led to the revision of regulation to support SME lending in 2013. A further SME programme, the 'PM Youth Loan Scheme', was launched in 2013,[139] as well as the Export Finance Facility, which mandated commercial banks to offer concessional conditions and interest rates on long-term loans to exporters.[140]

The Low Interest Rate Experiment

Yet the boldest move made by the SBP to arrest disintermediation was the low interest rate experiment that it undertook in 2012. By this time, the 2008 loan from the IMF had been prematurely terminated due to the state's inability to implement a series of unpopular reforms, including reform of electricity subsidies and of the tax system.[141] Free of IMF conditionality demanding high interest rates, the SBP was able to experiment with new approaches. The SBP struck out on a low interest rate path, dropping rates from over 13 per cent to almost 8 per cent over a year and a half and including two leaps of 150 basis points (bps).

The new, low interest rate environment attempted to address the collapse in intermediation by tackling competitiveness in the banking sector. For the SBP, the root issue of the decline in intermediation was the lack of competitiveness in the banking sector, fed by the ample, low risk and high profit supply of government debt that was being held by the banking sector.[142] By dropping interest rates, the SBP could at once reduce the burden of debt servicing on government finances and force the banks back into retail intermediation to supplement lower profits on government debt. At the same time, it was expected that private sector lending demand would rise in response to lower rates. It was hoped that this, combined with the fortified floor on savings deposits, would lead to increases in both deposits and loans. By enhancing the role of the interest rate in the economy and enhancing the SBP's capacity to track economic and financial change for constructing policy targets, recovering bank intermediation could support stronger monetary policy transmission.

The low interest rate experiment endorsed the conventional approach to monetary policy insofar as it focused on the banking sector in its efforts to strengthen transmission. Yet it also posed a head-on challenge to conventional policy by effectively contesting the conventional relationship between interest rates and inflation. With inflation back over 10 per cent in 2011, the SBP effectively declared lower interest rates to be non-inflationary. Citing SBP research[143] that found inflation was rooted not in the interest rate on rupees, but more importantly in key prices in the economy such as fuel, electricity, wheat and the exchange rate (which is itself a proxy for global prices on key commodities), the SBP argued that low interest rates would address disintermediation without posing a threat of higher inflation (SBP 2013f).[144] This position poses a radical break with inflation targeting convention by denying the efficacy of the interest rate as a policy lever, despite the apparently contradictory commitment that the SBP maintained (and continues to maintain) to moving towards a comprehensive regime of inflation targeting. As discussed further in later chapters, the proposition that lower interest rates will not fuel inflation effectively denies the rupee the status of complete money. The insignificance of the interest rate to inflation was tentatively posed at first but became increasingly explicit.[145]

Persisting Low Deposits

Inflation did indeed drop sharply over these years, but the same policy success could not be claimed of the low interest rate experiment with regard to bank intermediation. The SBP's various support schemes for private sector deposits and credit continued unabated, yet by 2014, private sector credit was down to just 15 per cent of GDP, half of what it had been in 2007. On the deposit side, improvements were posted after 2011, but even by 2014 they had not regained their 2007 levels.[146]

Survey data over these years portrayed a decline in the use of deposit facilities to match the abysmal performance of private sector credit. The World Bank's Global Findex survey found that the number of adults with accounts at financial institutions actually dropped from 10.3 per cent to 8.7 per cent between 2011 (which was already a low base) and 2014.[147] Similarly, the Financial Inclusion Insight survey found that the percentage of respondents who actively used bank accounts had dropped from 7 per cent to 6 per cent between 2013 and 2014 (FII

2015: 11). In 2014, the Findex survey found that, although some one-third of the population save, only 3 per cent do so in a formal financial institution. On the credit side, although almost half of the adult population borrows, only 1.5 per cent use formal financial institutions.[148]

At the same time, the failure of branchless banking to attract deposits was being raised by industry commentators, who lamented the overwhelming reliance on agent-assisted full cash withdrawals of branchless banking transfers rather than the upkeep of 'mobile wallets'.[149] This prompted further relaxation of regulations over small deposit facilities (primarily around 'Know Your Customer' regulations) in an effort to make deposit accounts more attractive to the public. In 2015, 'basic banking accounts', which had been launched in 2005 but received little uptake,[150] were repackaged as *'asaan* accounts' (*asaan* translates from Urdu into English as 'simple'). These new 'simple' accounts offer lower documentary requirements on what was already a fee-free account with no minimum ongoing balance and free withdrawals. Similar reductions in regulation were made on 'mobile wallets' in 2016.[151]

These same years saw a resurgence in the informal economy that could explain some of the drop off in deposits. Yet at the same time, growing informality in the economy also implies that declining deposit statistics are, in fact, more severe than statistics suggest. Currency in circulation had doubled between 2011 and 2015,[152] contributing to mounting evidence of significant growth in the informal sector.[153] In 2015, the SBP reported that the informal economy more generally was growing faster than the formal economy and that informal credit markets were 'vibrant' (Ministry of Finance/SBP 2015: vii, 10).

Growing informality and declining bank intermediation suggest that the formal banking sector is losing ground to informal financial service providers through irregular financial instruments. Moreover, the decline and stagnation of deposits is even more severe than statistics suggest if it is occurring not in the conditions of slow but steady recovery that formal GDP statistics suggest, but in the buoyant economic conditions that are implied by huge informal sector growth.[154]

In any case, where a growing informal sector may induce a decline in deposits if businesses seek to hide undocumented wealth, the same logic does not apply to small deposits held by individuals. And yet, despite the huge push for financial inclusion undertaken by the SBP, statistics suggest that small deposits have in fact declined significantly. Deposits of less than 50,000 rupees in 2015 terms (about four months of the average wage) have decreased by some 25 per cent on their 1995 levels.[155] Even if the entire 60 billion rupees deposited in private microfinance banks is included in this figure, a drop of between 10 and 15 per cent remains in small deposits between 1995 and 2015. Neither have the NSS or postal savings seen an increase since the 1990s. As a percentage of GDP, postal savings stood at 0.7 per cent in 2015, just short of their 1992 levels. NSS holdings stand at 10 per cent, as compared to 18 per cent in 1990.[156]

This significant decline in small deposits is particularly striking given the decline in head-count poverty over these years and the huge growth in workers' remittances. One of few 'good news stories' over these years, remittances grew from a value of around US$4 billion in the mid-2000s to almost US$20 billion by 2015.[157] The boom in remittance flows has driven down poverty rates yet has not been reflected in deposit statistics. According to World Bank data, there were over 9 million more people earning over US$3.10 per day in 2013 as compared to 1996.[158] The US$3.10 benchmark is certainly not an income that could be considered too low for savings practices to be occurring, as the seminal contribution of Daryl Collins and colleagues show in their extensive field-based study 'Portfolios of the Poor'.[159] In fact, US$3.10 per day is about equivalent to the average wage in manufacturing and construction in Pakistan and is much higher than average wages in the agricultural sector.[160]

Described by the World Bank as the 'Pakistan enigma',[161] the slow pace of financial inclusion in Pakistan poses a consistent puzzle to conventional analysis: small deposits have not increased – despite huge efforts on the part of the SBP and the international community, despite the growing ranks of the population living above the poverty line, and despite the huge growth of incoming remittances. Adding to this is the upswing in macro indicators after 2013. GDP growth had tracked steady improvement since 2010 and the World Bank's 2012 prediction of firm recovery over the coming year[162] had materialised by 2014. The external account stabilised, foreign exchange reserves posted a significant improvement and the rupee strengthened. Yet combining steadily improving formal macro indicators with evidence of a buoyant informal economy in which jobs and growth were being generated suggests that even the low figures of official deposit and lending statistics as a percentage of GDP are overinflated.

The financial inclusion agenda frames low levels of small deposits as a problem of access to the financial system for the poor. From this perspective, the poor are not discouraged from financial inclusion by the interest rate environment, given that the poor are known to access informal deposit and credit services that leave a significant margin for informal dealers. Rather, the problem is conventionally understood to be that financial products fail to meet the needs of the poor on issues like documentation and the small amounts of money that the poor deal in. Addressing these kinds of issues has clearly been a key objective of the central bank in its vociferous efforts to enhance banking sector engagement.

Answering to the needs of the non-poor, however, who may be more sensitive to the return on deposits, has also been an important central bank policy response to the persistent low levels of deposits in the banking system. Yet the predicament of disintermediation and low deposit rates specifically can also be framed not as a problem of interest rates providing too low a return or banking products being too inconvenient, but as the consequence of money and finance having moved elsewhere. As taken up in later chapters, disintermediation may, in fact, reflect a more nuanced rejection of the rupee as money and thus a deep-seated set of problems for money, the monetary environment and monetary governance. Here the predicament faced by the financial inclusion agenda comes into view.

Conclusion: A New Economy of Instability and Opacity

No longer a low-inflation economy, the Pakistani economy has become characterised by monetary instability, encompassing the exchange value of the rupee and its interest rate, as well as the key prices that give everyday meaning to the usefulness of the rupee as money. These kinds of issues were already in evidence in the mid-1990s, when inflation surged and poverty rose as prices were set to float on the market. As the decade closed, the float of the currency itself was soon to be achieved. With this milestone, an increasingly familiar set of policy issues became recurring themes. Later chapters draw on the history of the rupee recounted here and argue that these persistent tensions between openness and stability reveal a more fundamental set of problems for money and the monetary environment in Pakistan than a conventional reading suggests. As the final chapter shows, a conventional reading consequently misreads the predicament of financial inclusion in Pakistan in significant ways.

This chapter has explored the dynamics by which liberalisation has driven a new volatility in the money and prices of Pakistan's new economy. Although rarely articulated as issues of monetary governance, the state's persistent hesitancy around the release of key commodity prices to market dynamics implicitly reveals policy recognition of the link between key commodity prices and instability in money and the economy at large. This concern was given voice in the justification of the low interest rate experiment in 2012. By dropping interest rates at the same time as seeking lower inflation, the SBP denied the anchoring role of interest rates and pointed to the significance of key commodities in inflation dynamics. This recognition of crucial shortcomings in the capacity of the rupee to anchor the economy effectively eschews the inflation targeting strategy that the SBP has pursued before and since.

The significance to the monetary environment of those commodities that carry anchoring attributes, over and above their impact on the central bank's capacity to manage money, is returned to in Chapters 6, 7 and 8. For now, the point is that the efficacy of monetary governability has been cast into doubt as anchoring problems have become increasingly obvious. That is, the years since liberalisation have been characterised by the SBP's struggles to limit the carry through of global price volatilities in commodities and dampen volatility in the rupee on exchange markets in its efforts to harness the rupee as a policy lever under open markets.

Yet monetary conditions are not only much more volatile in the post-liberalisation period, but the monetary environment has also become much more opaque. As informality in money and in markets has blossomed, the weight of instability and opacity, as argued in later chapters, has fed uncertainty. Drawing on the description of the rupee and its liberalisation undertaken here, later chapters develop the proposition first outlined in Chapter 2, that instability and opacity in the rupee undermines the trust upon which state money is dependent.

This chapter has shown that the central bank is putting a great deal of policy attention into enhancing the governability of the rupee – not least through efforts to expand financial inclusion – in the face of a multi-faceted assault on monetary policy transmission: from the collapse of statistical reliability, to the carry through of interest rates, the evidence of alternative non-rupee anchors, and the unknowable extent of dollar and other non-rupee liquidity in the economy. Later chapters develop a reading of this predicament that contrasts with conventional analysis by recognising the possibility of rupee contestation. By this reading, disintermediation is less an issue of interest rates being too high or financial products that are inconvenient to their users, and more a question of monetary contestation. Here we face the critical contradiction entailed in the financial inclusion agenda, which pivots on the valorisation of the rupee as a risk management tool in the midst of a monetary environment that detracts in crucial ways from the soundness of state money. In these conditions, later chapters argue, financial inclusion is drawn into the central bank's toolkit not as a tool of poverty alleviation but as a tool of rupee governance.

For this possibility to be explored, we must now turn to an examination of how the contestation of money might be recognised in patterns of money use amongst the local population. Informal foreign exchange markets, with which the infamous *hawala* trade is intimately tied, have become a key outward expression of the disruption of state money in Pakistan. Yet any number of alternatives to local state or foreign exchange money may in fact be thriving where state money itself has become compromised and central bank control over state money contested. In these circumstances, the state's attachment to money is opened up to question and the potential for non-state money use arises as a salient potential marker of monetary change.

Notes

1. The developmental state model entails strong state intervention and extensive regulation and state planning that is directed towards rapid industrial development. See Naseemullah and Arnold (2015) and Zaidi (2015) for a discussion of how Pakistan fit this definition prior to liberalisation and especially in the 1960s.

2. For a thorough review of the economy over the period, see Zaidi (2015), and for conditions relating more specifically to money and banking, see Meenai and Ansari (2010).

3. See Dorosh and Salam (2007: 10) and Salam and Mukhtar (2008: 84).

4. See Chowdhury (1969), Ministry of Finance (2001) and Meenai and Ansari (2010).

5. See Hasan et al. (1995), Zaidi (2005: 293) and Hamid, Nabi and Nasim (1990: 17).

6. See, for example, Hamid, Nabi and Nasim (1990: 22), Nabi (1997) and Dorosh and Salam (2007).

7. As well as Hamid, Nabi and Nasim (1990), see Zaidi (2015) for a comprehensive analysis of the macroeconomic history of Pakistan.

8. On foreign exchange management, see Mirakhor and Zaidi (2004). See also Meenai and Ansari (2010).

9. See especially Chowdhury (1969) and Ministry of Finance (2001).

10. See Chowdhury (1969) and Islam (1972).

11. See Chaudhry and Sahibzada (1995), Salam (2001, 2012) and Dorosh et al. (2016).

12. See Meenai and Ansari (2010), Zaidi (2005: 284), Hamid, Nabi and Nasim (1990) and Salam and Mukhtar (2008).

13. The 1970s were a particularly difficult time in Pakistan, with civil war leading to the independence of Bangladesh, formerly East Pakistan, in 1971, and a military coup in 1977 leading to the state execution of former prime minister Zulfikar Ali Bhutto in 1979.

14. The persistently restricted nature of the economy is reflected in the World Bank's assessment in 1988 that, despite some reform efforts, the Pakistani economy continued to exhibit a bias towards import substitution (World Bank in Zaidi 2005: 173). See also Mohsin Khan in Zaidi (2005: 344).

15. See Hamid, Nabi and Nasim (1990: 22).

16. That is, economic management was redesigned away from the previous approach to controlling the build-up of current account deficits through direct controls (for example, through issuing limited import licences) to letting the rupee float under the assumption that demand for imports would drop off as imports became relatively more expensive when the rupee devaluated due to high current account deficits.

17. See especially Zaidi (2005: 440).

18. See Mahmood (1999) and WTO (1995).

19. See World Bank (2006) and Nasir (2012).

20. See Hasan et al. (1995), Zaidi (2005: 293) and Hamid, Nabi and Nasim (1990: 17).

21. Zaidi (2005). See also Gera (2007), Mahmood (2012) and Nasir (2012).

22. See Sayeed and Abbasi (2015), also Arby (2004).

23. See Akhtar (2006, 2007), Meenai and Ansari (2010: 85), Sayeed and Abbasi (2015: 8) and Ministry of Finance (2015: 122). Also, M. A. Choudhary, interviewed by the author, Karachi, 20 May 2016.

24. See H. A. Khan (2012).

25. See Mirakhor and Zaidi (2004).

26. That is, the Authorised Money Changers system provided a legal framework within which small companies that exchange rupee cash for foreign exchange could operate, although these small firms were excluded from legally participating in the remittance trade. See Meenai and Ansari (2010: 185) and Siddiqui (2014: 88).

27. See Khan and Burki (2005).

28. This is notably the case with cotton, which is key to the textiles industry. See Salam (2009).

29. See M. H. Khan (1994), Faruqee and Colemand (1996), Mustafa, Malik and Sharif (2001), Salam (2001), Salam and Mukhtar (2008).

30. See Mahmood (1999: 16) and WTO (1995).

31. See Parish (2006) for a comprehensive analysis of the ADB's engagement in the power sector in Pakistan.

32. See Chaudhry and Sahibzada (1995) and Ahmad et al. (2006).

33. See World Bank (2006).

34. A detailed review of the IPP project can be found in Fraser (2005).

35. As Fraser explains, there were a number of developments behind the financial difficulties experienced at this time at the Water and Power Development Authority, which pays the IPPs for the power that they put into the grid. Two key issues were inflation, which made tariff setting more difficult, and rupee depreciation, which made the US dollar indexed payments to the IPPs more expensive than envisioned. See Fraser (2005).

36. See Haider, Ahmed and Jawed (2014: 497) and Hasan et al. (1995). For examples, see Hossain (1990) and Nasim (1995).

37. See Salam (2001: 5, 2016) and Dorosh and Salam (2006).

38. For example, see Haider, Ahmed and Jawed (2014), Khan and Ahmed (2014) and Hanif, Iqbal and Khan (2016).

39. See, for example, Abbas, Beg and Choudhary (2015) and M. Khan (2015).

40. Government transfers (such as IMF payments) are conducted outside of the foreign exchange markets, through SBP reserves. These payments, however, indirectly affect the exchange rate because they function as a key indicator for speculative sentiments (see Khalid 2014: 5). The relationship between reserves and speculative pressure on the exchange rate explains the link between IMF payments and the exchange rate that is standard in Exchange Rate chapters in SBP Annual Reports and in the business press.

The same applies to oil payments during periods where they have been transferred onto the books of the SBP to minimise pressure on the foreign exchange markets (see, for example, SBP 2005b: 135; SBP 2007: 147).

41. For example, the liberalisation of foreign exchange allows access to foreign exchange cash and foreign exchange bank accounts, which offer venues for holding positions that effectively 'bet' against the rupee. Another example pertains to the liberalisation of trade, with which those involved in the import and export trade can hold out on processing foreign receipts in expectation of a favourable shift in the exchange rate.

42. More specifically, the Standby Agreement abolished the explicit exchange rate band that had helped to stabilise the rupee as it moved towards a free float. At the same time, IMF demands relating to reserve adequacy limited the ability of the central bank to buffer exchange rate volatility by drawing down reserves through foreign exchange intervention. The SBP was therefore forced to raise interest rates and implement a series of measures that attempted to reduce the speculative pressure that was bearing down on the rupee. See SBP (2001a: 158).

43. See, for example, SBP (2001a: 157, 2007: 146, 2006: 151).

44. See respectively SBP (2007: 124) and SBP (2005a: 152).

45. For details of the *hawala* trade in Pakistan, see Khalid (2014) and Siddiqui (2014). A detailed examination of *hawala* focusing on Afghanistan is offered by Thompson (2011). See also El-Qorchi, Maibo and Wilson (2003).

46. That is, if the SBP had have purchased the required dollars on the formal exchange market, the surge of demand for the dollar and excess supply of the rupee that would have been generated by the exchange would materialise as a sharp decline in the value of the rupee in the formal market. By purchasing dollars on the informal market, exchange rate effects of large US dollar purchases could be circumvented altogether, since the exchange rate in the informal market is not a published, official rate.

47. The concern here is about state support for a multiple exchange rate system and is articulated in the IMF's Articles of Agreement, which strives for a unified exchange rate. See IMF (2001).

48. SBP (2004b).

49. SBP (2001a: 160).

50. Ibid., 159.

51. Ibid., 158.

52. See Mirakhor and Zaidi (2004).

53. Pakistan did, in fact, default in late 1998, but the default was relatively contained due to Pakistan's compliance with creditor restructuring. Pakistan missed an interest payment in November 1998 but rectified the payment within the grace period. When default occurred again shortly thereafter, conditional restructuring was undertaken. See Moody's Investors Services (2012).

54. For example, see IMF (2001: 20).

55. This is reflected in the local press. See, for example, The News (2011), Dawn (2013), and Miraj (2015).

56. On the history of *hawala*, see Thompson (2011) and Siddiqui (2014).

57. See Kar (2010).

58. See Khalid (2014).

59. That is, if remittances flow through formal markets then they appreciate the rupee because they materialize as a purchase of rupees for foreign exchange in the market in which the exchange rate is recognised by official sources. This also strengthens the national accounts by improving the current account, itself a key indicator for credit rating agencies and other commentators (note that remittances are recorded on the current account, not the capital account, in Pakistan).

60. On the SBP's use of monetary aggregates, see Khan and Hussain (2005) and Jan, Haider and Hyder (2013).

61. The scale of this netting out is potentially very large indeed given the scale of remittance flows into Pakistan as well as the scale of illegal capital flight out of Pakistan, which does not necessarily net out by being sent to the same market from which remittance flows originate. See El-Qorchi, Maibo and Wilson (2003), Siddiqui (2014) and Khalid (2014). Edwina Thompson's in-depth research on *hawala* in Afghanistan involves a series of examples of the very complex ways in which *hawala* transactions are netted out across networks of dealers and through a whole series of formal and informal transactions (Thompson 2013).

62. For some examples of this pressure, see SBP (2003: 147), Aazim (2003) and SBP (2005b: 152, 2007: 146).

63. See, for example, Lopez-Acevedo and Robertson (2012).

64. Eurobonds are bonds issued in foreign currency, in this case Pakistani government bonds denominated and paid in US dollars. Eurobonds signal confidence in the issuer, given that these entail much more risk because the state is not able to 'print' the currency in which the bond must be repaid.

65. See SBP (2013a: 91)

66. See World Bank (2014b). On FDI flows, see Khan and Khan (2011).

67. See SBP (2006: 142, 2007: 123).

68. See IMF (2006).

69. See IMF (2005: 15).

70. Ministry of Finance (2008: vi). See also Akhtar (2007).

71. See, for example, Burki (2007).

72. On the government's concerns around commodity price liberalisation, see Faruqee and Colemand (1996).

73. Support price programmes pertained to crops including wheat, rice, cotton, sugarcane, potato, onion, gram, sunflower, soybeans and canola. See Salam (2001).

74. See ADB (2010) for details.

75. See Khan and Burki (2005) and Salam and Mukhtar (2008).

76. See Kinder (2010: 6).

77. See, for example, ADB (2014).

78. See World Bank (2003) and (ADB 2014: 12).

79. See World Bank (2003).

80. See Kessides (2013: 274).

81. See, for example, Naqvi et al. (1994) and Hasan et al. (1995).

82. This is spelled out in a World Bank discussion paper by Faruqee and Colemand (1996).

83. See SBP (2007: 146).

84. On the persistence of concern over speculative pressure, see Hamid, Nabi and Nasim (1990) and Zaidi (2015); on the shift of oil payments onto the SBP's books, see SBP (2004a: 26, 2005b: 135).

85. While this strategy was deemed to be helpful for quelling speculative pressure (SBP 2007: 147), it was not an entirely successful solution. Putting oil payments onto the SBP's books shifted the shock of large payments on to reserves, which generate their own speculative dynamics (Khalid 2014: 5).

86. See Zaidi (2015: 536); see, for example, Sayeed and Abbasi (2015: 13).

87. See SBP (2007: 154, 2005a: 178).

88. See, for example, SBP (2005a: 181).

89. See SBP (2007: 171).

90. For example, SBP (2007: 75), Ul Haque (2011) and Sayeed and Abbasi (2015).

91. See Khwaja, Mian and Zia (2008).

92. See Ul Haque (2011) and SBP (2005a: 163).

93. See SBP (2005a: 160, 2006: 143, 2007: 124).

94. See, for example, M. Z. Khan (2013).

95. See Asghar (2012).

96. See SBP (2005b: 129).

97. See A. A. Usmani (2003). See also Siddiqui (2014).

98. See Khalid (2014).

99. See SBP (2007: 146).

100. See, for example, Ul Haque (2010) and SBP (2012: 86).

101. See UNCTAD (2012b: 49) and Cheng and Xiong (2014).

102. Central bank borrowing refers to the government's use of the central bank to fund its own debt. Otherwise known as 'monetising government debt', using the central bank as a funding stream for government expenditure is conventionally understood to be highly inflationary. This because it equates to 'printing' money (that is, producing new money) to distribute in the economy through government spending, rather than borrowing from the public by selling bonds (which takes existing money out of the economy). Although the inflationary implications of central bank borrowing are disputed

by Post-Keynesian economists, central bank borrowing is fiercely disapproved of by the IMF and has been one of a series of problem issues in negotiations between the IMF and Pakistan.

103. See SBP (2008a: 57, 2009a).

104. See, for example, Pesnani, Saleem and Rahooja (2008: 8).

105. See SBP (2008a: 107).

106. See Rafique (2015). See also Fair and Watson (2015).

107. That is, increasing evidence was coming to light that parts of the Pakistani military were supporting the Taliban at the same time as it was collecting funding from the United States and its allies for fighting the Taliban. A useful historical reference to this enduring issue is provided by Rashid (2000). On concerns being raised in the United States, see, for example, Jones (2007) and Fair (2008).

108. See SBP (2007: 119).

109. See, for example, SBP (2011b: 113, 2014: 117).

110. See Sayeed and Abbasi (2015).

111. See Hyder (2012) and Nasir (2012).

112. See P. I. Rana (2008).

113. See Settle (2012).

114. See Amjad, Arif and Irfan (2011) and Qureshi (2016).

115. See SBP (2009a: 165).

116. Ostensibly a guarantee of multi-year aid designed to increase aid to parts of the Pakistani economy that lie outside of the military, the Kerry-Luger Bill stepped up accountability over how US aid money could be spent. The Bill faced severe criticism from Pakistan's Army chief, who deemed it 'insulting' (The News 2009a), amidst broad criticism of the bill in Pakistan as patronizing and belittling of Pakistan's sovereignty. See, for example, The News (2009b).

117. In the years to come, the US–Pakistan relationship only became increasingly fraught, with stern rhetoric and insistent condemnation declared in the public domain on both sides. The United States withheld and cut off aid on a number of occasions over the following years. This persisted up through 2015 and beyond, when Coalition Support Funds were withheld because of Pakistan's failure to clamp down on the terrorist group known as the 'Haqqani network' (Syed 2015, 2016). The Pakistanis, for their part, sent US troops stationed on Pakistani soil home at one point, and closed off the NATO supply route from Karachi to Kabul for some seven months at another. A key flashpoint in deteriorating Pakistan–US relations after 2008 included the US seizure of Osama bin Laden in 2011, who was found apparently living under the protection of the Pakistani army across the road from an army base in the garrison town of Abbotabad. Another such incident was the accidental killing of 24 Pakistani military personnel by US air fire, also in 2011.

118. This concern is raised by Mishra and Montiel (2012) in their review of monetary policy transmission in low-income countries.

119. This argument is made at the research department of the SBP itself. See Choudhary, Naeem, et al. (2011).

120. See Mahmood in Sayeed and Abbasi (2015: 24).

121. See Kharal (2012).

122. See SBP (2010a: 135, 2009a: 165, 2009e: 76).

123. SBP (2009a:168).

124. See El-Qorchi, Maibo and Wilson (2003) and Thompson (2011).

125. Mohammad Hanif Akhai, interviewed by the author, Karachi, 20 May 2016.

126. The PRI makes payments to formal sector banks and exchange companies that effectively subsidise remittance transfers in an effort to make formal sector prices of remittance transfers more attractive to remittance senders and receivers than informal transfers. For details, see Qureshi (2016). See also Amjad, Irfan and Arif (2013).

127. These statistics are taken from the World Bank's Global Financial Development database.

128. This includes sharia compliant 'profit and loss' accounts. See SBP (2009b: 169–71).

129. See SBP (2008b: 70).

130. The Benazir Income Support Programme is Pakistan's premier cash transfer programme. It reaches over 5 million beneficiaries with a monthly payment of 1,500 rupees (around US$14). See www.bisp.gov.pk. For details on the routing of government payments through the branchless banking network, see Pasricha and Revzi (2013).

131. See FII (2015).

132. See SBP (2011d).

133. Details about the financial literacy programme are available under the 'financial inclusion' tab on the SBP's website www.sbp.org.

134. Choudhary, interview, 20 May 2016. See also SBP (2010c).

135. See SBP (2013e).

136. See respectively SBP (2009c, 2009d) and SBP (2011a: 54).

137. See Ministry of Finance/SBP (2015: vi).

138. See SBP (2011c).

139. See respectively SBP (2013d) and SBP (2013c).

140. See SBP (2013b)

141. see Hyder (2012).

142. See, for example, SBP (2013f: 37), A. S. Khan (2014) and Choudhary, Khan, et al. (2016).

143. Specifically Choudhary, Naeem, et al. (2011).

144. Also Choudhary, interview, 20 May 2016.

145. Compare, for example, SBP (2012: 59) to Abbas, Beg and Choudhary (2015), M. Khan (2015) and Hanif, Iqbal and Khan (2016).

146. These figures are taken from the indicators 'bank deposits to GDP (%)' and 'domestic credit to the private sector (% of GDP)' in the World Bank's Global Financial Development Database, available at www.data.worldbank.org (World Bank 2014b).

147. This indicator, coded in the Findex database as 'account at a financial institution', contrasts with the indicator coded as 'account'. The 'account' indicator plots an increase from 10 per cent to 13 per cent between 2011 and 2014. However, the 'account' indicator is inconsistent across the survey years insofar as it includes mobile accounts in the question in the 2014 survey but not in 2011 survey. Moreover, the SBP notes, in its Branchless Banking Newsletter from October 2014 (available at sbp.org.pk), that the bulk of mobile accounts in 2014 were inactive. Hence, the 'account at a financial institution' indicator is used here. See World Bank (2014b).

148. See the World Bank's Global Financial Inclusion Database (World Bank 2014a).

149. See, for example, FII (2015), Kafeel (2015) and Kumar and Radcliffe (2015).

150. See Nenova, Niang and Ahmad (2009).

151. See respectively SBP (2015b) and SBP (2016).

152. Currency in circulation went from 1.5 trillion in June 2011 to 2.9 trillion in December 2015. See SBP Monetary Statistics available at www.sbp.org.pk.

153. See, for example, Zaidi (2015: 814).

154. Note that the deposit statistics quoted earlier are as a percentage of GDP, which is the most common way of presenting deposit statistics because it is the easiest way to make deposits comparable over multiple years and between countries (unless, as is evident in Pakistan, those GDP statistics are not reliable).

155. The comparison of deposits over time is calculated by the author to adjust scheduled banks' deposits categorised by size to the SBP's consumer price index (CPI). Note that this includes federal and provincial microfinance banks but not private microfinance banks. When calibrated to CPI, deposits of less than 50,000 rupees in 2015 are comparable to deposits of less than 10,000 rupees in 1995. The aggregate amount in deposits of these comparable sizes are then adjusted to CPI. In constant 2015 rupees then, this calculation produces a drop from just over 550 billion rupees in 1995 to around 410 billion rupees in 2015. Deposit by size statistics for 2015 are taken from chapter 3.5 of the SBP's Monthly Statistical Bulletin for February 2016; and for 1995, from chapter 4.3 the SBP's Banking Statistics of Pakistan 2004–5, both available at ffwww.spb.pk.org. Average wage data can be found in the Pakistan Bureau of Statistics' Labour Force Survey at www.pbs.gov.pk.

156. With a huge network of offices offering a series of financial services including deposit facilities for small savers, Pakistan Post has been seen as an important potential venue for financial inclusion, especially in remote areas (Nenova, Niang and Ahmad 2009: 86). Similarly, the NSS has long served small savers with bond-like products issued directly by the government, although data on NSS holdings amongst small savers is complicated by the openness of the scheme to institutional investors for certain periods.

Postal and NSS statistics are available in the SBP's M3 monetary statistics (available at www.sbp.org.pk) and have been calibrated by the author against official GDP statistics.

157. These statistics are taken from World Bank data. However and as argued above, statistics of remittance flows are particularly vulnerable to misreporting.

158. The World Bank calculates a poverty headcount ratio at US$3.10 (2011 purchasing power parity), which produces a figure for the percentage of the population living below US$3.10, at 60.5 per cent in 1996 and 36.9 per cent in 2013. The 9 million figure referred to here is arrived at by calibrating this data against population statistics, which suggests that 67 million people lived below the US$3.10 benchmark in 2013 as compared to 76 million in 1998. These data are taken from the World Bank's World Development Indicators available at www.data.worldbank.org.

159. Collins and colleagues show that those living on less than US$2 per day engage in complex financial practices, including considerable saving (Collins et al. 2009).

160. The equivalence noted here is calculated using the average exchange rate for 2011 to convert the US$3.10 rate, itself in 2011 dollars, into a monthly figure, which is compared with sectoral wages that are taken from the 2010–11 Labour Force Survey, available at www.pbs.gov.pk. The monthly figure comes to just over 8,000 rupees, higher than the average wage in agriculture, which is around 5,500 rupees, and just below the average wages for construction and manufacturing, at 8,272 and 8,472 rupees per month respectively.

161. See the blog entry 'Pakistan Enigma: Why Is Financial Inclusion Happening So Slowly?' written by Stephen Rasmussen on the CGAP (Consultative Group to Assist the Poor) site. CGAP is a partnership of private, public and multilateral development organisations housed at and administered by the World Bank. It is a major player in the financial inclusion landscape in Pakistan. The same concern of uptake by the public incongruent with the state's huge efforts to promote financial inclusion is raised in the Financial Inclusion Strategy, which was released by the Ministry of Finance and the SBP in 2015.

162. See World Bank (2012a).

4

Exploring Monetary Change amongst Households

Chapters 1, 2 and 3 explored increasing complication in the monetary environment. In Chapters 1 and 2, monetary change was depicted in terms of how traditional norms and theories by which state money is understood as money – its conditions of creation, its reliability, its pliability and plausibility as a policy object, its role amidst the myriad of financial instruments and its capacity to fulfil the traditional functions of money more generally – is being challenged by globalised markets. In Chapter 2, this was accompanied by a mapping of the monetary environment in the specific context of a frontier economy. Emphasising the importance of perceptions of stability, this mapping delineated economy-wide foundations on which trust in money stands and in which monetary contestation may conceivably arise. This framework served to inform the history of the rupee recounted in Chapter 3, which emphasised growing uncertainty within the monetary environment by drawing out instability, informality and increasingly visible anchoring issues as the post-liberalisation period progressed. These chapters have thus set out a macroeconomic context in which state money is revealed as suffering a deficit in the stability and reliability that credible money demands. This predicament suggests a potential reallocation of state money from its classic Keynesian function of the risk-free asset, to a subject of risk management, a reading that is consistent with Pakistan's 'enigma' of slow progress in financial inclusion (Rasmussen 2018).

Drawing the focus down to the level of microanalysis, the next two chapters shift the focus onto ordinary people and their utilisation of money in the everyday economy. This chapter lays out the terms in which household money use is explored in the study and Chapter 5 applies these terms through a household survey. At issue is the identification of changing money use patterns that might reflect the shifting status of the rupee from risk-free asset to subject-of-risk, and thus point towards everyday acts of monetary contestation that might reveal the kind of distrust in money that is so central to sociological theories of money.[1] If changes in daily economic transactions – amongst households and in bazaars – can be identified in connection with financial conditions that have undergone change with the liberalisation of money and markets, then substantive meaning attached to the liberalisation of money on the ground, amongst ordinary Pakistanis, can be pinpointed. Rather than an abstract proposition of meaning, a focus on daily practices brings the everyday impacts of liberalisation into relief, thereby translating the abstract notion of financial inclusion into the everyday economic experience of ordinary people. This chapter sets out the terms in which the study bridges the abstraction of theoretical and policy debate to carry the analysis of state money and its usefulness into the domain of the mundane transactions of everyday life. In order to do this, the chapter turns to finance theory.

The chapter builds an analytical apparatus for interrogating monetary change at the level of the household by drawing on notions of risk and risk management that have been developed in finance theory. Specifically, finance theory identifies risk as a cost, and draws on notions of liquidity and diversification in identifying risk management practices. This chapter explores how these ideas, and the balance sheet thinking that finance theory is built upon, can be applied to households in order to explore the experience of monetary risk in the everyday economy so as to link the broader theoretical analysis of money in Pakistan and everyday money transactions. As demonstrated in its application in Chapter 5, this approach facilitates an assessment of the riskiness of money and explores the inverse of trust in money – that is, monetary contestation – in an analytical framework that is grounded in the empirics of money use.

The second part of the chapter then sets out a full mapping of the study's theoretical structure. Here the finance theory that guides the household-level analysis in this chapter is set alongside the framing of instability, uncertainty and monetary contestation that serves the macro analysis undertaken in Chapters 2 and 3. This, in turn, is set out in terms of Keynesian monetary theory, which designates state money as the safe asset and provides the foundational definition of money that is relied on throughout the study. This chapter is consequently the key theoretical chapter for the book as a whole insofar as it maps out how each level of analysis – from the heights of global finance, to the dilemmas of macroeconomic management, to the everyday use of money amongst ordinary, generally poor, households – fit together in a distinct analytical frame. It is within this framework that Chapters 6, 7 and 8 explore the complexity of Pakistan's frontier money and the problems that it poses for a development strategy that hinges on financial inclusion.

Principles of Finance

At the heart of the discipline of finance is risk. Although risk may be intimately linked to uncertainty, itself by definition indeterminate, interpreting the sort of monetary change associated with globalisation *as risk* gives analytical form to this change. That is, although certainly not free of its own methodological problems,[2] finance theory offers a way to calibrate and compare the impact of different instances of volatility as degrees of risk, which, in turn, are designated as costs. This approach to volatility as risk and risk as a cost is evident in asset pricing models, for example, which include a measure of an asset's volatility as an input in the calculation of the value of that asset. Finance theory also identifies practices that attempt to manage risk on the part of investors as distinct risk management strategies. This study applies these principles of finance theory to the everyday portfolios of households' economic transactions by exploring the way that volatility imposes a cost on household balance sheets and identifying where risk management strategies might be in use. These, in turn, point towards the experience of substantive financial risk.

The Cost of Risk

Finance theory most often poses risk as a problem of costs imposed by volatility. Although volatility does not capture the complexity of uncertainty in the terms of Knight, Keynes or Shackle,[3] it does offer a quantification of risk that permits comparison between different risks. This study does not seek out a dollar cost of risk through quantification, but it utilises the idea that volatility carries a cost where it is borne. By utilising the idea of volatility as a cost burden, this approach can demonstrate why risk is a problem for ordinary people.

For example, volatility imposes costs in simple balance sheet terms insofar as price volatility increases the risk of asset-liability mismatches.[4] In circumstances of volatility, a funding shortfall is more likely to arise because the value of an asset might suddenly drop or the value of a liability might increase sharply. In this situation, finance would have to be drawn from elsewhere to pay out the liability when it becomes due because the asset's value falls short. The cost of the volatility that generates the risk of under-funding here is the cost of undertaking a hedge that would neutralise that risk.

The dynamics of risk as a cost can be clearly demonstrated through a stylised example of interest rate risk born by banks. A bank exposed to interest rate volatility faces the risk of the interest rate on its short-term liabilities (its short-term borrowing) rising, which would create a funding gap by which the return on long-term lending (on the asset side, for example, mortgage lending) falls short of the new, higher cost entailed in paying out its liabilities (that is, of funding its short-term borrowing with proceeds from its long-term lending). That is, if the (short-term) interest rate on the bank's funding source unexpectedly goes up, then the bank will need to pay more to maintain its short-term borrowing even though the interest rate remains unchanged on the funding stream that the bank uses to pay out that short-term borrowing, which comes from the money paid to it by households on long-term mortgages. This interest rate risk can be hedged, for example, by purchasing an interest rate derivative that will lock in a future interest rate and thereby neutralise the threat of volatility in the interest rate. The cost of neutralising volatility in this case would be the cost of the derivative contract.

Alternatively, the bank could seek a 'matched book' hedge, by matching the maturities on the asset and liability side of the balance sheet. That is, the bank could match long-term liabilities (long-term borrowing) with long-term assets (long-term lending, such as mortgage lending). Given that long-term interest rates tend to move together across different assets, just as short-term interest rates do, any shock to the cost of borrowing in long-term markets will likely be countered by a commensurate rise in profit derived from owning a long-term asset (long-term lending). The cost of mitigating volatility in this case would be the opportunity cost[5] generated by the fact that there would usually be a lower spread (that is, profit) between long-term assets and liabilities than there would have been between long-term assets and short-term liabilities. The cost is thus the lost profit (and the lost profitable opportunities to which that profit could have been applied) from choosing a low-risk, low-profit strategy.

For a household, interest rate volatility also demands risk bearing. Interest rate volatility, for example, poses a risk that the change in the cost of servicing liabilities such as mortgage or car payments will exceed change in the value of received wages on the asset side. Similarly, volatility in wages (for example, through insecure employment contracts) threatens the value of the asset (future wages) falling short of the liability (future mortgage and car repayments), even if the liability value does not change. In this case, a hedge could be effectively purchased through the maintenance of 'precautionary balances' (savings) that could be accessed if volatility in either the future asset value or the future liability value created a funding gap. The hedging costs of volatility in this case is the opportunity cost of holding large cash savings, that is, not profiting from the commitment of that money to an investment that carries a greater return than liquid savings (the return on which is low, such as in the case of demand deposits, because they can be accessed at short notice).

In the context of Pakistan, a funding gap imposed by volatility in the household balance sheet typically arises where, for example, wheat prices rise. A higher wheat price increases the value of the household food bill (on the liability side of the balance sheet). An effective hedge could be in the shift from cash to 'in kind' wages in wheat itself (on the asset side of the balance sheet), which can then match price changes on both sides of the balance sheet (that is, a 'matched book hedge') – as the cost of wheat for consumption goes up so too does the value of wheat earned as wages. The cost of volatility in this situation lies in transaction costs related to converting in and out of wheat, the possibility of the wheat wage being less than the cash wage (which imposes an opportunity cost), and potential price changes between wheat and other prices on the balance sheet in the future.

The nature of the household balance sheet, however, limits hedging options. Unlike a company that can move in and out of different asset classes, or even liquidate its entire portfolio in the event of bankruptcy, the household cannot survive without subsistence goods, such as housing, food and transport. Effectively, this means that significant portions of the household balance sheet are illiquid, which poses considerable hurdles to the capacity of households to hedge their portfolios.[6]

Even for banks, which can undertake sophisticated statistical analysis that measures standard deviations in historical prices in order to quantify risk, not all risk arising from volatility can be hedged perfectly or even hedged at all. Here risk becomes uncertainty, its costs incalculable and its potential hedges ambiguous. Uncertainty was raised in Chapter 2 as pervasive in the frontier economy context, and explored in Chapter 3 in relation to instability and opacity in money and markets in Pakistan. It is, however, left to one side of the discussion for the time being. For the analytical frame constructed in this chapter and applied to Pakistani households in the next, we will stay within the bounds of finance theory, thereby considering money in terms of risk and leaving the question of uncertainty to be revisited in the final three chapters of the book.

Diversification and Liquidity for Risk Mitigation

Finance theory has developed a set of principles that relate to microeconomic risk management under conditions of volatility, which expand upon the kind of hedging strategies mentioned above. Two such principles from the discipline are liquidity and diversification. The theoretical developments to which these pertain, however, provide not only a useful set of risk management strategies, but also demonstrate developments in how the financial sector thinks about risk and finance. These developments in finance theory thereby make a dual contribution to the analytical framework that is developed in this chapter to examine household risk bearing. On the one hand, designation of liquidity and diversification as risk management strategies offers analytical tools for identifying risk management amongst households (which, in turn, point towards the presence of risk borne by households). On the other hand, the historical developments in finance theory to which these risk management principles pertain paint their own picture of the historical growth of risk in global financial conditions as financial flows became increasingly liberalised. These developments in finance theory thus contribute an additional facet to the story of international monetary change that was recounted in Chapter 1, which provides the big-picture frame for the consideration of the rupee and its amenability to the financial inclusion agenda.

The first of these key risk management strategies is the principle of diversification, which was first established in the Modern Portfolio Theory of the 1950s and developed further in Capital Asset Pricing Models (CAPM) in the 1960s. The key insight of portfolio theory was its conceptualisation of assets not as idiosyncratic risk profiles but as constituent components intrinsically linked to the market as a whole. This perspective views a portfolio not as a collection of individual assets but as a combination of risk-to-return profiles carefully chosen from the web of relative prices that link assets across the scope of the market. Just as constituent assets in the market as a whole are linked, the constituent assets of a portfolio are meaningful primarily in relation to one another. A shift in one asset's value thus invites coordinated adjustments in other assets in order to maintain optimality in the portfolio.

Markovitz's (1952, 1959) formulation of this perspective in Modern Portfolio Theory formalised the diversification strategies that investors were already intuitively undertaking by identifying how constituent assets in a portfolio can complement, or hedge, one another so as to offset the risk profiles of each asset in an optimal portfolio allocation. CAPM (Treynor 1961, Black and Scholes 1973) took this portfolio view a step further, identifying not individual assets' risk exposures, but market risk exposure as the locus of both risk and profit.[7] Leaving debates about the efficacy of CAPM aside, the point here is that these innovations in finance theory formalised core principles that remain central to risk management in the financial sector.

Another important principle of finance theory in relation to risk management under conditions of volatility is that of liquidity. Expressed by Keynes (1936) in terms of liquidity preference in the 1930s, he proposed that heightened uncertainty produces a greater preference for liquid over illiquid assets. That is, investors tend to shift from less liquid assets (like long-term lending) into cash and bank deposits in times of heightened uncertainty because state money, as a product of the state, is the embodiment of safety and liquidity. This could be seen in the wake of the global financial crisis of 2008 with investors proving unwilling to invest in long-term markets, shifting their investments, instead, into shorter-term, more liquid investment.

Indeed, liquidity provides a hedge against volatility by allowing investors to quickly move in and out of positions. As one investment firm describes, 'In a volatile market, liquidity is crucial. If you owned Enron stock in 2001 and suspected that it was in trouble, you needed only call your stockbroker and tell him to dump it. Two minutes later, you're out. No need to ride it from $100 down to five cents' (Players Captial Group 2014). Alternatively, a portfolio of liquid assets means that assets can rapidly be summonsed for unexpected market opportunities, which are more likely to arise in volatile conditions.

These developments in early theory have remained pillars of finance. Yet the way that these early contributions have segued into later developments in finance theory in turn reflect change in financial conditions. Following the breakdown of the Bretton Woods system of fixed exchange rates, early contributions to finance theory that focused on uncertainty took on a new importance. Over the ensuing decades, deregulation, disintermediation,[8] innovation and sharply growing liquidity in the global economy generated new financial conditions that made risk management a major focus in the discipline in the 1990s.[9]

By this time, the frictionless markets of CAPM were being revised.[10] Responding to empirical findings of surging liquidity premia in periods of increasing uncertainty,[11] new theoretical developments in the 1990s set out to augment CAPM with parameters for liquidity and uncertainty in an attempt to align CAPM theory more closely with real market dynamics.[12] By bringing uncertainty back into theory's evaluation of assets, the liquidity-augmented CAPM echoed Tobin's earlier adaptation of Modern Portfolio Theory, which had effectively incorporated Keynes' liquidity preference into portfolio theory. For Tobin, an optimal portfolio allocation would balance uncertainty (which was defined in terms of the degree of uncertainty of future interest rates) with cash holdings. That is, Tobin's optimal portfolio allocation included risk-free asset holdings (cash) in direct proportion to uncertainty so as to express a time-varying liquidity preference: higher uncertainty was reflected in a higher proportion of cash holdings in the portfolio. Although the relationship between uncertainty and liquidity was retained from Tobin's augmented portfolio theory in the new iterations of CAPM, the liquidity premium in these models was no longer attached solely to cash.[13] By the 1990s, sentiments of uncertainty were modelled as affecting liquidity premia in an array of assets, thus implying that not only cash but any number of highly liquid assets can be utilised in risk mitigating strategies. This retraction of cash as the core custodian of risk-free liquidity, and thus the sole proxy for uncertainty as it had been in Tobin's work, reflects how cash was already losing its privileged position amongst other assets by the 1990s.

Applying the Principles of Finance to Household Portfolios

Whilst developments in asset price modelling may reflect disruptions to Keynes' liquidity preference theory that are expressed in the nuances of finance theory's evolution, the tradition of interpreting cash as the risk-free asset remains well entrenched in monetary and macroeconomic theory and feeds into central bank policy, as shown in the final chapters of the book. Conversely, in this study, state money is interpreted as itself a potential locus of uncertainty. This has been the contention of the first three chapters, in which a context of monetary disruption at the heights of global finance offered a backdrop to the problematic conditions of money in the frontier economy context, and specifically in Pakistan. As elaborated in Chapters 6 and 7, given that the rupee is unstable and the monetary environment uncertain, state money is unlikely to remain the safe and stable lynchpin of the broader economy that Keynes had written about in the 1930s. As such, in Pakistan it is far from clear that liquidity should be attached uniquely to the rupee. Liquidity thus becomes far more complex than Keynes' depiction because no asset is the unique custodian of risk-free liquidity.

Amidst this muddying of the waters, this study draws on the crucial insights of Keynes' liquidity preference, Modern Portfolio Theory and CAPM in order to construct a methodology for exploring monetary change at the level of the household. To this end, the rest of this chapter arranges ideas of risk, diversification, liquidity and the balance sheet framework into a methodology for exploring if and how households experience greater risk attached to state money, a methodology which is then applied in Chapter 5 in household interviews. This methodology focuses the household interviews on patterns of household money use (and therein the possibility of substantive monetary contestation in day-to-day transactions), which are analysed by utilising both the portfolio view that looks beyond the individual asset as a discreet risk exposure, and the principles of diversification and liquidity as core responses to uncertainty.

Yet in order for the question of liquidity and diversification to be meaningful in a frontier context, conventional categories of assets and liabilities need to be recast. Here portfolio analysis must be adapted to the 'unbanked', and asset classes and measures of liquidity re-assessed. The key contributions of liquidity preference, Modern Portfolio Theory and CAPM therefore need to be recalibrated in application to the local monetary environment in a frontier economy. This section undertakes this set of tasks, thus developing a set of indicators which are applied in the following chapter in order to identify the burden of growing monetary risk through household interviews.

In order to identify indicators of growing risk attached to state money in household money use patterns, we must first consider how to falsify the notion that state money functions as the risk-free asset in everyday household money use. This is tackled by looking for monetary behaviour amongst households that reflects the relegation of state money from the unique role as the money object, to just one of many liquid and risky instruments. In doing so, we are able to observe in household strategies implicit recognition that state money is not the risk-free asset of Keynesian theory. This could occur where liquidity preference is not expressed as the standard formulation of flight to liquidity in terms of cash but where liquidity preference seeks greater liquid holdings in other assets that offer comparable monetary attributes of liquidity and durability. That is, state money evidently is no longer the unique refuge of safety when it is no longer the destination of a flight to safety.

In a stronger interpretation of the relegation of state money from its traditional role as risk-free asset, state money itself could become the object of diversification strategies. That is, state money could become the source of uncertainty that prompts a shift into safety and liquidity. This would represent liquidity preference theory turned on its head: in these circumstances, state money is not only no longer the refuge of safety but is, in fact, the locus of risk.

By formulating interview questions that attend to these possibilities, the survey's approach to analysing the monetary behaviour of households draws on the portfolio view, by which constituent assets in a diverse portfolio are examined not in isolation but in terms relative to one another. The implication here is that any change in risk attached to state money can prompt adjustments across the entire portfolio in order to hedge the new risk attributes included in the portfolio.

More specifically, this methodology opens up two possible money strategies that indicate the experience of greater volatility (and thus greater risk) embedded in state money, thereby offering two empirical markers in household behaviour that flag perceptions of riskiness in state money. One is of state money holdings being reduced and the second of portfolio adjustments being undertaken that seek to hedge the new risk attributes of state money through reconfiguring other assets in the portfolio. However, state money cannot realistically be abandoned altogether given its dominance and legal status as a means of exchange. This suggests that hedging necessary holdings of state money by rebalancing other assets in the portfolio may become a dominant strategy. Hence, a portfolio view suggests that the question becomes not only how is cash avoided as a store of value asset under new volatility, but what kinds of assets are used to maintain the balance of a portfolio – or hedge new risk – when state money becomes risky?

Yet in order to explore liquidity and diversification in household monetary behaviour, we must adapt portfolio analysis to accommodate the 'unbanked', and asset classes and measures of liquidity so as to be applied in an environment of incomplete rupee monetisation, 'shallow' financial markets and entrenched informality. Hence, it is the effective operationalisation of finance theory's liquidity and diversification *principles* rather than the use of specific forms of financial *instruments*, such as derivatives or insurance products, that constitutes the probe through which risk exposure and management can thus be explored in household interviews. This construction allows the study to explore potential responses to volatility without making misplaced assumptions about which instruments these strategies are carried through. This is particularly important in Pakistan, where local conditions clash with the formal sector institutions that prevail in the advanced economies. Indeed, given the largely 'unbanked' nature of Pakistani households the traditional categories of finance theory are unlikely to yield meaningful conclusions on risk management strategies.

In these circumstances, the analysis must be open to the 'moneyness' of a broad array of assets and liabilities so as to be able to identify money use amongst non-state money instruments. That is, if households effectively relegate state money from its unique role as risk-free asset in their everyday transactions, and other assets with similar money attributes are consequently enrolled in the kinds of functions that state money would traditionally execute, then those alternative instruments may be usefully considered as money instruments. Enquiry into household practices therefore emphasises not what the instrument *is* so much as *how it is used*. Household interviews must thereby be open to a rethinking of the distinction between money and commodity, financial instrument and consumption good. At issue is the necessity of considering a much broader set of instruments as potential proxies for state money. Here the question for households (as will be discussed in greater detail in Chapter 5), becomes not only 'have you minimised your exposure to the rupee?' but also 'what kinds of highly liquid stores of value do you use alongside the rupee?'

In recognising the potential for money functions to operate amongst different kinds of goods, this analysis answers to that put forward by Keynes in chapter 17 of the *General Theory* (1936). Keynes' exploration of the defining attributes of money, in turn, grounds state money within finance theory. The analysis also draws on opposing definitions of money offered by money theory more generally (and discussed at length in Chapter 7). Thus attuned to the importance of liquidity, of safety and of stability to the constitution of money, monetary functioning amongst the various components of the household balance sheet comes into relief. This perspective facilitates a rereading of monetary engagement that takes in a much more diverse set of non-state money instruments than cash, bank money and various formal financial products offered by the formal financial sector.

More importantly, however, by adjusting the scope of money to the kinds of assets and liabilities available in local markets, ambiguity within and between money instruments becomes visible. Discussed extensively in Chapters 6 and 7, the issue here centres on state money losing its unique definitional attributes of safety and stability and thus looking much more like any other liquid asset. A consequence of this relegation of state money from its unique role as risk-free asset could be the development of greater liquidity attributes in various near-monies where markets evolve to offer the monetary attributes that are demanded by the public, but are not demanded in the form of state money. In such circumstances, debates within money theory inform a nuanced view of the various attributes of different assets that picks up both on how state money itself is changing and how markets for non-state money assets are transforming over time. This casts emphasis upon how the space between state money and other assets is becoming increasingly ambiguous and how this predicament further expands the money space for non-state money instruments.

This recasting of money extends to notions of monetisation and barter: if the exercise of monetary functions is recognised amongst non-traditional assets, then rupee-denominated monetisation is no longer necessarily a measure of financial sophistication. Similarly, the use of non-traditional money objects in money strategies is no longer necessarily associated with barter and, as such, should no longer be considered a precursor to modern exchange. Instead, an openness to money use in non-state money instruments offers an unconventional reading of the monetary environment in which new risks can be revealed and change in money observed quite in contrast to the conventional view. As Chapter 3 suggests, an analysis that is limited to traditional tools of finance such as cash, bank deposits and derivatives would observe in Pakistan unhedged exposures amidst financial shallowing and even demonetisation in recent years. In the standard theoretical framework, this would imply regression to simpler economic formations with minimal credit, poolings of savings and risk hedging activities as people regress to one-to-one trading and a survival, subsistence economy. In contrast, by identifying where non-state money is used as money, complexity in monetary management becomes apparent. Barter can be recast as not necessarily a defining characteristic of a subsistence moneyless society but potentially as a means to conceive of an alternative commodity money held intentionally separate from state money and therefore as financial innovation itself.

This approach focuses on greater monetary instability as a key expression of financial change arising from the liberalisation of money and markets in Pakistan. It is hypothesised herein that being 'unmonetised' provides no buffer from the vicissitudes of global finance. In these circumstances, it is suggested that monetary instability prompts new demand for a range of non-official money in the form of highly liquid goods. At issue is the use of hedging practices through the exercise of diversification and liquidity preference within these highly liquid but traditionally non-money goods. These strategies are predicated on the hypothesis that if finance is framed in terms of liquid tools of risk management, even the 'unbanked' may be observed undertaking complex financial strategies, although not necessarily those centred on the conventions of official banking and state money. Where this leaves financial inclusion is taken up in Chapters 6, 7 and 8.

Conclusion: A Complete Theoretical Mapping

Finance theory's identification of volatility as a cost burden of risk, of liquidity and diversification as risk management strategies, and of a portfolio-wide perspective of the household balance sheet constitutes the third layer of theory which the analysis traverses, from the heights of global finance, through the macroeconomic challenges of monetary control, to the everyday economy amongst households and in the bazaars of a frontier economy. This framework centres around Keynes' description of money in chapter 17 of the *General Theory*, which, in turn, grounds the orientation of money in finance theory, by which state money is the cornerstone of risk and liquidity: the top of the pyramid of money, the destination of liquidity preference, the guarantor of the risk-free status of sovereign bonds – at the interface of every transaction across the economy and into the future as the medium of exchange and the denominator of credit.

By setting out the distinct characteristics of state money that mark it out as unique amongst other potential monies, Keynes develops a rich description of the attributes of money. Keynes' description of money centres on liquidity and stability, which is referenced back to the state's unique provisioning of state money. For Keynes, state money (not wheat or gold) trumps all rivals because it uniquely can be the risk-free asset. This conception of state money reflects a historically distinct institutional environment, with set exchange and interest rates and protected markets for finance as well as goods and services. In this environment, money could be safe and stable and could be controlled by the state.

'Keynesian money' thus offers a benchmark against which change in state money can be assessed. This benchmark was applied in Chapter 1 in a consideration of cutting-edge change at the heights of global finance, where deregulation and financial innovation have transformed markets for money and finance. By casting the contemporary monetary environment against Keynes' 1930s description of state money, change in money and the monetary environment comes into relief. So too does the challenge that contemporary monetary conditions pose to the notions of money embedded in finance theory and economic thinking more broadly.

Keynes' description of money in the *General Theory* also offers a useful discussion on the nature of money insofar as it can be utilised in a methodology for assessing the 'moneyness' of potential rivals to state money. That is, Keynes' description, along with the lengthy money theory literature to which it contributes, offers a set of principles that guide the consideration of how monetary attributes might be embodied in different assets. This is undertaken in the final section of the book, where monetary attributes of different assets are explored in order to evaluate their potential to be applied to money functions in the context of Pakistan's post-liberalisation monetary environment.

A second layer of theory draws the focus back from specific monetary attributes to the broader environment in which money is embedded. Taken up in Chapter 2, the theoretical framework developed here brings together a set of key insights from social studies of money and central banking to set out a distinct perspective on money's grounding in the everyday economy. It is proposed that perceived stability – not just in money but across macroeconomic indicators – is crucial for money's uncontested functioning. This framework thereby links money into its wider economic context and posits the potential for money to become contested. Specifically, following the Keynesian lineage of the underlying conception of money as the safe asset, this framework sets out how instability feeds uncertainty and how uncertainty undermines trust in money. Exactly what monetary contestation looks like where trust in money fails, is left to Chapters 6, 7 and 8.

This framework – of notionally risk-free state money embedded in the broader economy and dependent on trust – is applied to the consideration of the monetary environment in frontier economies in general in Chapter 2 and, in greater detail, in the specific context of Pakistan from Chapter 3 through to the end of the book. In Chapter 3, this framework informs which macroeconomic and monetary developments are examined. Hence instability and opacity, as core drivers of uncertainty and thus key issues for the maintenance of social trust in money, are key themes that guide the description of the rupee's liberalisation. Rather than a conventional focus on the evolution of the formal regulatory regime, the history recounted here emphasises the rise of the threat of inflation in the post-liberalisation economy, the way that instability generated through the open current and capital account ripples across the broader economy, and the obfuscation of basic economic and monetary trends with growing informality in money and markets. How this instability generates uncertainty and how uncertainty feeds the substantive contestation of money is then taken up in the final chapters of the book.

The third layer of theory, described in the first part of this chapter, applies finance theory to the everyday uses of money, which informs the field interviews and the selection of secondary sources. Here finance theory provides a methodology for the examination of monetary behaviour which both identifies how the burden of risk that is generated by instability imposes costs at the household level and how risk mitigation strategies can be recognised. This third layer of theory completes the analytical bridging, from the heights of the global economy, to frontier economies in general, and then to the household experience, itself set within the national context of monetary change. That is, more specifically, how liberalisation makes money unstable, how this predicament poses specific challenges in frontier economies, and how this predicament plays out in Pakistan, both from the perspective of the central bank and from that of households.

The theoretical framework in which the study of the monetary environment in Pakistan is undertaken is thus strongly influenced by Post-Keynesian themes. Specifically, the study is oriented around themes of uncertainty as an economic problem; of the interconnectivity between economic and monetary spheres; and of how the institutional environment garners (or undermines) trust in money. The view of money itself that this entails combines the financial characteristics of money emphasised by Keynes and operationalised in finance theory, with an interpretation of money as a deeply social phenomenon. Specifically, the analysis of money focuses on its instrumentality: how liberalisation and globalisation has impacted how money (including state money) is and is not used in the everyday economy, and what this means for the central bank's capacity to control money in the economy. Where the analysis identifies the contestation of conventional money practices, the sociality of money is invoked. Taken up in the last three chapters of the book, this analysis gives concrete form to the idea that money relies on trust and that, where that trust is undermined, money may become contested.

The final stage of the analysis is to apply these findings to theory and to policy, specifically to the money theory literature and to central bank policy as it engages with financial inclusion. The conclusions drawn offer a distinct reading of money and central banking in an open, low-income economy, and of how ordinary, generally poor people engage finance. Here we see a shift from financial inclusion pursued as a tool for household risk mitigation under the volatility of open markets, to financial inclusion pursued as a tool for enhancing money's governability in an ambiguous and unstable monetary environment.

Notes

1. For a detailed discussion on the role of trust in sociological theories of money, see Chapter 7. The social studies of finance and central banking, discussed in Chapter 2, is one offshoot of this literature.

2. See, for example, Davidson (1993) and Shackle (1972).

3. That is, risk is probabilistic and thus calculative whereas uncertainty is not. Knight (1921), Keynes (1936) and Shackle (1973) all elaborate extensively on the idea of uncertainty as distinct from risk.

4. As noted in the introduction, the balance sheet terms used in this book are not the strict balance sheet terms of formal accounting standards but rather those of the financial inclusion literature (for example, Collins et al. 2009), in which cash-flow items are considered as balance sheet items.

5. The opportunity cost refers to the profit that an investor misses out on by choosing one particular path. Here, for example, the opportunity cost is the profit that could have been yielded by keeping long-term assets and short-term liabilities on the balance sheet, rather than choosing to match long-term assets with long-term liabilities.

6. For an illuminating discussion on household risk and liquidity, see Bryan and Rafferty (2018) and Bryan, Rafferty and Jefferis (2015).

7. In contrast to Modern Portfolio Theory, however, CAPM *proposed* a strategy of optimisation in its specific formulation of an optimal set of exposures, rather than formalising the general principle of diversification that was *observed* in existing investor behaviour.

8. That is, the decline in traditional banking as households and firms move away from banks for holding savings and for making loans. The term is grounded in the 'intermediation' that the banking sector traditionally undertakes between depositors and lenders.

9. Malz (2015) offers a very accessible introduction to the reorientation of finance around growing risk in the post–Bretton Woods era.

10. CAPM is constructed upon assumptions of frictionless (or perfect) markets, in which the market is completely liquid and there are no transactions costs or other 'distortions'. Frictionless markets will price two assets of identical cash flows identically regardless of liquidity attributes. That is, a more liquid asset will not attract a higher price because there is no advantage to holding liquidity in a perfectly liquid frictionless market.

11. That is, markets were observed to be putting a higher cost on assets with liquidity attributes in times of uncertainty, which posed a contrast to the frictionless markets of CAPM.

12. For a review of the literature on how CAPM has been adapted in accordance with changing conditions attached to liquidity, see Adler (2012).

13. See, for example, Acharya and Pedersen (2005).

5

Fieldwork Findings

As discussed in Chapter 4, finance theory informs the approach taken by this study to households by identifying volatility as a cost burden of risk and identifying potential risk management strategies through portfolio allocation. In applying this micro-level analysis to households in Pakistan, evidence of monetary volatility as a substantive concern for ordinary people is sought out. Where found, such findings help to substantiate the argument that the liberalisation of money and markets and consequent exposure of money to global liquidity has generated meaningful change in money and the monetary environment.

This chapter discusses how, by drawing on field interviews, the study seeks out evidence of the substantive experience of risk attached to the liberalised rupee amongst households and in local bazaars. The chapter opens with a review of existing methodologies for interrogating household finances before setting out the methods utilised in field interviews for this study. The second part of the chapter systematically lays out the findings from field interviews in raw form. Worked in with the macro analysis from chapters prior, secondary fieldwork and newspaper articles, these findings are analysed in Chapter 6 to produce the conclusions of the final two chapters.

The field interviews thus inform the analysis of the monetary environment in Pakistan yet the interviews do not seek to unambiguously prove certain findings. The intention is not to fully scope the dimensions of alternative 'currencies', but to identify the ways in which the conventional understanding of the pre-eminence of state money as means of exchange, store of value and unit of account is being challenged in often ad hoc but quite comprehensive ways. Hence, the field interviews do not seek to establish a schema of risk management strategies through proportional sampling and a rigorous quantitative survey. Neither do they seek to develop an ethnographic description of the subjective and culturally mediated experience of financial risk. Rather, the field interviews seek to open up the question of money and globalisation to further analysis by exploring disruptions to mainstream assumptions about money and its governance in the field. By offering a view into the workings of the everyday economy, findings from the field interviews do not offer unequivocal truths about how the rupee is engaged across the economy but do suggest a complexity in money strategies that defies conventional assumptions about money and, ultimately, about the usefulness of financial inclusion as a poverty alleviation measure.

Methods for the Analysis of Household Finances

As the financial inclusion agenda has become increasingly dominant within development thinking, it has spawned its own empirical literature and methods, which explore the financial engagement of households in the everyday economy. The primary innovation of this literature has been the widening of the scope of the analysis to include informal financial engagement amongst households. Two key methods stand out: financial diaries and large-scale surveys.

The seminal contribution of Collins, Morduch, Ruthven and Rutherford (2009) crafted the financial diaries approach to studying household engagement with finance. Tracking household cash flow, leverage and savings through entries made to 'financial diaries' over a period of months, and including an array of informal and in-kind transactions, the financial diaries method has produced a level of detail that far surpasses that of conventional statistics relating to household savings and debt with the banking sector. Specifically, this approach has identified complexity in financial engagement even for those living on less than US$2 per day. By producing evidence of capacity amongst the poor for strategic financial behaviour, these findings have disrupted the assumption of 'hand to mouth' living amongst the poor and provided crucial backing for the financial inclusion agenda. Recognition of high turnover, high levels of leverage and sophisticated diversification of assets and liabilities amidst diverse networks of family, neighbours, local shopkeepers and moneylenders implies a potential market for improved financial products aimed at poor households and produced by the private sector.

The financial diaries method complements the large survey studies on household finance that were being undertaken at the same time as the study by Collins and her colleagues (2009). Although household surveys, such as the Household Integrated Economic Survey in Pakistan, had long been undertaken by national statistical bureaus, a new generation of household surveys were launched in the late 1990s and early 2000s, which sought to measure financial inclusion through representative sampling and lengthy, structured surveys. Most significantly, the World Bank and Bill and Melinda Gates Foundation's 'Global Findex Database' incorporates internationally comparative surveys on household finances in over 150,000 interviews in some 148 countries. The key finding of the Findex study relate to the massive scale of informal savings and borrowing amongst households in developing countries (Demiguc-Kunt and Klapper 2012). Again, these findings are employed to justify the expansion of formal finance in developing countries in order that superior microfinance products become available to better service the financial needs of households.

These new approaches to household finances have spawned new literature and a wealth of new data over the last decade or so that interrogates household financial practices. In Pakistan alone, CGAP's smallholders dairy project was undertaken in 2014,[1] which followed three large-scale household surveys examining household financial practices undertaken intermittently from 2008, as well as a rural household panel survey focusing on finance and safety nets.[2] These studies have produced a wealth of detail on household finances that have hugely advanced academic knowledge about financial and economic precariousness amongst ordinary, generally poor households in Pakistan and the rest of the world, developing and advanced alike.[3]

The key limitation of these kinds of studies, however, is that their structured nature remains inflexible to probing the outer limits of their findings. The Findex study, for example, finds that more than half of savers in 55 countries save in ways unaccounted for by the survey methodology, even though that methodology explicitly seeks to engage informal practices (Demirguc-Kunt and Klapper 2012: 34). This reflects a methodology ill equipped to recognise the full scope of potential financial instruments for inclusion in the dairy and survey format, in part due to the inflexibility inherent to the structured methods entailed in both financial diaries and large surveys, by which the researcher is unable to probe beyond the set categories of the study. These restrictions are inherent in such large-scale field-based projects, which rely on uniformity in order to protect reliability and comparability of results but lose the flexibility that allows research to penetrate deeper into the ambiguities of household finances.

The kind of flexibility that can carry research further into the nuances of household financial engagement is offered by ethnographic methods. From Jane Guyer's work on exchange in Atlantic Africa (2004) and Clifford Geertz's 'thick descriptions' of the Moroccan *suq* (1979), to more recent applications to microcredit and informal mortgage products in squatter settlements,[4] ethnographic research offers unrivalled depth of analysis. Generally undertaken through intensive participant observation, ethnographic research offers the researcher a method which allows the time and flexibility to probe the responses offered by respondents to the researcher's questions, exploring new questions as they arise. The product of ethnographic research consequently moves beyond the categories into which financial behaviour is slotted in research utilising survey and financial diary methods. At the cost of the direct comparability facilitated by the structured methods of surveys and financial diaries, ethnography produces rich individuated descriptions of the subjective experience of households in navigating the everyday economy. Ethnography consequently carries with it a burden of interpretation, which is complex at the best of times but particularly challenging in inter-cultural research.

At the opposite extreme is secondary quantitative analysis. Not tainted by the possibility of self-reporting bias that attaches to survey data nor the reflexivity concerns that accompany ethnographic methods, quantitative data analysis offers an alternative method for the examination of household financial engagement. Primarily, the data used in quantitative analysis is provided by service providers, such as commercial banks, microfinance institutions and mobile money providers. Typical of central bank analysis, this kind of quantitative method informs the construction of various indices of financial inclusion[5] and constitutes the vast bulk of the data collected by, for example, the SBP, in its statistics on the geographical penetration of bank branches, the cash-to-deposit ratio and the use of 'mobile money wallets'. The key database for this kind of data is the IMF's Financial Access Survey, which tracks more than 150 data series for up to 189 economies in a comparable format that relies heavily on secondary quantitative data like the number of ATMs to population, per capita deposit accounts, the number of monthly withdrawals in deposit accounts and mobile money balance values as a percentage of GDP.

For Pakistan, these kinds of data raise a series of issues. Misreporting plagues household surveys, banking statistics, price indicators and national accounts, rendering uncertain the financial statistics and the macroeconomic indicators that are commonly used as the denominators. From investment, consumption, output, employment and even population, to remittances, deposit levels, inflation and kerb exchange rates, a series of factors undermine the reliability of these kinds of quantitative data. These include capital flight, tax evasion and the netting out of flows through *hawala*, which disrupt remittances, investment, GDP and the import and export of goods in the national accounts;[6] a lack of trust over anonymity relating to household surveys[7] and political engineering of census data collection;[8] political interference, poor sampling and unreliable data collection techniques in monetary statistics;[9] and inappropriate categorical schemas in data collection. Examples of the latter include the dominance of highly casualised labour and work not reimbursed by cash in relation to employment statistics, or the exclusion of informal savings and credit practices in financial inclusion statistics.[10] These conditions detract from the efficacy of conventional indicators and propose alternative, potentially more relevant sites of key indicators. For example, for economic decisions made by actors in the economy, the kerb exchange rate may be more important than the official exchange rate, or the black-market interest rate more important than the bank rate.

This book argues that this context of incomplete and disputed quantitative data amidst growing informality in money and markets, combined with the persistent but unexplained failure of households to respond to longstanding policy efforts to enhance financial inclusion, demonstrates a pervasive ambiguity and complexity in the monetary environment. For present purposes, however, the problem of uncertain data is considered in terms of the methodological challenges it poses to tracking the monetary behaviour of households in particular. This very hazy monetary and financial context suggests a lack of clarity around how far financial instruments and financial strategies stretch beyond conventional categories. In this context, qualitative methods may help to overcome data collection problems, such as the inflexibility demonstrated in the inability of the Findex survey to account for the kinds of practices used by the majority of savers in a large portion of countries. In-depth and semi-structured interviews are more open to following unexpected paths of enquiry and thereby exploring where the unknown boundaries of money meet any array of unorthodox practices and objects. Moreover, household financial practices are a sensitive topic, deemed by most as very personal information. The sensitive nature of the subject matter reinforces the suitability of the qualitative approach. In-depth interviews offer the cultivation of rapport through face-to-face engagement and the flexibility to probe further where a respondent appears comfortable, or to pull back where a respondent appears to be discomfited by the nature of the question or suspicious of the interviewer's motives.

Choosing Methods for Field Interviews

The field interviews undertaken for this study sought to contribute to the existing literature by combining the small sample and social embedding characteristic of ethnography with a focus on empirical indicators more characteristic of survey methods. This is in contrast to the subjective interpretations more typical of ethnography. This approach seeks to bring the analysis into the fringes of household financial practices, exploring the outliers of money strategies so as to open up conventional assumptions about money to question rather than construct a rigorous schema of household practices. The strength of this approach is its capacity to access information about how money and finance is engaged at the outer reaches of conventional practices. This comes at the cost, however, of being unable to firmly establish proportionality of unconventional practices within the economy.

Not dissimilarly to the portfolio approach taken by financial diary studies, the field interviews focused on the instruments and strategies of money and finance amongst households and in bazaars. Yet, rather than seeking to simply document strategies and instruments, the interviews sought to uncover evidence towards a distinct set of questions that attempt to identify transgression from the incontrovertible money that lies implicit in central bank and development policy. At their core, the field interviews sought to engage the possibility of monetary contestation. Do people unequivocally rely on money as the safe asset in terms of their everyday transactions? Or is there evidence that state money's robustness – the unthinking trust in money that is shared across a community – is in fact contested? Can instances of new money strategies be found that reflect perceptions of growing riskiness in money? Or is money found to be used just as it always has been? That is, is there evidence in the everyday money economy of instances of departure from the conventional notions of state money as legal tender – as unit of account, means of exchange, and store of value; as the safe asset and the conduit of monetary policy, that is, the thread that connects every transaction in the economy, across time and across space; and as a tool for risk mitigation for the denomination of savings and investment that can both smooth consumption and function as an emergency fund in times of financial distress?

This enquiry was taken up in field interviews through indirect questioning. Seeking not to explore how ordinary people *felt* about the rupee's credibility or their *opinions* of monetary risk, the interview questions instead sought out empirical *practices* that reflect the complication of the rupee as money in concrete ways. Specifically, where new money practices are taken up as risk management strategies, they make visible the experience of risk by representing responses to that experience of risk. Indeed, where we find that the new risk profile of the rupee is the central feature driving its contestation, we find a predicament not only of theoretical interest but also of significant policy salience.

The simplest entry point to contestation of the rupee's core money functions is identification of the use of alternative stores of value. This is most distinct where new stores of value explicitly replace rupee holdings. Similarly, the use of alternative means of exchange and units of account were the target of interview questions, but an openness to any manner of potential money strategies was crucial in keeping with the study's aims to venture where conventional analysis could not go. The interviews thereby sought to decipher each informant's current money strategies, as well as explore money strategies that had been used in the past. They centred on questions about the storage and liquidation of sums to meet costs such as wedding costs, school fees, the purchase of a motorbike or a piece of land, or inventory purchases amongst shop keepers.

By seeking out empirical handles that reflect risk management techniques, the field interviews sought to minimise the complications of interpretation related to cultural differences between interviewer and interviewee. These complications could play out in terms of the interviewee adapting their answers in recognition of any of various structural roles embodied in the researcher/interviewee relationship; or could play out in terms of misunderstanding rooted in the difference in cultural schemas around money, risk, responsibility and humility, or indeed a myriad of other specific cultural differences between researcher and interviewee. That is, through contrasting cultural perspectives, the contrived nature of the researcher/interviewee relationship could prompt misunderstanding in the interpretation of the question on the part of the interviewee as much as of the answer on the part of the interviewer. Keeping the interviews focused on the concrete, rather than the abstract, helped to manage these issues. This is of even more relevance to the field interviews because the interview questions took a second order approach to the experience of financial risk by seeking out evidence of counteracting risk management strategies rather than directly addressing that risk itself. Already one step removed from the study's core focus on risk, the questions maintained an emphasis on empirical information, specifically on money instruments utilised by interviewees and time frames in which different instruments were used, that could signal changing experiences of risk. These data were deemed easier to interpret than more abstract and personally mediated information, such as personal narratives of the experience of financial insecurity or risk mitigation.

As for accessing respondents, the bulk of interviews relied on either snowballing or the existing networks of experienced researchers in the field, who collaborated in the field interview process. These strategies for accessing interviewees essentially rely on the social trust within the networks of respondents and between established local researchers and different members of the community. Although this approach does not offer the benefits associated with random, representative sampling, it promises rapport between researcher and respondent that is beyond the grasp of studies with larger samples. The socially embedded nature of the process by which interviewees were identified thus constitutes a core strength of the study, appropriate to both the sensitive nature of the interview subject and to local sociality, which tends to cast outsiders and formal authorities as untrustworthy amidst thick reciprocal social bonds amongst extended family and clan networks. In fact, the most fruitful interviews tended to be those that essentially exercised the social capital of the experienced researchers who collaborated on the fieldwork side of the study. Whilst interviews with strangers tended to simply fail to elicit engagement with the interview questions, those with respondents accessed through existing social networks often led to lengthy and candid discussion of very personal (and sometimes illegal) financial details.[11]

Details of the Field Interview Methods

Two field trips were undertaken by the author in 2014 and 2016. The field trips focused on a primary set of interviews with respondents who were selected to loosely reflect different geographical regions and ethnic groups, and to include representatives from key economic groupings. Snowballing contacts led to the over-representation of some groups and under-representation of others. However, the role of the field interviews was to identify the uses of alternatives to state money and thereby open the space for discussion around potential shifts in money rather than unambiguously prove certain findings. This approach accommodates an uneven sample as well as the unpredictable nature of field research in Pakistan.

The fieldwork design sought to include representatives from rural households because of their demographic weight, with the agricultural sector reported to employ some 45 per cent of working Pakistanis (Pakistan Bureau of Statistics 2015). Another key group for the sample was bazaar-based traders. Here again we find a key employment category, at 15 per cent according to the official data, that traverses income levels (ibid.).

As purveyors of consumer goods, including core subsistence commodities, bazaar-based traders were interviewed not only in their capacity as citizens that are subject to the post-liberalisation monetary environment, but also as key stakeholders who could discuss their views as to how their customers may have changed their practices over the years. This was especially the case for money changers, whose views were sought out less with regard to how they themselves may have shifted their strategies in response to unstable money but rather to how they perceived the public's engagement with the money-changing sector to have changed over the years.

Interviews were conducted in homes and in the bazaar, and included interviews with traders in bazaars in Peshawar, Charsadda, Hyderabad, Karachi and Quetta; agricultural workers, dealers in agricultural inputs, agricultural land owners and rural low-income salaried workers in Rajanpur, Charsadda, Mirpurkass and the fringes of Lahore and Khanewal; money changers and gold dealers in Lahore, Hyderabad and Peshawar; commercial bankers in Peshawar and Karachi; as well as dealers, developers, planners and customers involved in land markets in Charsadda, Peshawar, Islamabad, Rawalpindi, Karachi, Quetta, Zhob and Mirpurkass.[12]

The interview questions had to be constructed in a manner sensitive to taboos around discussing money in an Islamic society. Specifically, Islamic thought frowns upon speculation in favour of productive investment.[13] This principle casts a shadow over active strategies that respond to nominal instability in money, such as inflation and exchange rate depreciation, because of the connotations of speculation that they entail. Accordingly, the interview questions were designed to avoid direct questions about what strategies were being taken up in response to monetary instability, probing instead how money strategies may have changed in the more recent, post-liberalisation years. To this end, periodisation was loose. In many interviews, periodisation was identified in terms of 'Musharraf' or 'Zardari time', referring to the era of the Musharraf presidency from 2001 to 2008 and that of Zardari from 2008 to 2013. This broadly recognised periodisation corresponds to that proposed in Chapter 3, by which the post-liberalisation period is identified as the years after 2008 – that is, from 'Zardari time' onwards.

As mentioned earlier, the interview question sought to remain open to any array of potential money objects and money strategies. However, the interview questions deliberately avoided the consideration of jewellery as a potentially alternative money form because of the traditional role that jewellery plays in dowries. It was deemed that jewellery may have a cultural significance that complicates its role as an asset, making its role in the portfolio harder to understand to an outsider. As such, changes around practices with regard to jewellery may be more difficult to decipher. Instead, the interviews focused on ordinary assets and liabilities such as wages, housing costs, staple food commodities and consumer durables whilst simultaneously being attentive to further alternative assets and liabilities. The field interviews were thereby designed to identify instances of the cultivation of money attributes in non-state money markets. This meant that the experience of financial risk was assumed where certain shifts in money practices could be deciphered.

In sum, the methods chosen for the field interviews mark the fieldwork out as a distinct contribution to the structured studies on household finances in Pakistan that have been published over the last decade. The interviews were able to probe the outer limits of money practices because of the embedded social networks within which the bulk of the interviews were undertaken, the flexibility of the in-depth interview format and the openness to unconventional money objects and practices inherent to the research aims themselves. This approach allowed the interviews to explore outer limits of money that are inaccessible to larger, structured studies.

The nature of the field interviews was such as to produce indicative results, rather than conclusive facts. The small sample limits the findings' generalisability just as the social embedding of the interviews provided valuable access to taboo information while simultaneously detracting from the kind of proportionality and generalisability that are the strengths of large, structured surveys. The reflexivity issues associated with qualitative research undertaken with small samples were tempered by the empirical handles at which the interviews grasped. A richness in the experience of risk is clearly lost when it is whittled down to its bare material bones. However, greater reliability in the eventual analysis is promised by a focus on information that is less ambiguous and more empirical. This is particularly so given the inter-cultural nature of the interviews and the cultural and religious taboos around just the kind of strategies that the fieldwork was designed to explore.

Contextualising the Field Interviews

In order to strengthen the analysis of the primary field interviews and collect further data on the broader context of monetary liberalisation in Pakistan, a secondary set of interviews with key stakeholders was undertaken.[14] These interviews were with senior SBP officials, policy makers and academics. Key stakeholder interviews helped to substantiate the findings and to build a richer picture of the policy landscape. On the one hand, these interviews offered an opportunity to receive feedback on the analysis from those at the centre of the policy, research and practice of money management in Pakistan. On the other hand, these interviews permitted some exploration of how key issues had played out 'behind the scenes', offering a richness to the analysis by allowing it to absorb a diversity of perspectives beyond those exhibited on the public record.

Taken together, the primary and key stakeholder interviews offer important primary data that build up a cohesive picture of the rupee – as an everyday fact of economic life for ordinary people and as the evolving subject of a governance problem for the central bank. These data, and the analysis that follows, do not contradict the key studies on household finances in Pakistan but rather fill in a gap – or, money – that is left dormant in the underlying assumptions upon which those studies are predicated. Specifically, the three large surveys on access to finance in Pakistan over the last decade tell a story of the persistence with which the population has failed to respond to the state's longstanding efforts to engage households in formal finance. These surveys show very slow take-up of formal finance despite the development of significant incentives, amidst stagnation and even decline in some indicators.[15]

Alternatively, the panel study on rural households undertaken by the International Food Policy Research Institute (IFPRI) in 2012 and 2013 and the smallholder diaries project undertaken by CGAP at around the same time tell a story of financial precariousness amongst households.[16] This precariousness is explored in much greater detail in the work of Haris Gazdar, Hussain Bux Mallah and Mysbah Balagamwala, whose fieldwork on the food economy and coping strategies in the face of food inflation paints a rich picture of how an economy of social obligation sustains the poorest households through times of adverse shocks.[17]

The contribution of the present study is to link the precarious economic reality of households revealed in the work of Gazdar and his colleagues, the smallholder diary project and the rural households panel survey into a broader monetary context. By focusing on money, the present study explores what role monetary change might play in the financial precariousness of households by rethinking where the food economy meets the monetary economy. This, in turn, answers to the questions left open by the survey-based studies. Here the present study steps in to explore some of the practices that might be keeping people out of formal finance. Deliberately embracing an openness to unconventional money objects and strategies, the study looks beyond the limited scope of these financial inclusion surveys to engage the outer limits of money strategies. The unique contribution of the present study thereby helps to build a richer picture of the low levels of financial inclusion that characterise Pakistan's formal finance sector. The rest of this chapter lays out the findings from field interviews in a raw but systematic form. Analysis of the findings is not undertaken until Chapter 6.

Findings from the Field Interviews

This presentation of findings from the field interviews is organised in a schema of money functions, describing what sort of non-state money instruments are being used as store of value assets, as a means of exchange and as units of account. Reference codes attached to each interviewee are used, which correspond to the interview list in the Appendix. The following section discusses how interviewees talked about their use of state money and bank accounts in the pre-liberalisation era in contrast to the post-liberalisation era. Discussion of how these findings are linked to the book's key argument is taken up in Chapters 6, 7 and 8.

Cash and Bank Accounts, Before and After Liberalisation

Constituting state money itself, cash and bank deposits offer a starting point for the presentation of the findings from the fieldwork. Interviewees reported significant change in how their money strategies utilised both cash and bank deposits across both the pre- and post-liberalisation period. These changes suggest a shift away from reliance on the rupee as a store of value towards greater dominance of cash and bank accounts as means of exchange.

Cash

Predominant amongst low-income rural interviewees, vivid descriptions were offered in field interviews of hiding places for cash holdings in the home in years past. These interviewees consistently described how those in their own family had kept cash in various places in the home, such as the wheat store, in brickwork, in secret pockets sewn into linen and in jars buried underground. Some of these interviewees recounted memories of cash that had suffered water damage due to poor storage,[18] of notes stored for so long that they had become demonetised,[19] and of Hindu neighbours in years past who were known to bury cash in jars in the ground.[20] One interviewee reported that his uncle had kept thousands of dollars' worth of rupee cash, which was discovered when he died.[21]

As with many other cases pertaining to changed practices identified in these interviews, the time frame in which practices had changed was difficult to define. When directly asked, almost all interviewees across all key groupings claimed not to have changed their practices around cash holdings. Yet the recent nature of some of the stories of cash storage reported by interviewees and the consistency of sentiments around old and new practices suggest that cash had been held until quite recently. This proposition is supported by detailed fieldwork on store of value assets undertaken by Shahina Waheed in the mid-1990s. In field interviews in a village geographically and culturally close to the rural field sites referred to in this book, Waheed identified a series of traditional savings strategies, such as using cattle, but found cash savings to be predominant.[22]

By contrast, the present field interviews found that in each case, low-income rural interviewees consistently declared that, as was the case with other people, they no longer held cash as a savings instrument. When they were asked at the outset of the interview if the rupee's condition had become worse these interviewees complained of rising prices, but none of the low-income rural interviewees made the direct connection between rising prices and the sharp decline in popularity of cash as a savings instrument, even though they themselves contradicted tradition by choosing not to hold cash.[23]

These sentiments were substantiated by the manager of a commercial bank branch in Peshawar, who explained that 'people are worried about depreciation. In the old days, people used to keep their money under their pillows but they don't do this now.... Investing in gold, gems, wheat, sugar and rice are practices that have increased over the years'.[24]

Bank Accounts

Amongst traders, medium–large agricultural landowners and those in the property market, holding savings in bank accounts appeared as rare as holding savings in cash at the village level. Around half of the traders interviewed stated that they did not have a bank account at all. Those that did have an account reported that these were only kept for transactional rather than savings purposes, and specifically for transferring funds to other accounts. This was the case for both regular deposit accounts and sharia compliant 'profit and loss' accounts.

One trader described how in recent years he had started to rent out his account to others to make bank transfers.[25]

Almost half of the traders interviewed put an explicit time frame around when they themselves, or people in general, had stopped using bank accounts for holding money. This time frame correlated with the denigration of the rupee in the years after 2008. For example, the two interviewees that were probably the wealthiest of those interviewed explicitly stated that while they continued to use bank accounts to transfer money to other people, they had themselves stopped holding balances in bank accounts since 2009 or so and had replaced these holdings with other asset forms.[26] Amongst lower income groups it was difficult to secure self-identification of prior reliance on banks for holding savings rather than simply for transferring money. Yet explicit time frames around the general shift away from bank accounts were also given by these less wealthy interviewees. For example, in the 2016 interviews, a bazaar-based trader in a working class suburb of Karachi explained that 'bank accounts had been more popular in the Musharraf years',[27] just as another in the same suburb noted that 'people use bank accounts less since Zardari time ... [because] they give less profit'.[28]

A general decline in deposit holdings can be seen in banking statistics. As discussed in Chapter 3, the deposit base dropped in 2008 and has been unable to recover, despite vigorous efforts by the central bank and the improvement in monetary and economic indicators. Reflecting upon this predicament, one senior SBP official stated in an interview with the author that 'we are regressing in terms of intermediation'.

Alternative Store of Value Assets

In discussing their money strategies, interviewees raised a series of instruments in which store of value functions are exercised. These ranged from traditional money objects like cattle to elaborate instruments such as informal and short-term land holdings.

Cattle

Each of the interviewees who resided in rural areas reported that rather than holding value in cash, they prefer to purchase cattle as a store of value. Some of these interviewees offered sophisticated explanations of the different costs of different types of cattle (from a baby goat to a buffalo) and of differing sale prices depending on the age of the animal. One urban trader confirmed that cattle are purchased and held for resale in urban areas as well.[29]

Wheat

Some of the low-income rural interviewees also discussed the purchase of wheat as a store of value instead of cash. These findings are supported by research by Gazdar and his colleagues at the Collective for Social Sciences Research Karachi, which found low-income households stockpiling wheat as a response to food price inflation.[30] Although one small farmer proposed that he himself would buy either wheat or a small animal to hold and sell if he wanted to store value of some 3,000–4,000 rupees (the equivalent of some US$30–40 at the time, or two to three weeks of the average agricultural wage),[31] other low-income rural interviewees referred to the purchase and resale of wheat with disapproval.[32] In these cases 'hoarding' wheat was described as a strategy undertaken by other, less reputable members of their community. Taboos around wheat hoarding are identified by other researchers in the field.[33] In any case, further evidence of stockpiling of wheat was expressed in interviews with traders in Balochistan and Hyderabad, who reported that rather than the daily purchases of grain common in decades past, bulk household purchases had become a norm.[34]

Fieldwork undertaken by Gazdar and his colleagues also offers a sense of the ease with which wheat can be sold into the market. This research includes interviews with those from traditional beggar families, who receive wheat as charity but subsequently convert it to cash in order to make cash purchases of other goods.[35] This suggests that wheat stockpiling at the household level may be not only for later consumption but also for later sale.

Inventory and Other Storable Commodities

As for holdings in grain amongst wealthier interviewees, a large landholder in Sindh described how he, like other landowners in his area, had built new warehousing facilities so as to store agricultural commodities to hold and sell.[36] He explained that in 2009 or 2010 he started to invest in agricultural commodities as store of value assets, such as wheat, rice, sugar, spices, oil and pulses. Whilst previously all wheat grown on his land had been sold at harvest with the proceeds held in bank accounts, he now stores not only some of the produce from his own land but buys produce from the market to hold and sell. This interviewee explicitly described these practices as a substitute for the use of bank accounts, which he stopped using as a store of value in 2009. Reports of increasing capacity for commodity storage amongst landlords after 2008 are suggested in media reports as well as in the field-based research of Asif Saeed Khan on the wheat sector.[37] Similarly, older work on the wheat sector shows that 'hoarding' was not practised in the 1990s, largely because price stability throughout the season did not offer opportunities for profitable arbitrage.[38]

Amongst traders, enhanced storage of agricultural commodities was described by a number of interviewees as a way to facilitate the storage of value without relying on the rupee. A small trader in Karachi, for example, described commodities like rice, sugar and cattle as alternative assets to bank deposits that had become popular since the Zardari years.[39]

For traders, any non-perishable stock can act as a store of value. One gem dealer, for example, when explaining why he did not have a bank account, pointed at gems on display in his shop and said 'this is my bank'.[40] A branch manager of a bank in Peshawar explained how gem dealers manage their stock as a portfolio, rapidly reinvesting in gems from cash and shifting between different types of gems as their values fluctuate. Referring to the liquidity in a gem portfolio and the attentiveness with which dealers respond to market signals, he noted that dealers will shift portfolio allocation 'at the first rumour' of future depreciation.[41]

For traders, however, commodity-related strategies extend beyond basic holding strategies that buy when prices are low and sell when prices are high. A tea merchant in Peshawar, for example, described how he had diversified his trade beyond tea as a risk hedge. 'When [the price of] one goes down,' he explained, 'another goes up.'[42] He now stocks a range of spices as well as rice, sugar and wheat. The same sentiment was identified in an interview with an agricultural commodity trader in Quetta, who described his long-term business strategy in terms of diversifying stock and customers, including a shift from dominant wholesale to dominant retail trade.[43]

Traders also reported daily purchases of new inventory, which effectively minimise overnight holdings of rupees. Recognition of this as a new strategy could not be confirmed, although the daily purchase of inventory was pervasive amongst trader interviewees.[44] The inability of the interviews to confirm whether daily stock purchases were new practices or not may be due to taboos around money and speculation, by which respectable Muslims do not want to be seen as if they are 'playing the market'. In any case, traders explained how they made frequent small purchases in preference to saving up rupee profits for less frequent but overall cheaper bulk purchases.

Dollars

Dollars were described by a carpet trader in Peshawar as an alternative to frequent stock purchases by traders in order to avoid holding rupees overnight as a store of value.[45] Money changers in Lahore, Hyderabad and Peshawar also reported the popularity of dollar purchases amongst traders.[46] A trader in the old bazaar in Peshawar described the emergence of 'commission agents', who visit shops in the bazaar at the end of the day to collect rupees and return them as dollars for overnight holdings.[47]

A more complex conversion of local into foreign currency amongst importers was described by a toy importer in Karachi.[48] This interviewee described how amongst those who import from China, he like others has opened a dollar and an RMB account in China. Whenever his rupee balances start to build up in Pakistan, he transfers rupees to China through informal money dealers and maintains his money balances in foreign currency there.

Money dealers also described how foreign exchange cash had become a store of value asset of choice for a broad sector of society. 'The situation is a new kind,' a money dealer in Lahore explained, '[in the late 1990s] people just exchanged money according to their needs [for example for money to take on the *Haj*].... [Now] people from every faction of society convert rupees into foreign currency.... Ordinary people see it as a viable option for profit as compared to the banking sector.[49] The dealer went on to compare the interest earned on 100,000 rupees kept in a bank account over a year, with the same earned on holding dollars in only a few days. As was the case with other money dealers interviewed in Peshawar and Hyderabad, the immense growth in the dollar business, the significant broadening of the clientele, and the purchase of dollars for speculative purposes were key to the description provided by this interviewee of how the foreign exchange trade had changed over the years. As to why people are buying dollars, the Lahore based money dealer stated simply 'there is no confidence in the rupee because it is not stable'.

Vacant Land

A further market that appears to compete with bank accounts for store of value assets is the land market, known locally as the 'plot' market. Interviews with key informants in the plot market (which include plot dealers, large and small plot investors and a private sector town planner) confirmed that the market had been static through the 1990s but had grown since 2001. Key informants agreed that the market had become extremely active since around 2009. This time frame correlates loosely with the structure of the sample interviewed in relation to the plot market. Of the 13 market participants interviewed, 7 had entered the market since 2009, including 3 of the 6 dealers interviewed.[50] Three further participants did not clarify when they entered the market.[51] Thus the number of participants who entered the plot market only since 2009 could be as high as 10 out of 13.

Further evidence of the expansion of the plot market and therein the diversification of market participants arose during the field interviews. The plot market was found to be extremely active even in remote areas. An interview with a plot dealer in Zhob,[52] a remote district centre of 25,000 people with some of the worst development indicators in the country,[53] reported brisk market liquidity. He explained that his customers included those from low-income backgrounds, such as families of migrant labourers in the Gulf. Reflecting the informal nature of the market, the dealer received a large sum of cash wrapped up in a ladies' shawl during the interview.

The broadening of access to the plot market across income groups is suggested by other sources. The website zameen.com, which advertises plots for sale, carries listings for plots as small as 1 *marla* (25 square metres) for as little as a few hundred dollars. 'Even for a man who doesn't have electricity in his hut,' a commercial banker in Karachi explained, 'if he gets money he will have the option of buying one marla of land.'[54] An interview with a town planner and draftsperson in Peshawar further reinforced this point.[55] This informant described a trend towards smaller plots in more recent developments. In the interview, he presented plans for a development on the semi-rural edge of Peshawar. The plans showed large plots, a commercial district, schools, a mosque and parks constituting the centre of the development, which was ringed by small plots, of 125–250 square metres, targeting investors. The peripheral location of these investor plots promised that the central part of the development, where homes would be built and people would live, would be less affected by the investor plots, which could remain vacant for significant periods. Plot dealers agreed that the market was no longer dominated by the rich and the salaried classes, but that a more diverse customer base had become a norm in recent years.

A salient focus of the interviews with key informants from the plot market, which were largely undertaken in 2016, was the undocumented and short-term transactions that had been reported as popular by informants in the 2014 interviews. Detailed and consistent descriptions of the process by which informal purchases can be transacted through the plot market were offered by a number of plot dealers and key participants.

In short, informal transactions are facilitated by dealers who work on a 1 per cent commission and arrange the 'agreement to sell' document to be signed by seller and buyer when payment (usually cash) is made. Further documentation, however, is not completed. That is, the purchaser does not obtain the primary proof of ownership, a document known as the *fard*, from the local land administrator, known as the *patwari*. Nor does the purchaser pay stamp duty, capital value tax, transfer of immovable property tax or any registration fees. No mutation documents (*intiqal*) are issued by the state to confirm the transfer of ownership.

When the purchaser sells the plot in the informal market, a new 'agreement to sell' document is signed between the undocumented holder of the plot and the new purchaser. The full documentation is only completed when a purchaser chooses to shift the plot back into the formal market. At this point, the purchaser completes the full documentation and the plot is signed over from the original seller (that is, the person who first sold the plot into the informal market) to the final buyer. Thus, although a chain of individuals may have purchased and sold the plot on, their names will not appear on any formal documentation. On the official documentation, the plot will appear as sold and purchased by only the person who first sold the plot from the formal into the informal market, and the person who finally brought the plot back from the informal into the formal market.

In contrast to the formal market, informal transactions thus make settlement in the plot market instant. Exercise of such a short-term facility was apparent in the interviews. For example, an auto parts dealer in Peshawar described his shortest plot holding as spanning only half an hour.[56] An agricultural land owner in Sindh interrupted the field interview to take a phone call pertaining to a plot that he had purchased 20 days earlier and was on that day trying to liquidate.[57] He described the plot market in his area as being characterised by the agricultural cycle, so that when capital was needed to be put into agriculture, for example, with the purchase of inputs, plot prices dropped as capital was drawn out of the market. Later, when agricultural profits were realised, plot prices were driven up as capital returned to the market.

This informant, in common with the property investor in the affluent countryside near Islamabad,[58] described short-term plot holdings as an alternative to bank account holdings. Moreover, these informants confirmed that short-term, informal plot transactions had only appeared in the market in the years since 2008. Consensus on the growth in market liquidity after 2008 supports this proposition, given that informal transactions are more likely to go smoothly in a highly liquid market. Specifically, informal transactions need to be liquid because the original seller (who first sold the plot into the informal market) needs to sign the official documentation when the plot eventually returns to the formal market through the final purchaser's registration of formal land ownership. Hence, the longer it takes to liquidate a plot, the greater the risk is that the original seller will no longer be willing to participate in the official documentation process. This problem was explained by a plot dealer in Charsadda in terms of problems he had had with an informal transaction when the original seller went abroad and was not able to complete the documentation when the plot finally re-entered the formal market.[59]

Alternative Means of Exchange and Units of Account

Alternative means of exchange and unit of account functions were identified in interviews pertaining to US dollars and wheat. Although it was difficult to gauge the degree to which these money functions had been taken up as new strategies in wheat, the use of dollars to denominate value in the carpet industry offered a clear shift away from rupee denomination coinciding with the post-liberalisation years.

Dollar Denomination

The most striking evidence of a shift out of the rupee as a means of exchange and unit of account came from a set of interviews with Afghan carpet dealers in Peshawar in 2014. These dealers explained that, since the rupee had become unstable in the years after 2008, the carpet trade had shifted out of rupees and into US dollars. 'We didn't use US dollars 20 years ago,' one dealer explained, 'we started to use US dollars 5 or 6 years ago.'[60] These dealers explained that rupee instability had become a major issue in their industry. Both were concerned by the long lag times between ordering a carpet and receiving the delivery. They explained that previously, the transactions between wholesalers and retailers had been denominated and paid in rupees, which is a dominant form of money in parts of Afghanistan. The dealers explained that since around 2009, pricing in the industry had become denominated in dollars, and payments with suppliers carried out in dollars. 'We deal in US dollars to protect ourselves,' one dealer explained.[61] Although retail sales continue to be often conducted in rupees, he noted, they are based on conversion from a US dollar price at the day's conversion rate. These dealers explained that the rupees received from sales are generally changed immediately into US dollars.

Wheat Denomination

A subtler reference to change in means of exchange and the unit of account could be detected in rural interviews with regard to wage payment and debt denomination. Although a time frame could not be established that could show distinct transition, the persistence of non-rupee rural practices around wage and debt payment and denomination may be influenced by the kind of rupee instability that appears to have prompted the changed practices in the carpet industry. Specifically, rural respondents reported the persistence of in-kind wages, not only for direct cropping labour, but also for agricultural services wages. Consistent across the interviews were reports of the preference for wheat as payment, and especially so for low-income households. It was noted that wheat can be used as a means of exchange, for example, in grocery stores, in both rural and urban areas. These findings are supported by those of the Collective for Social Sciences Research Karachi.[62]

Rural respondents reported that cash was often paid for wages associated with the cultivation of cash crops. As one farmer explained, labourers preferred to be paid in cash for the cotton harvest because small quantities of cotton could not be exchanged for a good price.[63] Rural respondents also described the denomination of loans in agricultural commodities, be it between farmer and supplier, or between neighbours. These findings are confirmed by an International Growth Centre study on informal lending in agriculture, which found a dominance of in-kind lending, neither denominated nor paid in the rupee.[64]

Perceptions of Volatility

When asked specifically about volatility, recognition of monetary decline coinciding with the post-liberalisation period was extremely consistent. All interviewees were able to identify a period of transition to greater price volatility that roughly coincided with the deterioration in the rupee and inflation in food prices that occurred after 2008, as described in Chapter 3. This was as much the case for illiterate members of low-income rural households as for traders and other groups. 'People have lost confidence in the rupee,' one commercial banker explained, 'because it devalued from 45 rupees to the dollar to more than 100.'[65] Similarly, a money dealer in Lahore explained that 'there is no confidence in the rupee because it is not stable'.[66]

Certain interviewees expanded upon this description of monetary volatility with other observations of growing volatility in recent years. A farmer near Khanewal, for example, observed that it is not only the rupee itself that is losing value, but that gold and land are now more volatile than before, prices of which 'can even go down'.[67] Others in the agricultural sector noted greater volatility in agricultural prices in general. For a fertilizer dealer in Charsadda, the greater volatility in fertilizer prices since 2002 reflected both a burden of risk and an opportunity for profit.[68] A young landowner near Mirpurkass complained of the greater volatility in the wheat price as compared to that in the time of his father. Complaining at once of higher prices and of the disruption to predictability in prices, he said, '[The price] has gone up 50 rupees today and it's now harvest time.'[69] The same concerns were raised by a gold dealer in Peshawar. He said that while the gold price changed on a weekly basis in the late 1990s, 'there is now a morning price and an afternoon price'. Moreover, the dollar and gold prices, he reported, no longer move in tandem but have become unpredictable vis-à-vis one another.[70]

Conclusion: Multiple Money Instruments Serving Multiple Money Functions

Although far from conclusive, these findings proffer evidence of changing money practices, which draw on a whole array of money functions, whether overnight holdings of transactional balances, medium-term savings instruments, the denomination of debt and wages, and even the means of exchange. Moreover, although it is clearer in some cases (such as land, cattle and foreign exchange) as compared to others (such as wage denomination in grain), the sources considered in this chapter suggest a newness in the take-up of these money strategies that sets them apart from traditional practices and pegs them specifically to conditions associated with the new economy. The findings from the field interviews thus cannot reveal the degree to which people use new money strategies or exactly how new these strategies are, but they do suggest a change in money use that disrupts the static and unconscious reliance on state money that is implicit in conventional analysis.

As such, these observations raise a series of analytical issues. If the kinds of instruments raised in the field interviews are linked to the decline in deposits raised in Chapter 3, and these money strategies are cast not as going 'backwards' to barter, but going 'forwards' to liquid and diversified asset markets, then where does that leave the central bank? What does that mean for money theory, either in its academic incarnations or its technical forms, as operationalised by central bank practice? And what about financial inclusion? The three chapters that follow explore these questions and thereby bring themes from Chapters 1, 2 and 3 – of the changing relationship between the state and money and of volatility entrenched in money itself – into engagement with findings from the field of new money practices that detract from the dominance of state money.

Notes

1. CGAP is a partnership organisation at the World Bank and a major player in the global financial inclusion space. CGAP's smallholders study (Anderson 'and Ahmed 2014) was undertaken in Pakistan, Tanzania and Mozambique.

2. The three household surveys were undertaken by the Bill and Melinda Gates funded Financial Inclusion Insights initiative; the World Bank's Global Findex; and Gallup's Access to Finance survey conducted in partnership with the SBP. See Naeha Rashid's brief comparison of the three on the CGAP blog (Rashid 2015). The rural household panel survey (IFPRI/IDS 2016) was undertaken by the International Food Policy Research institute and the Institute of Development Studies.

3. The push for new household data in developing economies finds a parallel in the advanced economies, where there has been a great deal of new interest in household finances, particularly since the recent financial crisis. The IMF's 2005 *Global Financial Stability Report*, for example, called for greater data collection on households, which was taken further in the IMF and Financial Stability Board 2010 Financial Crisis and Information Gaps report, prompting Deutsche Bank's Panel on Household Finances Survey in 2010, The European Central Bank's Household Finance and Consumption survey in 2013, and the Fed's Survey of Household Economics and Decision making in 2013 in the US.

4. See respectively Kustin (2015) and E. Taylor (2013).

5. On the construction of financial inclusion indices, see Park and Mercado (2015).

6. As discussed in Chapter 3. See El-Qorchi, Maibo and Wilson (2003) and Thompson (2011).

7. For example, see de Zeeuw (1996), Dorosh, Niazi and Nazil (2006) and Malik, Nazli and Whitney (2014).

8. For concerns about the most recent census, see Zaman (2017) and Hussain (2017).

9. See Malik, Nazli, Mehmood and Shahzad (2014). With regards to deposits and kerb exchange rates, data can be misreported by market operators and remain unverified by the SBP. For example, anecdotal evidence suggests that banks artificially raise their deposit levels at the end of the month in order to reduce the amount of capital demanded by capital requirements; and kerb dealers report lower rates to the SBP than they are actually dealing in, in order to avoid further pressure being placed on them by the SBP to reduce kerb premiums. Underreporting of kerb premiums is noted by the SBP (2008: 132).

10. Demirguc-Kunt and Klapper (2012: 34).

11. The ethics process undertaken ensured that interviewees' information was well protected.

12. More specifically, primary interviews were undertaken with fifteen traders in bazaars in Peshawar, Charsadda, Hyderabad, Karachi and Quetta; five agricultural workers near Khanewal and Rajanpur; one fertilizer dealer in Charsadda; two low-income salaried workers near Khanewal and in Karachi; five money changers and a gold dealer in Lahore, Hyderabad and Peshawar; medium–large agricultural landowners in Mirpurkass and the fringes of Lahore; three commercial bankers in Peshawar and Karachi; and eight people involved in the land market (dealers, developers and planners)

in Charsadda, Peshawar, Islamabad, Rawalpindi and Zhob. The interviews included five customers in the land market, in Karachi, Peshawar, Islamabad, Quetta and Mirpurkass. Rural representatives are present in each category, except money changers and commercial bankers. The majority of interviewees were male, which reflects the male dominance of bazaar trade and public society at large; however, three of the six low-income rural interviewees were female. The interviews spanned the country and included each province, with the exception of Gilgit-Baltistan. Interviews were undertaken in Urdu, Sindhi, Seraiki, Punjabi, Pashto and English, with the support of a translator in all cases except for those interviews undertaken in English. In order to cultivate rapport, the interviews were not recorded in audio. Rather notes were taken by hand, directly in the small number of interviews conducted in English, and from the translator's oral English translation in the bulk of interviews. Although some of the interviews lasted for only around fifteen minutes, the majority lasted for a period of between half an hour and an hour. Some of the most informative interviews were spread over a number of hours.

13. See, for example, Kuran (1986).

14. See Appendix for names and dates of key stakeholder interviews.

15. See Settle (2017).

16. See, respectively, IFPRI/IDS (2016) and Anderson and Ahmed (2016).

17. See Gazdar and Mallah (2013), Balagamwala and Gazdar (2014) and Gazdar (2015).

18. Interviewee AW#5, interviewed on 27 April 2014, near Khanewal.

19. Interviewee SW#1, interviewed on 27 April 2014, near Khanewal.

20. Interviewee AW#1, interviewed on 24 April 2014, near Rajanpur.

21. Interviewee FD#1, interviewed on 14 May 2016, in Charsadda.

22. See Waheed (1996). Waheed's interviews were taken in a village near Sargohda.

23. Interestingly, when asked why cash is no longer held, interviewees most often cited security concerns. One farmer explained that 'these days, the children would steal it' (Interviewee AW#4, interviewed on 27 April 2014, near Khanewal). These comments go unexplained here; suffice it to say that the study's focus on (self-reported) empirical behaviour rather than self-reported motive is an important aspect of the methodology that guides the field interviews.

24. Interviewee BM#1, interviewed on 22 April 2014, in Peshawar.

25. Interviewee T#14, interviewed on 21 May 2014, in Karachi.

26. Interviewee LO#1, interviewed on 3 May 2014, near Mirpurkhass; and PI#1, interviewed on 13 May 2016 in Islamabad.

27. Interviewee T#15, interviewed on 21 May 2016, in Karachi.

28. Interviewee T#14, interviewed on 21 May 2016, in Karachi.

29. Interviewee T#14, interviewed on 21 May 2016, in Karachi.

30. See Gazdar and Mallah (2013) and Balagamwala and Gazdar (2014).

31. Interviewee AW#1, interviewed on 24 April 2014, near Rajanpur.

32. Interviewee SW#1 and AW#5, interviewed on 27 April 2014, near Khanewal.

33. See A. S. Khan (2014).

34. Interviewee T#10, interviewed on 10 April 2014 in Quetta; and interviewee T#8, interviewed on 29 April 2014, in Hyderabad.

35. See Balagamwala and Gazdar (2014).

36. Interviewee LO#1, interviewed on 3 May 2014, near Mirpurkhass.

37. See respectively Z. Khan (2008) and Aazim (2014); and A. S. Khan (2014: 90).

38. See Khan and Burki (2005).

39. Interviewee T#13, interviewed on 5 May 2016, in Karachi.

40. Interviewee T#1, interviewed on 21 April 2014, in Peshawar.

41. Interviewee BM#1, interviewed on 22 April 2014, in Peshawar.

42. Interviewee T#5, interviewed on 22 April 2014, in Peshawar.

43. Interviewee T#10, interviewed on 10 April 2014, in Quetta.

44. The nature of daily purchases was discussed at length with interviewee T#13, interviewed in Charsadda on 4 April 2016; and interviewees T#7 and T#8, interviewed in Hyderabad on 29 April 2014.

45. Interviewees T#3 and T#4, interviewed on 22 April 2014, in Peshawar.

46. Interviewee MD#1, interviewed in Lahore on 19 April 2014; Interviewee MD#2, interviewed in Hyderabad on 29 April 2014; and interviewee MD#3, interviewed in Peshawar on 15 May 2016.

47. Interviewee T#5, interviewed on 22 April 2014, in Peshawar.

48. Interviewee T#11, interviewed on 14 May 2014, in Karachi.

49. Interviewee MD#1, interviewed on 19 April 2014, in Lahore.

50. Specifically, these new entrants were dealers PD#2 and PD#3, interviewed on 13 May 2016, in Islamabad, as well as PD#5, interviewed on 14 May 2016, in Charsadda. The customers of plot dealers who were new entrants to the market included interviewee LO#1, interviewed on 3 May 2014, near Mirpurkhass; interviewee T#15, interviewed on 21 May 2016, in Karachi; interviewed on 22 April 2014, in Peshawar; and interviewee T#12 interviewed on 15 May 2014, in Peshawar.

51. Specifically, MC#3, interviewed on 15 May 2016, in Peshawar; and T#10, interviewed on 10 May 2014, in Quetta.

52. Interviewee PD#1, interviewed on 8 May 2014, in Zhob.

53. Government statistics find that for Zhob district, around 60 per cent of the population is illiterate, over one-third of households have no access to sanitation facilities and infant mortality is far higher than in war-torn Afghanistan. See Government of Baluchistan and UNICEF (2011).

54. Interview with Mushtaq Khan on 12 May 2016, in Karachi.

55. Interviewee TP#1, interviewed on 15 May 2016, in Peshawar.

56. Interviewee T#12, interviewed on 15 May 2014, in Peshawar.

57. Interviewee LO#1, interviewed on 3 May 2014, near Mirpurkhass.

58. Interviewee PI#1, interviewed on 13 May 2016, in Islamabad.

59. Interviewee PD#5, interviewed on 14 May 2016, in Charsadda.

50. Interviewee T#3, interviewed on 22 May 2014, in Peshawar.

61. Interviewee T#4, interviewed on 22 May 2014, in Peshawar.

62. See Gazdar and Mallah (2013) and Balagamwala and Gazdar (2014).

63. Interviewee AW#5, interviewed on 27 April 2014, near Khanewal.

64. See Haq, Aslam et al. (2013).

65. Interviewee BM#1, interviewed on 22 April 2014, in Peshawar.

66. Interviewee MD#1, interviewed on 19 April 2014, in Lahore.

67. Interviewee AW#2, interviewed on 27 April 2014, near Khanewal.

68. Interview with FD#1, interviewed on 14 May 2016, in Charsadda.

69. Interviewee LO#1, interviewed on 3 May 2014, near Mirpurkhass

70. GD#1, interviewed on 22 April 2014, in Peshawar.

6

Unstable Money and Risk Mitigation in the New Economy

As Chapter 3 shows, the liberalisation process has shifted the pricing regime on money and on key commodities from set pricing and comprehensive intervention towards a market float. This process has by no means been absolute. The rupee itself, together with the key prices of wheat and electricity, continues to be subjected to intervention that seeks to smooth volatility. The wheat price is influenced by the continuing but much pared-down programme of state procurement. Electricity is still priced in accordance with tariffs set by the state, although these have moved much closer to global prices, both in terms of the rupee price and in terms of much more frequent tariff revision. Regardless of these vestiges of the pre-liberalisation era, however, transformation in the economy has been significant and this transformation extends to the monetary environment – the governance of money and of the prices that give everyday meaning to the usefulness of money.

Applying the analytical framework developed in Chapter 2, this chapter contends that the new economy is characterised by complex and persistent instability. This instability reaches into the everyday transactions entailed in maintaining the consumer basket and thereby imposes very real implications for money. Building on the description of the transformation of the rupee relayed in Chapter 3 with a description of attendant transformation in alternative monetary forms, which were raised in Chapter 5, the chapter presents a conception of frontier money as entailing multiple money forms, each with its own profile of risk and liquidity, that include the transformed open economy rupee as well as an array of alternative money forms.

This analysis is premised on the changing risk profile of the rupee in the post-liberalisation environment of the new economy. If state money is not the 'stable pole', then it carries risk of volatility in its value relative to subsistence goods, as well as the risk of long-term depreciation. In these conditions, the risk-free status of state money is undermined as the monetary environment becomes more complicated. In these circumstances, state money's distinction from other liquid assets becomes less pronounced: the once clear line is increasingly blurred between state money – as an embodiment of key monetary attributes and thus a unique money instrument – and ordinary commodities and assets which may carry similar profiles of risk and liquidity.

This chapter proposes that key markets have evolved to service demand for highly liquid money instruments. This market development presents a monetary environment characterised by a series of money instruments, which offer varying degrees of 'moneyness' in different combinations of money attributes. These instruments may not necessarily be complete state money substitutes, but may be relevant to different applications of various money attributes across the balance sheet. Along with state money itself, these instruments constitute frontier money: a dynamic set of money instruments that fulfil conventional money functions where state money has become compromised.

This fracturing of the money object, in turn, suggests that economic agents utilise money in new ways. Specifically, multiplicity in money demands strategic money use. Amidst an array of alternative money options, agents must select the right money instrument to match the specific money function required. Such negotiation of the monetary environment is more complex than the use of money as habitual, or 'without a second thought',[1] that characterises uncontested state money in stable conditions. This chapter therefore casts the kinds of money strategies described in Chapter 5 as financial innovation: as dynamic strategies that respond to changing monetary conditions, which ultimately generate new money instruments. The implications for the financial inclusion agenda of this disruption to state money as unique and uncontested money in the economy are expanded upon in the final chapters of the book.

The first section of this chapter plots the liberalisation of the monetary environment in Pakistan, not just in terms of the rupee itself but of key anchor prices in the economy. It thus proposes that the monetary environment has become subject to a complex instability which undermines the rupee as money by undermining the 'working fiction of the monetary invariant' (Mirowski 1991: 580). The correlation between the strategies identified in the fieldwork and strategies known to be typical of hyperinflationary episodes is highlighted. It is argued that the 'discordance' of hyperinflation-like strategies in a rupee environment that falls far short of hyperinflation reflects a complexity of risk that is not captured by traditional monetary indicators. These strategies show how even relatively moderate instability undermines the rupee under open market conditions by generating uncertainty.

The second section elaborates upon each of the main instruments identified in the field interview in terms of their monetary attributes of liquidity and risk. This analysis reflects how the traditional functions of state money have become disseminated across an array of alternative money forms.

The third section argues that it is mistaken to see these sorts of strategies as a 'return to barter' or some kind of 'demonetisation'. The 'return to barter' reading suggests a digression into a simpler economy that could be remedied through the provision of access to savings and credit facilities, which are intended to give households the means to harness growth opportunities to escape the stagnancy of barter in moving away from subsistence and towards prosperity. On the contrary, the analysis put forward in this chapter suggests that the kinds of uses to which these non-state money instruments are put, in fact, constitute sophisticated monetary practices. Drawing on the most advanced forms of global financial liquidity, these strategies look more like the practices of hedge funds than of pre-capitalist barter.

The closing section describes frontier money. The concept of frontier money emphasises multiplicity and change in a monetary environment characterised by open markets and weak formal monetary governance. In a frontier monetary environment, the safety and stability of state money is eroded, with which state money loses its privilege amongst other assets. As a result, within frontier money, state money is but one of many risky money instruments.

Building on the analytical frame laid out in Chapter 2, the Pakistani context laid out in Chapter 3 and the household interviews discussed in Chapters 4 and 5, this chapter develops a picture of frontier money and the frontier monetary environment in Pakistan's new economy. This picture provides a critical building block in the argument posed in the final chapters of the book, which posits the financial inclusion agenda turned on its head – casting state money as the locus of risk more than a risk management tool and financial inclusion a better solution to the central bank's inability to control money under open markets than a solution to the stagnancy of poverty.

Growing Monetary Instability and the Liberalisation of Money and Markets in Pakistan

Based on long-run statistical analysis of Pakistan's key economic indicators, senior SBP researchers Ali Choudhary and Farooq Pasha (2013) find that generalised instability in Pakistan has become an economic norm over the last 30 years: 'The only "stable" stylized fact [for Pakistan's economy] is the instability that exists in key economic ratios and relationships.' Moreover, 'what is of more concern', they conclude, 'is that this instability has increased over the last decade' (ibid.: 34). These findings of greater volatility in key macroeconomic ratios and relationships (such as those between output and investment, output and consumption, and output and the external sector) support other statistical findings of heightened volatility. World Bank research on stylised facts in the Pakistani economy identifies increasing volatility in Pakistan's GDP in the decade since 2000.[2] SBP research identifies this as a 'four-fold increase in Pakistan's real GDP volatility over the past three decades coincid[ing] with the emergence of a deregulated financial sector since the 1980s' (Hussein, Saeed and Hassan 2011: 2). Moreover, Rashid and Husain (2010) find that intensifying inflationary pressure and exchange rate instability is linked to growing capital inflows over the same period. In this environment, it is unsurprising that recent research at the central bank finds very little price rigidity and weak wage rigidity.[3]

These studies make empirical contributions towards understanding how the Pakistani economy has changed through the relatively rapid years of transition to open markets. As described in Chapter 3, the Pakistani economy has shifted from a centrally controlled economy characterised by import-substitution and administered pricing, to an open economy with money and markets that were largely liberalised from state control by the mid-2000s. With this economic shift, the rupee has been released from administered interest rates, centralised credit allocations and a fixed exchange rate at the same time as access to foreign currency has been legalised, the current account has been liberalised and price controls have been removed.

Importantly, these changes have occurred in Pakistan in a context of significant long-run change in the global economy. As discussed in Chapter 1, the collapse of the Bretton Woods system of fixed exchange rates in the early 1970s is pivotal because the new degree of monetary volatility that accompanied floating rates established fundamentally new financial conditions. In these conditions, the liberalisation of money and markets can facilitate the kind of constant shocks to value that were discussed in chapters two.

These dynamics can be identified in the twists and turns of rupee governance described in Chapter 3. There we saw how interactions between liberalised money and open markets have generated an order of volatility that was unknown in the pre-liberalisation decades in Pakistan. The direct and indirect measures that the SBP has taken to limit the pressure placed on the rupee by price shocks to the balance of payments, as well as the direct and indirect measures taken by the SBP to limit the speculative pressure that exacerbates these rupee effects, attest to this set of problems. The wide-ranging nature of these measures – which include crackdowns on the kerb market, shifting oil payments out of the interbank market and onto the SBP's balance books, subsidising formal sector remittance flows, and concessional lending to the export sector – were all attempts to mitigate the disparate threats to the rupee under a regime of liberalisation. The translation of this underlying instability in the rupee into an uncertainty that undermines trust in money (as described in Chapter 2) is taken up here in the specific context of the rupee.

Monetary Instability after 2007

For Pakistan's transition to open markets, the float of the rupee in 2000 marked a crucial point. Yet, whilst instability in the rupee was a central policy problem right from the start of the float, the full brunt of open market conditions was only felt in the years after 2007. After 2007, extraordinary inflows linked to the War on Terror, the privatisation of state assets and more general conditions of excess in the global economy slowed. At this point, the international environment that had been described by the SBP as 'congenial' (SBP 2008a: 116) no longer allowed Pakistan comfortably to finance its external sector deficits through non-debt creating inflows and concessional loans. Up until 2008, these flows had helped to counter the impact on the rupee of the demand for hard currency that was being generated through the balance of payments, over and above the heavy pressures on the rupee arising through servicing foreign currency borrowing.[4] The predicament thereby exposed after 2007 was one of greater rupee volatility as the rupee bore the impact of external payments unbuffered by appreciation and foreign exchange reserve growth based in abundant and often geopolitical inflows. In 2012 the SBP complained that the value of the rupee had become 'more sensitive to geo-political and adverse market sentiments' than 'economic' factors (SBP 2012: 92). Here the central bank lamented the changing winds of the global economy: after years of benefiting from abundant inflows linked to its favourable geo-strategic position, the rupee was left reeling as speculative pressure responded to the eroding relationship with the United States.

Greater instability in state money is to some degree reflected in conventional data, notwithstanding the caveats around statistical data use described in Chapter 5. The greater exposure of the rupee to global markets (at least in terms of formal flows) is reflected in Figures 6.1 and 6.2. These show the transformation of key balance of payments flows as liberalisation has facilitated greater (and more volatile) engagement with the global economy. Yet asset and liability flows on the financial account are net figures using annual data points. These figures thus do not reflect the flows in and out of the financial account that cancel each other out in net terms, but which nevertheless generate real pressures on the economy on a day to day basis.[5] If gross flows were depicted, the significant branching out of financial account flows in the years after 2000 would be much sharper.

Figure 6.1 Balance of
payments, 1976–2014,
credit and asset side
(in US dollar,
thousands)
Source: IMF.

Figure 6.2 Balance of
payments, 1976–2014,
debits and liabilities
side (in US dollar,
thousands)
Source: IMF.

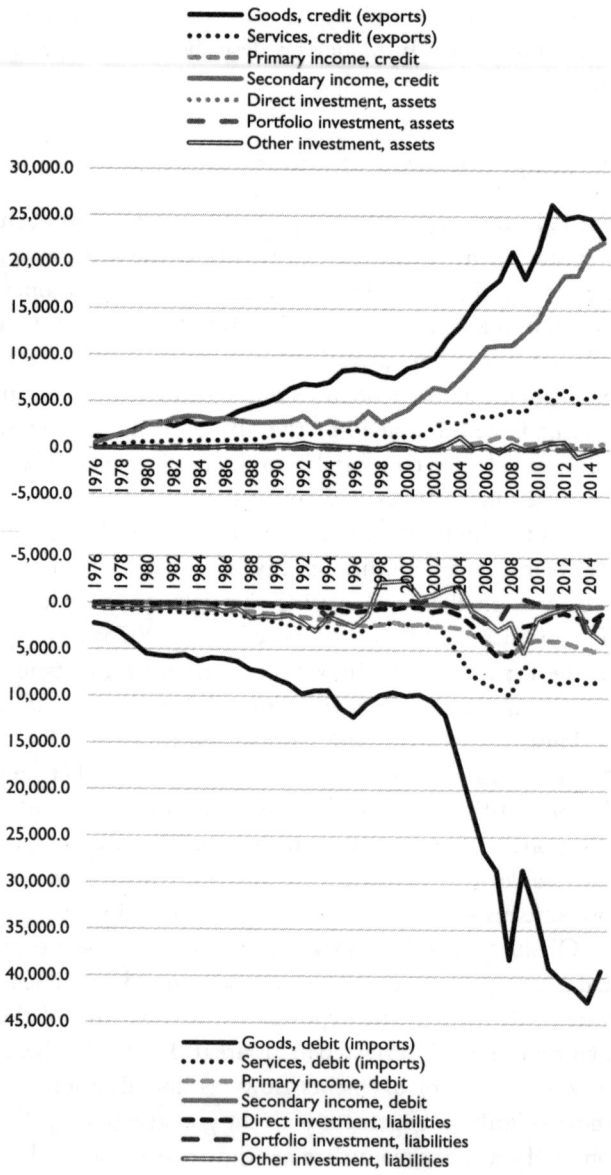

Figure 6.3 shows the official exchange rate between 1957 and 2016. The
gradual depreciation of the rupee though the 1980s and 1990s[6] – let alone the
flat line of the exchange rate before then – is in marked contrast to the much
more jagged peaks nd troughs of the rupee after the float and the marked decline
of the rupee in 2008 is visible.

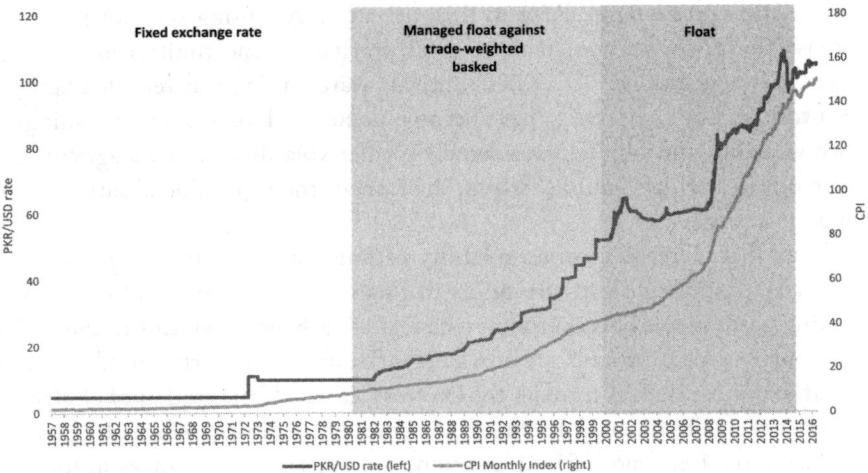

Figure 6.3 PKR/USD exchange rate and monthy CPI inflation, 1957–2016
Source: SBP; World Bank; IMF (2016a).

These statistics should, however, be treated with caution. At the very least, they do not capture informal flows.

An important aspect of monetary instability that is driven by openness is the liberalisation of prices on agricultural commodities and other subsistence goods such as energy. This has compounded the everyday experience of volatility in money by increasing the exposure of these crucial everyday prices to the vagaries of global market pricing. As discussed in Chapter 3, price supports in agriculture had been costly for the state to maintain but had been effective in providing stable prices for key commodities.[7] With liberalisation in the 1990s, direct price controls over agricultural commodities were removed and much of the indirect price supports provided by the state were dismantled. By the mid-2000s, agricultural prices had been almost entirely liberalised, although wheat procurement remained an exception and ad hoc interventions were sporadically taken across the agricultural sector when major threats to individual prices arose.

The substantive increase in agricultural price volatility in the wake of liberalisation is indicated by the increase of private wheat storage (itself a local taboo associated with 'hoarding') that occurred after 2008. Mushtaq Khan and Abid Burki (2005) show that instability in the wheat price was sufficient to attract the private sector to wheat storage in the aftermath of the 2001 liberalisation programme. Prior to this, private warehousing was not practised because the price was too stable to offer profitable opportunities for holding wheat between seasons.[8] After 2008, private warehousing was reported both in fieldwork and by the press to have become popular.[9] This suggests meaningful price volatility and implies considerably greater volatility in other agricultural commodities, which, unlike wheat, had shed their pre-liberalisation price supports entirely.

A marked increase in price volatility can also be identified in the cost of electricity. Exposing electricity prices to floating market rates had been a key sticking point in the liberalisation process after early price reforms in the 1990s had contributed to upward pressures on inflation and poverty rates.[10] After a hiatus under Musharraf through the boom years, the liberalisation of electricity prices was again pursued in the years after 2008. Price reform hinged on increasing the frequency of tariff revisions so as ensure that changes in the cost of production (notably in international oil prices) were carried into consumer prices.[11] These efforts were met with resistance by the public, by which both the frequency of tariff revision as well as the higher prices entailed have become the subject of popular protest.[12]

Yet the SBP has primarily considered the importance of electricity and wheat prices in terms of a one-dimensional concern with inflation. For this book, by contrast, the emphasis is placed on the everyday meaning that these prices give to the usefulness of state money in more fundamental terms. This analysis suggests that the liberalisation of agricultural and energy prices combined with the float of the rupee under a generally open capital and current account has generated new norms of volatility in money and pricing. As the rest of this chapter shows, these conditions have effectively generated monetary contestation in a fundamentally changed monetary environment.

Economic Uncertainty and the Rupee

Sentiments across the field interviews reflect a recognition of volatility that demonstrates the relevance of volatility in money and prices to the everyday economy of ordinary people. On the one hand, long-term comparisons were made by various interviewees between the present period and the vastly greater stability in prices in decades passed, such as in gold, in wheat, in fertilizer, in land and in the rupee itself. On the other hand, the sharp decline in monetary conditions in 2008 was recognised with exceptional consistency by interviewees. This was notable in the case of interviewees from low-income rural households, who are considered by many to be unlikely to be able to understand inflation.

Not simply a theoretical expression of greater volatility implied by the recalibration of the economy around market principles, these findings offer evidence that greater volatility carries substantive meaning for ordinary people.

It is the contention of this chapter and the study at large that this is not merely a one-dimensional volatility generated through the liberalisation of commodity markets due to the exposure of key prices to volatile market pricing. Rather, it is that liberalisation has generated a deep-seated instability that ultimately undermines the status of the rupee as money itself. By this reading, volatility in any single price in the economy is not experienced by economic actors as isolated price volatility. Rather, shocks to single prices are experienced as a series of related price shocks that combine to generate a deeper uncertainty around value that is intimately linked to economic actors' perception of the status of the rupee.

As set out in Chapter 2, the consideration of the threat of inflation entailed in inflation-targeting thinking does not do justice to the depth of volatility in a frontier economy such as Pakistan. Contrary to inflation targeting's singular attendance to core inflation, monetary deterioration can be fed by any number of shocks that are unrelated to both scarcity and 'overheating' in aggregate demand. Examples of such shocks include supply shocks in an important global commodity market, a 'friendly fire' incident amidst increasing antagonism in a key donor relationship, a sudden capital account gap with the last-minute cancellation of Eurodollar bonds in the wake of external crisis, or a much more mundane event like a forthcoming IMF repayment projected to adversely affect reserve coverage. These kinds of shocks can – and have – generated significant exchange rate shifts and speculation on the rupee's value that raises prices in the economy, especially in subsistence goods. They can also generate shocks to individual prices that quickly feed through into other prices, even though these kinds of price shocks are not deemed important in conventional thinking on inflation. In a monetary environment characterised by constant flux, the conventional approach of separating out the derivation of shocks, so as to form uniform inflation expectations that can distinguish core from headline inflation, is neither useful nor possible.

Rather, at issue is a deeper sense of uncertainty, which is fed by volatility in money and prices. From this perspective, unstable money and prices join with the instability in key economic ratios and relationships, identified as new stylised facts by Choudhary and Pasha (2013), to generate the 'knowledge surrogates' and the 'knowledge deficits' (Shackle 1972; Coddington 1975) that make up everyday perceptions about the economy. The economic uncertainty that is realised through these processes, it is contended in this book, in turn undermines the 'working fiction of the monetary invariant' (Mirowski 1991: 580). Under these conditions, economic agents 'think twice' about habitually relying on the rupee as money.

Hyperinflationary Responses as an Indicator of Uncertainty

The way that the changed strategies identified in the fieldwork pose parallels with hyperinflation supports the argument that price volatility has generated a deep uncertainty that feeds into the status of state money in the economy. Hyperinflationary episodes typically prompt a drop in bank deposits, increasing dollarisation and the expansion of barter transactions.[13] In Pakistan, although the potential expansion of the formal dollarisation of savings had been limited by the central bank in 2002,[14] the drop in rupee deposits has been distinct. 'Real' economy assets appear to be replacing the rupee as store of value assets through an expansion of barter transactions. Yet monetary conditions have fallen far short of hyperinflation. Hyperinflation is defined as inflation reaching over 50 per cent per month (Cagan 1956). As figure 6.4 shows, inflation in Pakistan barely hit 25 per cent and stayed over 20 per cent for only nine months.

Figure 6.4 Percentage change in consumer price index (over previous year)
Source: Pakistan Bureau of Statistics.

The severity of the response to deteriorating monetary conditions in Pakistan suggests that the experience of risk associated with the rupee exceeds that conventionally implied by the inflation level that has prevailed, even when rupee deterioration was at its worst. If monetary disruption in Pakistan is identified not as an isolated bout of inflation but as a problem of interacting instabilities spreading across prices and other macroeconomic indicators, then the hyperinflationary responses identified in Pakistan no longer appear disproportionate. In those circumstances, uncertainty is a far greater problem than 'menu costs' or 'shoe leather costs'.[15] Rather, non-monetary indicators combine with monetary indicators to generate uncertainty not portrayed by conventional monetary statistics. By this reading, hyperinflationary responses answer to a deep-seated uncertainty – a whole greater than the sum of its parts – that is only partly represented by inflation statistics.

Hyperinflationary responses to relatively moderate monetary conditions also show how volatility in the economy at large interacts with public perceptions about state money. State money bears the burden of uncertainty in the economy as a whole, as risk management techniques are applied through money strategies that are seemingly disproportionate to the monetary volatility at hand. This predicament poses a reversal of liquidity preference theory. Rather than a surge into state money, we see a decline in bank deposits. This reveals how money itself is perceived as a key locus of risk in an environment of heightened uncertainty, over and above the actual risk carried by state money as expressed in monetary indicators.

Given the comprehensive restructuring of the regulation of the Pakistani economy, the argument developed throughout this study is that the everyday financial volatility explored in the fieldwork is not rooted in a limited period of crisis, but rather reflects the condition of money under liberalisation. That is, in the post-2007 period, the extraordinary inflows that had protected the newly liberalised economy from exposure to global markets were removed. Without those flows buffering the economy, it experienced a new normal of instability. It is proposed here that volatility is an entrenched and permanent feature linked to the liberalisation of money and markets rather than resulting simply from the 2008 crisis and its aftermath. This explanation is consistent with the findings of Choudhary and Pasha (2013), of a 'new stylised fact' of growing instability across economic indicators and relationships.

It follows that improvement in macroeconomic indicators since 2013 does not signify an end to the problem of complex instability proposed here. Although macro and monetary indicators may achieve improvement and some degree of stabilisation, a more subtle, underlying volatility that is rooted in the liberalisation of money and markets persists. The implication is that the rupee is unlikely to resume its role in 'ruling the roost', even if improved macroeconomic indicators hold. Instead, open markets will persist in generating instability in key anchor prices, which fundamentally undermine state money. In these conditions, financial inclusion may be more useful to the central bank as a tool with which to generate greater governability over the rupee than to households to secure their own financial stability. This argument is developed further over the remaining chapters.

New Money Instruments

The rest of this chapter explores the monetary attributes of key commodities that were identified in the fieldwork as pertaining to money practices. It puts forward the proposition that the strategies identified in the fieldwork are best interpreted as financial innovation that responds dynamically to the shifting monetary environment.

Cattle

Changed practices around cash holdings that were reported by rural interviewees suggest a distinct and uncomplicated example of a shift out of cash and into more reliable money instruments for store of value functions. What was striking was the consistency of responses by interviewees, who assured the author that people simply do not save in cash any longer, even though this had been standard practice in the past. These findings are supported by detailed fieldwork on savings practices undertaken by Shahina Waheed in the mid-1990s. In field interviews in a village geographically and culturally close to the field sites referred to here, Waheed (1996) identified a series of traditional savings strategies, such as in cattle, but found cash savings to be predominant. Waheed's findings thereby offer a stark contrast to more recent fieldwork undertaken for this study, in which cattle was found predominant and cash unequivocally described by interviewees as no longer relied upon.

The unique risk profile of cattle explains its popularity. Cattle offer liquidity at all maturities and in a range of different 'denominations', from goats to buffaloes. Value chain research shows that the meat and dairy sectors in Pakistan are dominated by smallholders, who sell into the market locally. This implies extremely liquid markets. In dairy, for example, statistics suggest that some 95 per cent of all milk is produced from small-scale rural and peri-urban holding of 2–3 milking animals (Social Sciences Institute NARC 2003). These kinds of findings are supported by household surveys. The LUMS dairy survey, for example, finds that approximately half of the households engaged in selling milk have a herd of only 1–2 animals and a similar proportion are either landless or cultivate up to 5 acres (Burki and Khan 2011). Most of the milk sold, moreover, is informally marketed to traditional milk collectors, village and city milk shops and neighbours. This market structure accommodates non-standardised and occasional sales into the market, and includes very localised milk collection that feeds into the national market. A similar situation prevails in the meat sector, by which the market structure is well equipped for irregular and one-off sales that feed from local markets into national and export markets. On top of the additional markets that arise in time for religious festivals, cattle are easily encashed with end-users or village-level dealers, and can be deposited with others (including professional shepherds) for a fee to avoid the inconvenience of upkeep.[16]

Aside from these measures of liquidity, cattle also offer stability. Figures 6.5 and 6.6 show the price of the consumer basket of essential items over a four-year period.[17] In both figures, the price denominated in rupees is given by the black line. How much the basket is worth in terms of mutton and milk respectively is given by the grey line in each figure. That is, the slope of the grey lines show how much more or less mutton or milk is required to buy the basket in comparison to the week before. This shows that, once exposure to the rupee is stripped out of these 'prices', these derivative commodities of cattle show stability and appreciation as money forms. In other words, outside of a sharp drop in value of milk and mutton in mid-2013, there were very few periods in

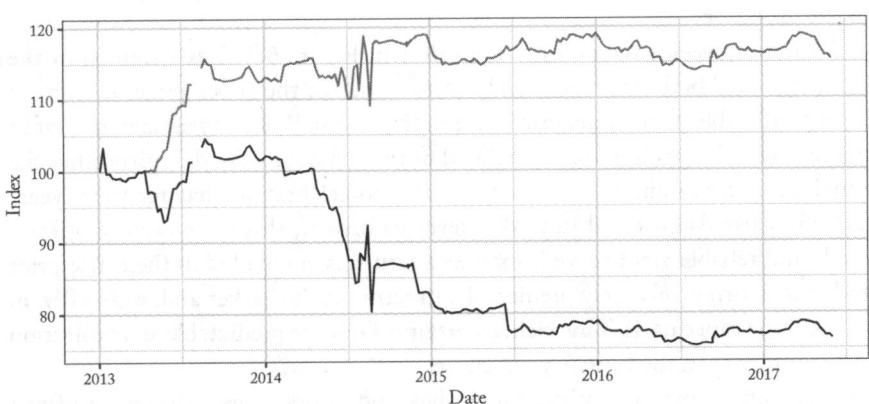

Figure 6.5 Weekly value of Essential Items basket denominated in rupees (black) and milk (grey), both standardized to start at 100

Source: Pakistan Bureau of Statistics, Consumer Prices of Essential Items, Annexure to Weekly Sensitive Price Index Reports. Available at www.pbs.gov.pk.

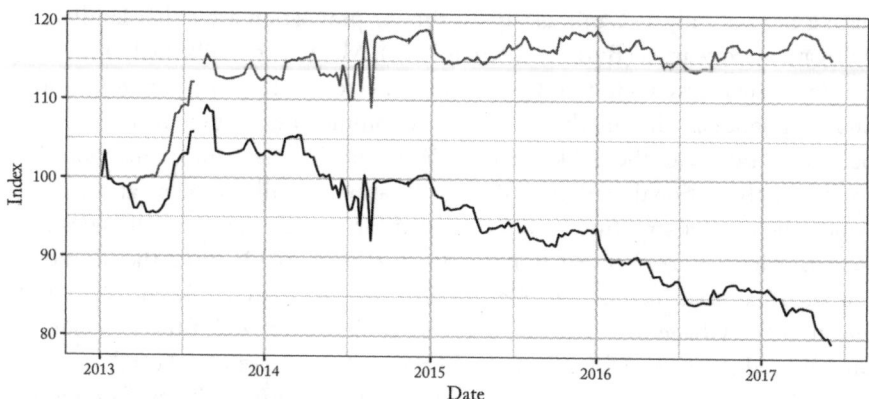

Figure 6.6 Weekly value of Essential Items basket denominated in rupees (black) and mutton (grey), both standardized to start at 100

Source: Pakistan Bureau of Statistics, Consumer Prices of Essential Items, Annexure to Weekly Sensitive Price Index Reports. Available at www.pbs.gov.pk.

which a household would have needed more mutton or more milk than the week before, in order to be able to afford the basket of essential items. In weeks where the value of the basket did go up, price rises were consistently duller in mutton or milk than in rupees. This is clearly visible in the milk price, where each upward tick of the basket's 'price' is exaggerated in the rupee price as compared to the milk price.

Moreover, weekly data on mutton prices in Figure 6.7 clearly show how the 'exchange rate' between rupees and mutton (that is, the rupee price of mutton) has a predictable price cycle: prices rise in the first half of the year and are flat in the second. This cycling may be related to the religious calendar, given that the ritual slaughter of animals associated with Eid celebrations has for these years fallen in early August and July. Whatever its drivers, this price cycling offers a stable and reliable yield curve insofar as a return is embedded in the cattle price and that return is relatively predictable, in terms of the basket and, especially, in terms of the rupee itself. This yield is certainly far more predictable as a projection of the future than the rupee's yield curve.

Transaction costs notwithstanding, these indicators suggest that cattle offer a reliable store of value asset, with minimal risk attributes, high liquidity and basically no down-side risk. This contrasts with national currency, the value of which is, at times, perceptibly undermined across the span of only weeks, let alone years.

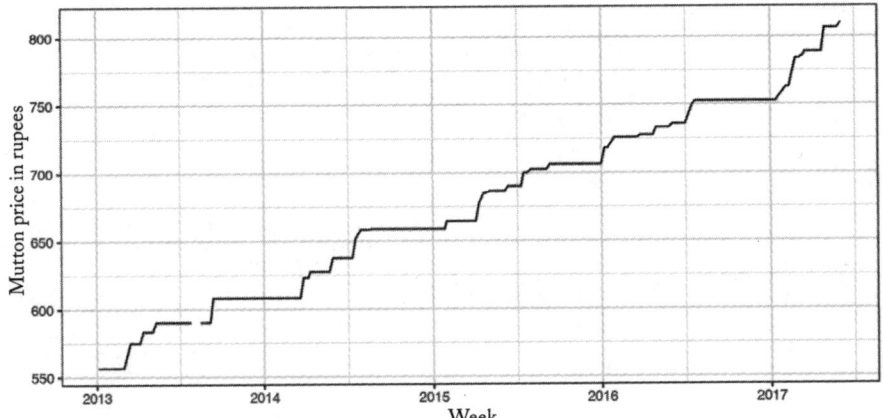

Figure 6.7 Weekly mutton price in rupees

Source: Pakistan Bureau of Statistics, Consumer Prices of Essential Items, Annexure to Weekly Sensitive Price Index Reports. Available at www.pbs.gov.pk.

Wheat

A more complicated example of monetary demand for non-state money instruments can be conceived of in the role of wheat in the Pakistani economy. Wheat plays a direct role in the daily economy of more or less all Pakistanis. This promises high and stable demand and high levels of liquidity in the market, which, in turn, implies reliability in pricing. Although the wheat price had been far more stable under the much more complete price controls of the pre-liberalisation years,[18] the much pared-down government intervention of the post-liberalisation years continues to dampen potential price movements.[19] This suggests that stability in the wheat price (relative to other commodities at least) is supported both by high liquidity in the market derived from consistent high demand and production, but also from the state's sponsorship of stability in the wheat market.

Analysis of weekly wheat prices between 2013 and 2017 shows that wheat has proven more stable than the rupee. That is, as Figure 6.8 shows, the price of the essential items basket in wheat terms is much more stable than the price of the basket in rupee terms. In wheat terms, the likelihood of a significant change in the affordability of the basket from week to week was thus significantly less than if the rupee were to be relied upon to secure the basket each week. This is further reflected in the standard deviation of the weekly price of the basket in wheat terms over this period, which is 0.75 per cent, in contrast to that of the basket in rupee terms, at 1.14 per cent.

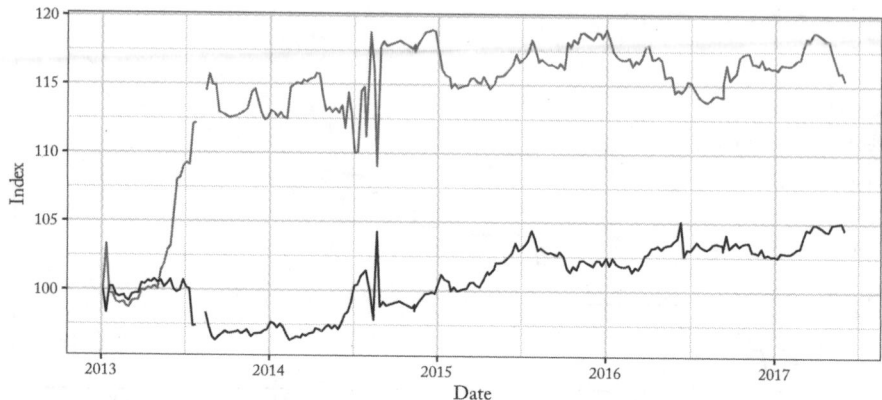

Figure 6.8 Weekly value of Essential Items basket denominated in rupees (black) and wheat (grey), both standardized to start at 100

Source: Pakistan Bureau of Statistics, Consumer Prices of Essential Items, Annexure to Weekly Sensitive Price Index Reports. Available at www.pbs.gov.pk.

Moreover, the close tracking of the basket as a whole in rupee terms (Figure 6.8) with the individual price of wheat in rupee terms (Figure 6.9) shows that it is the wheat price that drives inflation across the basket. SBP research suggests similar findings. As the head of the Research Department, Ali Choudhary,[20] points out, wheat prices influence broader pricing trends far disproportionately to wheat's share of either the consumer basket or the market.

This implies a strong anchoring role for wheat in the economy's broader pricing system, which, recalling Keynes, suggests quite specific monetary attributes. Keynes proposes that the economic community will demand that store of value assets and wages be denominated in the anchoring commodity, thus generating a feedback loop of self-reinforcing and interlocked monetary attributes in the anchoring commodity. Through this dynamic wheat lends itself to various money functions. Most obviously, wheat becomes a useful store of value asset[21] because its value (once stripped of volatility generated by rupee denomination) is less likely to change on a week-to-week basis. The increased incidence of private wheat storage identified in fieldwork interviews and corroborated by newspaper articles and other studies[22] reflects safety in the purchasing power offered by wheat.

More intriguingly, the persistence of wheat as a wage payment in Pakistan implies demand for the unique money attributes of wheat, which cannot be found in the rupee. These demands can be read into ongoing conflicts around the shift

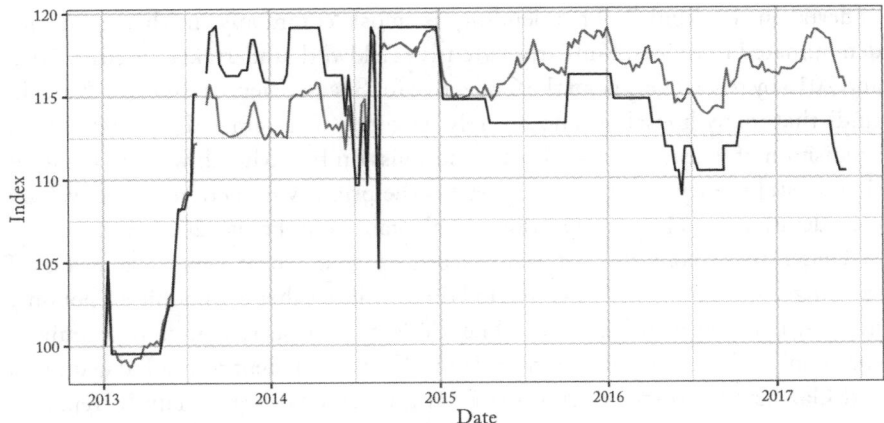

Figure 6.9 Weekly price of the Essential Items basket denominated in rupees (black), and weekly price of wheat (grey) denominated in rupees, both standardized to start at 100

Source: Pakistan Bureau of Statistics, Consumer Prices of Essential Items, Annexure to Weekly Sensitive Price Index Reports. Available at www.pbs.gov.pk.

from sharecropping to contracted daily labour, including the high profile case of the Okara Military Farm.[23] The conflict at Okara, like countless acts of everyday resistance amongst farm workers,[24] revolved around familiar themes of flexibility and insecurity. That is, the legally binding security offered by sharecropping, despite the otherwise poor conditions generally attached to that tenure, tends to be favoured by agricultural workers over the insecurity of contract day labour because the latter carries no obligation of continued employment outside of a day-long contract, even if that daily rate is higher.

In any case, where contractual day labour has nonetheless been instituted, wages often continue to be paid in kind. Similarly, wages for agricultural services, such as those of tradespeople linked to agricultural activities, continue to be paid in wheat. Indeed, the preference for wages in wheat is more strongly associated with those in the lower income brackets, where risks relating to securing basic subsistence are at their greatest. This persistence of in-kind wages despite the large-scale shift from traditional sharecropping practices to modern day labour contracts implies the increasingly important monetary role of key commodities such as wheat vis-à-vis declining safety and stability attached to conventional money. Here the anchoring role of wheat becomes crucial because it offers security in purchasing power that is undermined in wages denominated by an unstable rupee.

Moreover, wheat functions also as a unit of account. Grain loans from landlords and shopkeepers are common and the bulk of agricultural lending is undertaken in kind.[25] This lending is most commonly neither paid nor denominated in rupees. Similarly, extensive fieldwork undertaken in 2010, 2012 and 2013 by researchers from the Collective for Social Sciences Research Karachi finds that many households do not rely on rupee-denominated transactions for acquisition of wheat.[26] Haris Gazdar and Hussain Bux Mallah write that 'rather than [state] money … [it is wheat that] is the primary numéraire in the welfare considerations of a large proportion of Pakistani households' (2013: 36).

Under these conditions it is unsurprising that wheat acts as a means of exchange, and can be widely converted directly into other commodities, not only in rural but also in urban areas. The Collective's research finds that grain is commonly sold to shops for cash or goods. One respondent to the Balagamwala and Gazdar (2014) study, who was from a traditional beggar family, reported earning grain through begging and subsequently selling part of what was acquired to finance cash purchases. This is corroborated by value chain research and the IFPRI and CGAP studies, which show that wheat is commonly sold in small quantities and outside of regular contracts at the village level.[27]

These interlocking money functions suggest that wheat offers a superior hedging tool. In the same way that an index derivative tracks general price movements in the share market and thereby offers a hedge that can offset more volatile holdings in a portfolio, the linkage between wheat prices and general inflation inferred by wheat's anchoring role make wheat a distinctly useful hedge. Specifically, wheat is a good hedge for both potential downside volatility in other assets in the portfolio as well as generalised inflation. This explains why wheat is such a useful store of value. In addition, where wheat is earned as a unit of wage payment on the asset side of the household balance sheet it offers a perfect hedge to wheat as a consumption good on the liability side. Wheat therefore offers 'matched book' entries that protect the balance sheet from the potential of a funding gap arising through a mismatch in future asset and liability values.

Reliable data do not exist to determine a benchmark from which change in the status of wheat vis-à-vis the rupee as a monetary instrument could be measured over time. Nonetheless, these examples suggest how, by virtue of its central role in household balance sheets of assets and liabilities, wheat has become a key anchor to the economy at large, which in turn lends wheat to a series of other money functions. In this way, wheat appears to have transcended the role of a simple commodity in the economy to become a crucial money instrument that is supported by deep and liquid markets that are denominated in both wheat and the rupee.

In these conditions, wheat becomes an appealing denomination for wage payment, a low-risk store of value asset, a reliable *numéraire* of value and an everyday means of exchange. These functions are derived from its relatively reliable future value and its easy and low-cost conversion to other assets, which are, in turn, linked to the price inelasticity of demand for wheat, both in rupee terms and in wheat terms. Moreover, an implicit state guarantee over maintaining some kind of stability in the price of wheat has survived liberalisation. The value of wheat, as Keynes would agree, is consequently likely to maintain its value in step with prices in the rest of the economy, thereby posing wheat as a contender for Keynes' 'significant rate of interest' (1936: 236). As Chapter 3 has shown, this cannot be said for the rupee in the period since 2008.

Plots

The market for vacant plots of land offers a more unexpected set of monetary instruments which appear to cater to demand for short-term, transactional money holdings. In contrast to the wheat market, where a benchmark against which to measure change in the moneyness of wheat is not observable, the plot market has undergone distinct change that has increased the liquidity, and consequently the moneyness, of plot assets. These developments in the plot market appear to have occurred within a time frame that distinctly mirrors the post-liberalisation era as defined herein. Interview data report that the plot market has evolved to supply 'small denominations', by issuing smaller plots – starting from 25 square metres and worth as little as US$150 or US$200.[28] Key interviewees describe small plot sizes as a recent development. In addition, parallel transactions in plots through undocumented transfers are reported to have blossomed into a significant market over a similar time frame, thereby generating a greater supply of liquid instruments.

Indeed, the development of an informal market in plots suggests a distinct transformation in the land market. Here the time-consuming process of acquiring official documentation of ownership can be circumvented. The formal process involves a number of submissions to various organs of the state and takes a period of at least a month.[29] By contrast, an informal transaction in the land market requires only a single document signed between buyer and seller, and the transfer of payments, itself often undertaken instantaneously in cash. By transacting informally, as explained in Chapter 5, sale or purchase becomes potentially instant, thereby hugely increasing the liquidity of the plot as an asset. A position in the plot market can be – and is – reversed within an hour.

Thus, the increasing supply of 'small denomination' plots is complemented by near 'on demand' access to savings and low 'transaction costs' in terms of the burden of documentation. Whilst the plot market carries risk, it is the small risk of a large depreciation in the event of fraud rather than the large risk of a smaller but much more likely downside loss on state money held in bank deposits.

As such, for a remittance-receiving household seeking to store value for an intermittent period (for example, until school fees are due) the informal plot market could potentially be ideal. Depositing in banks can require considerable documentation[30] and a great deal of price risk, whilst an informal position in the plot market can be acquired rapidly, liquidated with little notice, free of the inconvenience of documentation and with little downside risk on the sum invested.

As discussed in Chapter 5, the rise of informality in the market in the post-liberalisation years suggests that plots are providing deposit facilities similar to those offered by bank accounts. Indeed, the interview data suggest that the growth of informality in the plot market arose as bank deposits were declining. At the same time, the clientele in the plot market broadened from the wealthy and salaried classes to much greater representation of those at the lower end of the income spectrum. Moreover, the timing of the introduction of informality to the plot market implies that the incentive for informal transactions may primarily reside in liquidity rather than tax evasion. After all, tax evasion has long been a popular principle of financial management in Pakistan, just as it has been at the heights of global finance. The imperative of liquidity insofar as it is linked to volatility, however, peaked in the same years that informality is reported to have appeared in the land market. Finally, the cycling of plots with agricultural prices reported in a rural, agricultural part of the country implies the same: a facility for the storage of transactional balances that is highly liquid and carries a satisfactory risk profile.

The analysis of land markets catering to demand for short-term financial instruments can potentially be taken a step further. Where dealers arrange for land to be informally transacted, they may settle the transaction as a net figure separate from the 'principal'. That is, A sells to B without transferring the title; and B sells to C, with the title settled between A and C. But rather than B paying A, and C paying B, the change in value of the land can be netted out and distributed between the three actors at the time of C's settlement. In most cases, the value of the land will go up, so C's settlement will be distributed between A and B, with B capturing the net increase in value and A taking the 'principal'. But in some cases, the value of the land will drop. If the value of the land drops, then C's settlement value is paid directly to A (as if the principal), on top of which B must also make a payment to A equal to the net change in value.

Where this kind of netting out of payments occurs, it is expressing not so much trade in land itself but trade in exposure to the market performance of land. The underlying asset is not actually changing hands either in a legal sense or in physical terms. Rather B is buying exposure to change in the piece of land's value over a certain period of time. As these periods of time can stretch from hours to days and months, a yield curve can be discerned, not unlike an interest rate yield curve expressing the different returns over different time periods. However, in the case of plots, it is not uniform across space or smooth over time.

This scenario demonstrates a more complex liquidity that can be facilitated by informally transacting land. Informality not only facilitates liquidity that allows land to act as a short-term store of value instrument that can take the place of a bank deposit, but also facilitates a degree of liquidity so great as to allow trade in exposure to an asset's market performance, much like a derivative product trades price movements on an asset without there being a formal trade in the asset itself.

Foreign Exchange

As shown in Chapter 3, the largely illegal foreign exchange market has grown rapidly since foreign exchange dealing was legalised as part of the liberalisation process. That is, although a small number of money dealers are registered operators, the bulk are not, and vast illegal trade is carried out including by registered dealers themselves. The size of this market suggests huge demand for what is in conventional terms money, albeit not local state money.[31]

The fieldwork interviews reported foreign currency, notably US dollar cash, functioning primarily as holdings for short-term transactional balances. This was apparent in the popularity of converting the day's profits into US dollars for overnight holdings reported amongst bazaar-based traders and money dealers alike. The popularity of overnight holdings of US dollars is also reflected in the emergence of 'commission agents', who visit stalls in the old bazaar in Peshawar to collect rupees and deliver dollars. Similarly, the dollar was reported as assuming the unit of account role, if not the means of exchange role, for the carpet industry. In both cases, these important money functions in the US dollar were reported as only becoming market norms since the post-liberalisation period.

In these transactions we see demand for reliability in value satisfied by dollar denomination and short-term holdings in dollar cash. These functions utilise the low default risk that is traditionally associated with state money, without the volatility risk that has become attached to the rupee.

Inventory

A final category of non-state money objects identified in the field interviews pertains to inventory and the potentially new ways in which stock is managed. Most striking is the rapid conversion of rupee profits by traders, where daily conversion of rupees to inventory takes place instead of weekly or monthly bulk purchases. The higher costs related to making frequent small purchases rather than cheaper bulk purchases at longer intervals are apparently weighed against the risk of holding rupees for longer periods.

Traders also reported diversification of their wares as a response not only to volatility in the rupee, but to unpredictable and uneven volatility right across the economy. In some cases, this was explicitly stated by traders who had expanded beyond the one or two commodities traded in the pre-liberalisation era to a whole array of different storable commodities in more recent years. Such diversification practices effectively hedge potential decline in the value of any of the components of the trader's portfolio of inventory.

Complexity in Money Practices

The fieldwork interviews thereby suggest that the rupee is no longer being unambiguously taken up as the default money object – as the uncontested form of money that is habitually relied upon as if 'without a second thought'. Rather, interviewees showed how they were effectively reconsidering their reliance on the rupee by using all sorts of non-traditional commodities and foreign state money, as money instruments. These money instruments are not necessarily offering a simple substitution for the rupee but appear instead as complex risk management strategies.

Instances of cattle holdings replacing cash holdings as a store of value asset demonstrate a simple substitution of cash for cattle. Where a trader starts to denominate trade in US dollars or agricultural workers demand wages in grain, we see alternatives to the rupee arise in particular money functions and in particular contexts. Much more complex than a simple reliance on the rupee for standard money functions, these constitute active negotiation of the monetary environment as people match different money instruments to their needs for different money functions. In these processes, the potential arises for a combination of strategies to hedge risk through a whole array of money functions. Examples include rapid conversion out of the rupee, holding overnight positions in the foreign exchange market, diversifying portfolios, matched book hedging, purchasing assets that track the general price level as do index derivatives, and holding transactional balances in market exposures.

Whether individuals take up one of these strategies or combine any number of them, by switching from the rupee to any non-rupee instrument for any single money function, they are effectively contesting the rupee as money. Rather than relying on the rupee by habit, ordinary people are observed as operating outside the rupee and negotiating the money environment by enacting risk mitigation strategies that draw on innovative applications of non-state money instruments in complex financial strategies. Here ordinary people are observed at the forefront of global liquidity, responding to the vagaries of global markets by juggling exposures – to the rupee itself as well as to the commodities that make up the consumer basket, all of which are heavily influenced by global market pricing. Under open markets, we see innovations in money practices that effectively forge new money instruments by rejecting the liberalised rupee as the economy's safe asset.

Conclusion: Frontier Money in Pakistan

The money instruments that are the subject of these new money strategies are referred to in this study as 'frontier money'. Yet frontier money includes the rupee, which remains an important if not exclusive form of money in the local economy. Frontier money is thus multiple and fluid. This section undertakes a closer examination of the ambiguity in money that forms the core of the frontier money concept.

Central to frontier money as it has been elaborated throughout is the issue of transactional balances and other liquid stores of value that stand outside of state money. By performing key money functions, short-term holdings of highly liquid alternative assets blur the line between what is money (traditionally considered to be state money) and what is a commodity (such as wheat). This is all the more so given that the fading distinction between state money and non-state money instruments is fed by changes in both sides: state money itself has become compromised (for example, by becoming unstable and consequently risky in the post-liberalisation environment) at the same time as markets for non-state money instruments have developed enhanced liquidity and thus 'moneyness' (for example, through the development of the informal market for vacant land). As the uniqueness of the monetary attributes in state money erode, state money becomes just another risky asset, rendering the line between money and non-money imprecise.

Moreover, as the privilege of state money as unique money in the economy erodes, monetary functions are dispersed across an array of assets. Here mutually reinforcing attributes of liquidity, stability in value and anchoring roles blur store of value assets, transactional holdings, wage units, and hedging instruments across an array of non-rupee money instruments each of which draw on all or some of these defining attributes of state money. Hence, we find in frontier money a complexity in liquidity whereby money functions are disaggregated and dispersed.

The case of instruments that are used for hedging monetary risk is a case in point. Hedging instruments cannot be neatly distinguished from money as conventionally conceived. The most important qualities in a hedging instrument are attributes of liquidity and thus stability in value, relatively costless realisation, physical durability and an anchoring role, which promises to track the general price level. These are the attributes of money that are described by Keynes as money's defining features. This suggests that the distinction between what can be fruitfully used as a substitute for state money and what can be fruitfully used as a hedge for price risk is blurred because an instrument that offers a good hedge, by definition, carries significant monetary attributes.

This is the argument posed by Dick Bryan and Michael Raffety (2006) with regard to derivatives offering an important new monetary role in the post–Bretton Woods environment, but is most evident in the present context in terms of wheat. Wheat may at once offer a matched book hedge, function as a store of value, provide a wage unit, and be used as a means of exchange. Wheat thereby embodies the whole gamut of monetary attributes – is it a hedging instrument or is it money itself? – yet wheat is not the only money object in use either. If we accept that the rupee is not the 'stable pole' proposed by Keynes and others, then there is no 'money proper' in the post-liberalisation environment. The stable pole of state money is here replaced by the spread of monetary functions onto a whole array of assets. This casts ambiguity over money by offering not one state money substitute but a whole series of instruments that offer various combinations of monetary functions. Frontier money is therefore fragmented. Not mutually exclusive categories of money and non-money, frontier money becomes a spectrum of moneyness, and state money (itself a changing category of money) can no longer unambiguously assume the position at the beginning of that spectrum.

This ambiguity in frontier money disrupts the notion of a linear progression from barter to money use that is found across the contributions from economics to money theory. From mainstream textbook versions of monetary development to Keynes (1936) to Post-Keynesian work, financial progress is charted from the simple one-to-one exchange of barter in a subsistence moneyless economy, to the more complex relations of leverage and risk management that accompany monetisation. This teleology is carried on, from shallow to deep financial markets, in the forward march of progress pursued in conventional thinking on economic development.

Embedded in that teleology is the assumption, long asserted in the monetisation literature, that 'the non-monetised sector is only remotely connected with the process of accumulation' (Chakravarty 1956: 703). Conventional notions of monetisation suggest that the use of non-state money as monetary instruments reflects an 'economic rationale [that] derives from the search by rural households for survival rather than maximizing algorithms in an environment of high risk and uncertainty' (Chandavarkar 1977: 655). This carries through in theoretical underpinnings of development economics that imply that state money offers the unequivocally superior efficiency by which income and capital formation are generated. By contrasting conventional monetisation to the clumsy tying up of factors of production in search of a 'double coincidence of wants',[32] the safety of state money is inferred just as the unsophisticated nature of exchange in non-state money is assumed. Herein lies a dichotomy between primitive exchange and a modern monetary economy that, as the next chapter shows, persists through the theoretical literature

Rather than comprising the vestiges of a primitive barter system, however, this study's findings suggest that individuals move in and out of state money as a portfolio choice, juggling a diverse set of exposures across assets and liabilities. To each of these is attached an 'own' interest rate (Keynes 1936) which reflects its liquidity risk. From this perspective, the persistence of wages in kind despite the shift to flexible daily-wage labour, short-term holdings of vacant land purchased in informal markets, overnight holdings of dollars, and transactional balances held in cattle or grain, can all be interpreted as not a necessity in a subsistence moneyless society but a means to conceive of an alternative commodity money, intentionally separate from state money. This suggests that state money has lost its privileged position in cash flow management, existing not as an exceptional asset that bounds and backstops the financial system because of its unique relationship to the state, but rather as one of many risky assets. Similarly, the banking system is not the only or even the privileged custodian of liquid 'near money' assets. To identify the persistence of in-kind wages, or the growing reliance on cattle and other stores of value as a return to more simplified, pre-capitalist forms would be to misread the evidence.

In light of the deterioration of the rupee in the new economy environment, these practices are posited as a response to new financial risk. These responses are made within a local institutional context, whereby risk management strategies are not operationalised only through the instruments of the formal financial sector but also through the tools at hand. A fund manager's portfolio allocation from money market holdings to real estate reflecting a change in preference regarding the ratio of risk to return would not be deemed as demonetisation, a return to barter or a regression to simplified survival strategies. In the same way, an agricultural worker's shift from cash to cattle, or preference for wages denominated and paid in wheat, may also represent a reallocation in regard to risk and return that seeks to counter new financial risks. Financial innovation that looks like barter can, it is contended here, be a dynamic financial response to the way that local state money has been affected by its exposure to global markets.

Notes

1. This characterisation of money as well functioning when it is taken for granted is emphasised by Carruthers and Babb (1996).

2. See Lopez-Calix, Srinivasan and (Waheed 2012).

3. That is, SBP research finds that prices and wages tend to be significantly less stable than those in developed countries. See Choudhary, Faheem, et al. (2016) and Choudhary, Mahmood, et al. (2013).

4. See, for example, the brief and accessible federal budget assessment offered by Rana, Settle and Khan (2010).

5. Previously known as the capital account (which, following convention, is the term used throughout this book, for example in terms of 'capital account liberalisation'), the IMF redefined the balance of payments in 1993, using the term 'financial account' for categories pertaining to cross-border trades of stocks and bonds. Consequently, the term 'financial account' is used here, in direct reference to the balance of payments categories that are represented in Figures 6.1 and 6.2, namely direct investment and portfolio investment flows.

6. The stepped exchange rate curve around 1998 reflects the multiple exchange rate imposed in the wake of Pakistan's nuclear tests. For the sake of brevity, this period has not featured in the present study. See Meenai and Ansari (2010) for details of exchange rate management through this period.

7. See Faruqee and Colemand (1996), Dorosh and Salam (2007) and Salam and Mukhtar (2008: 84).

8. See also Dorosh and Salam (2007: 10) and Salam and Mukhtar (2008: 84).

9. See respectively A. S. Khan (2014), and Z. Khan (2008) and Aazim (2014).

10. See World Bank (2006) and Kinder (2010).

11. See Ghumman (2009) and IMF (2016b).

12. See, for example, B. Usmani (2008) and *Pakistan Times* (2013).

13. An accessible discussion of hyperinflation is provided by Reinhart and Salvastano (2003).

14. Foreign currency deposits were capped at 20 per cent of rupee deposits in January 2002 in order to limit dollarisation. See Dawn (2002) and SBP (2002b).

15. In conventional textbook economics, menu and shoe-leather costs are commonly cited as the costs of inflation. Menu costs refer to the cost for firms of changing their own prices (for example, when a restaurant prints new menus to revise prices up). Shoe-leather costs refer to the cost of time and effort associated with the more frequent visits to the bank required if people chose to hold less cash (and visit the bank more often) in order to limit the decline in the value of cash holdings associated with inflation.

16. Some background on the livestock sector is provided by Bhatti and Arocha (2014), Sharif et al. (2009) and Rehman et al. (2017).

17. These calculations are based on weekly prices issued in the Consumer Prices of Essential Items, which is an annexure to the *Weekly Sensitive Price Index Report*, produced by the Pakistan Bureau of Statistics. The prices used for these calculations pertain to Rawalpindi and are calibrated against the low-income basket. These calculations were made possible by the work of Alun Pope at the University of Sydney.

18. See Faruqee and Colemand (1996), Dorosh and Salam (2007) and Salam and Mukhtar (2008: 84).

19. See Dorosh et al. (2016).

20. M. A. Choudhary, interviewed by the author on 20 May 2016, in Karachi.

21. See, for example, Gazdar and Mallah (2013) and Balagamwala and Gazdar (2014).

22. See Z. Khan (2008) and Aazim (2014).

23. The Okara Military Farm is a 17,000-acre tract of land that is formally owned by the military, but has for generations been sharecropped by families living on the land. Protected by the Tenancy Act (1887) from eviction, sharecroppers divide the cost of inputs and the agricultural output with the landowner (in this case, the military). When the military imposed cash rents in 2000, those tilling the land became exposed to the potential of eviction, sparking protests amidst violent repression from the military. See Human Rights Watch (2004).

24. M. Gaadi, interviewed by the author on 20 June 2013, in Islamabad.

25. See respectively Gazdar and Mallah (2013) and Balagamwala and Gazdar (2014), and Haq et al. (2013).77

26. Notably, Gazdar and Mullah (2013) and Balagamwala and Gazdar (2014).

27. See Anderson and Ahmed (2016), IFPRI/IDS (2016) and also Zia and Zia (2015) on the wheat supply chain.

28. See www.zameen.com, where plots are advertised for sale.

29. In field interviews, this process was described in detail by plot dealers and the period of time required confirmed by key market participants. The process is summarised in an accessible description at https://joshandmakinternational.com/legal-procedure-pertaining-to-selling-property-in-pakistan-excluding-federal-territory/ (accessed 1 September 2019).

30. As discussed in Chapter 3, the reduction of documentation required for opening and maintaining bank accounts has been a central pillar of the central bank's efforts to enhance the use of deposits. These efforts, however, conflict with the imperative of tightening 'Know Your Customer' rules, both in the interest of minimising tax evasion and limiting so-called terror financing. As a result, low documentation accounts are an exception amongst deposit products.

31. According to Shumaila Kafeel Siddiqui (2014), the Federal Investigation Agency estimates that in the largest money market in Peshawar, 400 dealers operate, only some 10 per cent of whom are licensed. Daily turnover in the market is estimated at US$12 million (ibid.: 101).

32. See Laumas (1990) and McLoughlin and Kinoshita (2012).

7

Money in Theory and Money in Pakistan

The analysis developed over the preceding six chapters offers a reading of radical monetary change in the wake of the liberalisation of money and markets. In Pakistan's new economy, the rupee and the everyday prices that express its usefulness are characterised by instability. Certainly, this is not the extreme instability of hyperinflation. But it is an instability substantive enough to prompt a series of hedging practices, which effectively contest the primacy of the rupee by dispersing money functions across an array of alternative assets. By using non-state money instruments for money functions, households seek to protect themselves from new rupee-related risk in an economic environment that is characterised by uncertainty.

This story of the loss of trust in money amidst the instability and uncertainty generated by open markets finds a natural home within Post-Keynesian thinking. After all, these issues express key Post-Keynesian themes, such as the contingency of money on social trust and the fundamental uncertainty that drives the imperative of stabilisation policies. Yet this reading of monetary change in Pakistan's new economy runs counter to certain key Post-Keynesian contributions to economic thinking. Specifically, the theoretical lineage of Post-Keynesian monetary thinking sets out a dichotomy between money and commodities that does not easily account for the kind of monetary change that has been observed in Pakistan.

At issue is the state theory of money that underlies much thinking about money. From a state theory perspective, money cannot be an ordinary market commodity because it is a social construction that is indelibly linked to the state. Be it the 'bank money' that is issued by the state-supervised banking system or the notes, coins and central bank balances issued directly by the state, conventional thinking about money posits money *by definition* as a 'creature of the state' (Lerner, 1947).[1] From a state theory perspective, the uniqueness of money amidst other assets lies herein: its defining characteristics are ascribed to the authority of the state under which it is issued.

To the contrary, this study has shown how the cornerstone role of the rupee as safe and stable can be compromised, and how certain uses of some commodities (primarily but not exclusively grain and cattle), can in fact be conceived of as commodity money. By this reading, the monetary environment in Pakistan's new economy is constituted not only by state money, which itself diverges in significant ways from conventional assumptions, but by an array of instruments that fulfil money functions in the local economy. This array of money instruments (of which state money is but one form) is described in this study as 'frontier money'.

This chapter explores how assumptions of a state theory of money are embedded in economic thinking and expressed in money theory, and how Pakistan's frontier money departs from these assumptions. The chapter's focus is on Post-Keynesian theory and literature. This focus engages the explicit grounding of Post-Keynesian theory in a state theory of money. Although dominant in neither policy circles, conventional textbooks nor mainstream academic journals, Post-Keynesianism has evolved out of broader Keynesian thinking into a coherent school of economic thought. Post-Keynesianism has developed into a credible and indeed dominant critique within academic debates, and is increasingly reflected in central bank and wider macroeconomic policy.[2]

The competing school of New Keynesianism by contrast *is* dominant in policy, teaching and academia. New Keynesianism is expressed as policy in inflation targeting and known in formal economic thought as 'the New Monetary Consensus'. Although less explicitly linked to a state theory of money than Post-Keynesian thinking, the incontrovertibility of state money that is assumed in policy practice reveals the assumptions of a state theory of money that underlie New Keynesian thinking. These assumptions play out in particularly striking ways in relation to financial inclusion.

New Keynesianism is addressed in the book's final chapter in terms of the policy implications of frontier money for Pakistan's central bank. This engagement with New Keynesianism in policy terms is congruent with the policy focus of New Keynesian thinking. New Keynesianism is less oriented towards qualitative enquiry and as such does not engage as deeply in the more sociologically grounded debates that are developed across the Post-Keynesian literature. The deeper social processes that enact monetary relations remain the domain of Post-Keynesian theory. Hence, for this chapter, the aim is to explore assumptions that are internal to Post-Keynesian theoretical thinking about money and the economy and thereby to develop the theoretical connotations proposed by frontier money. It is left for the next chapter to engage the domain of policy and thereby engage New Keynesian thinking.

In interrogating the break that frontier money makes with state theories of money, the chapter explores how the assumptions of a state theory of money make it difficult for economic analysis to engage with the problem of globalisation and monetary change. Specifically, it argues that Post-Keynesian thinking is well equipped to address changes in the monetary environment that are driven by globalisation. Post-Keynesianism consequently is the natural home for the kind of analysis of frontier money undertaken in this book. However, the chapter argues that certain flagship successes of Post-Keynesian monetary thinking have, in fact, also served to inhibit its propensity to explore monetary change. As explained later in this chapter, hard-won debates on the endogeneity of money, on the classical dichotomy and on the origins of money itself have bound Post-Keynesian thinking to a theory of money that cannot countenance non-state money forms and thereby has difficulty engaging with new complexity in money, both at the heights of global finance and amongst small, open developing economies.

This proposition is developed through the course of comparing and contrasting frontier money to key expressions of state theory in monetary thinking. The chapter first considers the embedding of the state theory perspective in the operational definition of money that is used by central banks to quantify the money supply (M0, M1, M2, and so on). Not only is this monetary schema a consensus tool used across central banks under the auspices of the IMF, but it draws on monetary thought that cuts across the ideological divide. The schema of monetary aggregates express both the characteristics of money identified by Keynes in the General Theory (1936) as well as those identified by Milton Friedman's Quantity Theory of Money (Friedman and Schwartz, 1963), itself a staple of monetary textbooks and a work that is conventionally understood to represent the antithesis of Keynes' position. In evaluating the applicability of monetary aggregates to frontier money, the analysis identifies a consensus state theory position in monetary aggregates as well a set of contradictory empirical challenges that have shaped the aggregates themselves.

From here, the chapter turns to chartalist theory. Chartalist theory offers a broadly accepted reading of the nature of money as a 'creature of the state', which is echoed across Keynesian thinking but is closely associated with Post-Keynesianism. This section maps out the definition of money offered by chartalism before considering how the monetary environment that was explored in Chapter 6 challenges basic chartalist propositions about the essential nature of modern money.

The next section considers a body of literature on money that comes from outside the discipline of economics. This section seeks to find in sociology and anthropology other lineages of theory that identify complexity and ambiguity in money and consequently may depart from the assumptions of state theories of money.

The final section situates frontier money in relation to Post-Keynesian thinking more generally. In this final section, the chapter explores the expression of a state theory of money in broader Post-Keynesian thinking and thus interrogates the contradictions that arise between frontier money and conventions of Post-Keynesianism thinking.

State Money and Monetary Aggregates

Monetary aggregates provide the operational definition of money by which central banks attempt to quantify exactly how much money is circulating in the economy. This accounting schema of money instruments reflects the assumptions of a state theory of money both in the parameters that define the different monetary categories that constitute monetary aggregates (M0, M1, M2, and so on) and in the fact that state money occupies M0 and M1 and thus is, by definition, the core of wider aggregates (M2, M3, and so on). Here we find state theory deeply embedded in operational thinking on money. This is of significance because monetary aggregates reflect a consensus on money, not only as the global norm for central bank accounting, but also insofar they draw on Keynesian theory as much as that of its otherwise adversary, Milton Friedman. Yet, even as monetary aggregates remain limited by their state money orientation, we also find a multiplicity and flexibility in money's operational definition that is congruent with frontier money.

Monetary aggregates are described in the IMF's *Manual on Monetary and Financial Statistics* but are in practice defined by individual central banks with national specificity. Monetary aggregates combine the so-called functional definition (Laidler 1969) and empirical definition (Friedman and Schwartz 1963) of money to construct the parameters in which different forms of money are allocated into 'M' categories and reported in central bank statistics (M1, M2, M3, and so on). These parameters hinge upon liquidity and stability in value on the one hand (the functional definition), and reliability in proportional relationships to income and the price level on the other (the empirical definition – so that as GDP increases, money also increases proportionally, and as prices rise, so too does the stock of money). Money is thus formally defined not only in reference to its liquidity and stability, which implies that money is an asset that is easy to store, cheap to realise and relatively riskless insofar as its future value can be relied upon, but is also an asset that acts as an anchor for the wider economy. The anchoring role is expressed in the statistical correlation of each monetary aggregate with nominal income (that is, GDP) and the price level (that is, inflation), which provides the basis for the monetary policy practice known as 'money supply targeting' via Friedman's Quantity Theory of Money. That is, the possibility of controlling inflation by controlling the expansion of each monetary aggregate is opened up by the anchoring role of money. In any case, here we see a consensus over money, not only insofar as monetary aggregates constitute the global norm for quantifying an economy's money supply, but also insofar as the characteristics that define money draw concurrently on Keynes and Friedman's characterisation of money as a stable anchor for the wider economy.

The M categories thus schematise money along a spectrum of moneyness, which by and large correlates to a hierarchy of liquidity. Central bank reserves (of which there are relatively few in the system as a whole) sit at the top of the pyramid and less liquid, privately issued securities (which constitute the bulk of money in the system) sit at the bottom. In this schema, M0, which is constituted by currency in circulation and central bank deposits (and is thus the money that is most directly produced by the state), best satisfies both the functional and empirical definitions of money: it is the most liquid money and the most stable in value and it should ideally carry a stable relationship with national income and the price level so that as GDP and inflation rise, M0 rises in step.

M1 sits below M0 in the hierarchy of money and is quantitatively greater than M0. M1 includes M0 as well as demand deposits in banks, which operate within the state-supervised banking system. It therefore represents an aggregate of money that is slightly less liquid, while maintaining a slightly less stable relationship with growth and prices in the broader economy.

M2 and M3 (and M4 and M5) are characterised by progressively less moneyness as monetary forms move further away from state control and entail less liquidity. In terms of the functional definition of money, the money instruments that constitute these later M categories typically are less liquid, reflecting the fact that they cannot be accessed instantly. Liquidation of these instruments may involve an overnight processing time and they may bear a term to maturity that incurs a financial cost to liquidate early. These money instruments also tend to be less stable, and to carry a less reliable anchoring relationship with broader macroeconomic indicators like growth and inflation, indicating a weaker expression of the empirical definition of money. These later categories include instruments such as time deposits, foreign currency deposits, money market mutual fund shares, short-dated commercial paper, and so on. The 'broad monies' of M2 and M3 (and M4 and M5) are thus included in the definition of money as an extension of 'narrow' or state money (M0 + M1).

A state theory of money is thus expressed in the structure of monetary aggregates. First, the parameters of moneyness that define money in each of its M categories closely resemble Keynes' characterisation of (state) money as both exceptionally liquid and a stable anchor for the wider economy. Keynes' chapter 17 in the *General Theory* (1936) shows how these characteristics are tied to the state's sponsorship of state money: according to Keynes, state money's exceptional liquidity and anchoring function reflect the uniqueness of state money amidst regular commodities insofar as state money is *not* a product of the market. In short, state money is more stable than regular commodities because the state controls the value of money by controlling its production and setting its interest rate. This unique stability then promises a unique liquidity: the stability of state money attracts its application to wage denomination and credit denomination, which cements the primacy of state money amongst other potential commodity monies by consolidating the denomination of value across the economy in state money terms. This in turn generates favourable conditions for the further use of state money as a store of value and, ultimately, as legal tender: exceptional stability generates exceptional liquidity as state money becomes key to economic transactions across the economy.

By effectively formalising Keynes' characterisation of money in the functional and empirical parameters of money, the schema of monetary aggregates enshrines an understanding of money that hinges on the stability and liquidity that is bestowed uniquely upon state money by virtue of the state's control over state money. This state-centric view of money is expressed more directly, moreover, in the designation of state money as M0 and M1 and thus the core of money from which further monetary aggregates, like M2, M3 and M4, emanate.

The primacy of an implicit state theory underlying monetary aggregates, however, is disrupted by the multiplicity of money entailed in monetary aggregates. This multiplicity, which can include everything from M0 to M5 in the definition of money, strikes a contrast to Keynes' depiction of money as a single instrument that evolves to achieve monopoly over its commodity rivals. Yet the multiplicity of money entailed in multiple aggregates is less a feature of design than of circumstance, and these circumstances tell their own story of monetary change over the decades since the collapse of the Bretton Woods system of fixed exchange rates. Until 1971, there was only one single aggregate for money in the United States: M1. This reflected the institutional context of a strong central monetary authority and of pre-globalised money, in which the volume of money in the economy resided in a narrow set of products and institutions. As financial innovation generated new highly liquid products in which to store value outside of the basic banking products that had been predominant in the post-war years,[3] the categories of money – if they were to maintain their policy relevance – had to be expanded to include a series of new instruments that were in various ways very similar to state money. The outcome was a series of new monetary aggregates, from M2 to M5, that expanded the definition of money for policy purposes.[4]

Over succeeding years pressure on the functional and empirical coverage of monetary aggregates intensified, demanding ever greater revision of exactly which instruments were covered by which aggregates. At issue was not just that the net cast by the Fed lost ground to an ever-expanding pool of new money instruments. In addition, liquidity within money was becoming more complicated. Rather than a linear expansion of money in each of the monetary aggregates which would track GDP increases, each aggregate in step with one another, aggregates behaved unpredictably and at times moved in opposite directions. At the same time, it was becoming increasingly clear that the geography of money was not the same as the geography of monetary governance, reflecting new globalised forms of money incongruent with established methods of aggregation.

These developments were reflected in the evolving practice of monetary governance. Money supply targeting, which had become official Fed policy in the 1970s, sought to control inflation by setting a target for the expansion of money in the economy as accounted for by the M categories.[5] Money supply targeting, however, became increasingly deemphasised in the 1980s as instability grew between aggregate measures and goal variables, such as growth and inflation.[6] Monetary aggregates were consequently increasingly relegated to the status of 'informational indicators' rather than direct policy tools, and their collection was wound down: the Fed stopped publishing M4 and M5 in 1980, and M3 in 2006, although monetary aggregates continue to be a key data source for policy in developing countries. As the governor of the Bank of Canada, Gerald Bouey, explained, 'We didn't abandon monetary aggregates, they abandoned us' (in Mishkin 2001: 4).

Nonetheless, the flexibility of the M category schema, which has been enacted through periodic revision of the different monetary aggregates since 1971, posits money as multiple. This position moves away from the static and singular notion of money as narrowly constituted by state money, which is implied by Keynes and carried further, as we shall see, in chartalist thinking. Monetary aggregates, by contrast, accommodate a multiplicity of money that poses a spectrum of moneyness in which state money (M0 + M1) is but the first of a series of classes of money. Moreover, the evolving nature of the different categories of monetary aggregates recognises that the relationship between liquidity in the economy and money is not static but rather changes over time, demanding periodic redefinition.

The discussion of the monetary environment in Pakistan undertaken in Chapters 5 and 6 is thus congruent with the conceptualisation of money that is formalised in monetary aggregates insofar as it identifies liquidity and anchoring roles – the functional and empirical parameters of money – as key monetary characteristics. However, this study also draws on the depiction of money as multiple and in flux, a fact which the schematisation of money as monetary aggregates has come to accommodate – by circumstance if not by design. By effectively realising the inadequacy of a static definition of money, the rise and fall of the policy of money supply targeting demonstrates change and evolution in money that offers a valuable perspective on money.

The monetary environment in Pakistan, however, also challenges the M category view of money in two distinct ways. First, the monetary instruments identified in Chapters 5 and 6 fall outside the traditional monetary aggregates insofar as they are found outside of regular financial markets. Non-traditional instruments, from grain and cattle to landholdings and undocumented foreign currency, are interpreted in this study as important money instruments in the economy. As a corollary, the banking system is not the central intermediary to economic activity that would be fitting to a measure of money in which central bank reserves and bank money are primary. The ill-fitting nature of a schematisation of liquidity that revolves around the banking system is reflected in statistics that show that the population in Pakistan is predominantly unbanked. Congruent with this reality, unconventional money instruments include those that are derived not only from outside of financial markets but outside of formal markets altogether.

Second, state money in Pakistan has itself been subject to significant change. That the Pakistani rupee is arguably too unstable to conform to either the empirical or functional definition of money poses one set of challenges to the schematisation of money as monetary aggregates.[7] The very fact that this contradiction remains largely unexplored reflects how a schema of money that centres on a state money core does not easily lend itself to analysis of how state money itself may be changing in relation to other forms of money. The M categories assume a static precedence of state money in which central bank reserves and bank money are by definition the best forms of money – the most liquid and the most stable whilst carrying a reliably proportional relationship to income and prices. This definition fails to account for change within state money or for change between state money and other forms of money. This is of particular salience for the analysis proposed herein, in which the appearance of commodity money is driven by qualitative change in state money itself.

The orientation of monetary aggregates around money produced by the state and the state-regulated banking system (which extends to its outliers in the wider financial system) reflect the assumptions of a state theory of money that are embedded in central bank operations and thinking on money more broadly. The implications for policy practice will be taken up in the following chapter. For now, the critical point is that a state theory of money appears in the state money core of monetary aggregates as well as in the parameters that define monetary categories through money's stable anchoring role and exceptional stability and liquidity, characteristics which effectively enshrine Keynes' description of state money in chapter 17 of the *General Theory* (1936). As a result, although monetary aggregates account for money as multiple and in flux, they are impervious to non-state money that may arise outside of the formal financial sector or to the changing risk profile of state money itself.

State Money and Post-Keynesian Theory

The schema of money expressed in the definition of monetary aggregates seeks functionality. Although this schematisation necessarily draws on a body of theory that is riven by theoretical debate, monetary aggregates are designed to undertake the ostensibly empirical task of quantifying money in the economy. The Keynesian agenda, alternatively, sets itself much broader goals. At issue is the theorisation of a comprehensive macroeconomic framework in which the conceptualisation of money is consistent with the broader theoretical structure. A coherent conceptualisation of money is particularly important in Keynesian theory, given that Keynes explicitly set out to reorient economic thinking around the peculiarities of monetary dynamics. This section shows how Post-Keynesian thinking engages a state theory of money and how that state theory of money is integral to wider Post-Keynesian thought. In demonstrating the binding of Post-Keynesian thinking to a state theory of money, this section considers three theoretical propositions that structure Post-Keynesian thinking: chartalism, endogenous money and Keynes' position on the classical dichotomy. It is left to the next section to explore the tensions between the expression of a state theory of money in the Post-Keynesian theoretical framework and frontier money.

Central to the argument developed across the chapter is the proposition that Post-Keynesian thinking is intimately tied to a dichotomy that Keynes set out between money and commodities. This 'money-versus-commodity' distinction rests upon a definition of money's uniqueness amongst other assets that is known as chartalist theory.[8] Chartalist theory grew out of nineteenth-century debates about epistemology[9] and draws together sociological, historical, legal and economic perspectives in fierce opposition to neoclassical interpretations of the origins of money. Known as 'metalists', in reference to the use of metals as money in the progression out of barter exchange, chartalists' opponents offer a simplistic history of money as a market innovation that grew out of barter exchange with the use of commodities, such as gold, to carry value in exchange.

Chartalism, by contrast, is derived from the Latin word for token (*charta*). Chartalists designate money as socially embedded – a token that is issued by the governing authority of a society, its value derived from the authority of that social system, rather than a commodity with intrinsic value that appears spontaneously out of market activity. Money is thus a 'creature of the state' not of the market, by which its acceptability is rooted in social relations, not in the calculative rationality of commodity exchange. Herein lies the explicit state theory of money that has become implicit in conventional thinking about money.

Keynes draws heavily on chartalism in the opening chapters of his *Treatise on Money* (1930) and is, as the rest of this chapter argues, fundamental to wider

Post-Keynesian thinking. Chartalism is not, however, explored deeply in conventional Post-Keynesian theory just as it had not been extensively examined in Keynes' own work. Although chartalism is evident across Post-Keynesian thought, the strongest expression of a state theory of money within Post-Keynesian theory is left to the so-called neo-chartalist theory, itself a controversial off-shoot of the main body of Post-Keynesian thinking.

Neo-chartalism extrapolates on the origins and nature of money in the course of building a macroeconomic policy programme on top of the foundations of sovereign money.[10] For neo-chartalists, governments have a largely untapped capacity to fund fiscal deficits, a capacity which is ultimately rooted in the power of states to define what is used as money by declaring the unit of account in which taxes are paid. By this reading, taxation was central to the historical process by which state money became the dominant form of money because it institutionalised each individual's 'need to acquire the means of settling their liabilities with the state' (Bell 2001: 157). That is, the dominance of transactions between disparate individuals and the state ensures widespread use of state money that effectively institutionalises legal tender. Perry Mehrling phrases this in terms of the state being the one entity 'with which every one of us does ongoing business' (2000: 402). Neo-chartalists extrapolate from the foundational premise of the state's power to control money via taxation to offer a policy platform that radically rethinks the role of sovereign debt and money creation in pursuit of the traditional Keynesian macroeconomic goal of full employment. This policy programme is not supported by all Post-Keynesian economists even though neo-chartalists claim a Post-Keynesian identity. Yet controversy within Post-Keynesian thinking pertains primarily to the policy programme that neo-chartalists posit as a logical corollary of chartal money, rather than to the premise of chartal money on which neo-chartalism is staked.[11]

Indeed Post-Keynesian theory unites around chartal money, which is consistent with endogenous money theory, itself the central expression of Post-Keynesian monetary theory and endorsed by Post-Keynesians of all stripes.[12] In endogenous money theory, we find a less strident expression of state theory but still a monetary theory that remains orientated around a conception of money as intimately bound to the state. Specifically, endogenous money theory builds upon the money-versus-commodity dichotomy by focusing on the role of the banking system in the production of money.

Similar to debates between chartalists and metalists a century earlier, endogenous money theory delivered a bold challenge to traditional monetary thinking, with Post-Keynesians fiercely contesting neoclassical claims about the very basics of monetary economics. At issue is the question of what drives money supply expansion, or, more specifically, what drives the expansion of bank credit.

For neoclassical economists, this expansion is controlled by the central bank's issue of central bank reserves, against which banks can leverage credit to businesses and consumers. This is the fractional reserve banking system of mainstream textbooks.

By contrast, endogenous money theory states that central bank reserves do not act as a constraint on lending but rather are issued automatically by the central bank to match the amount of credit issued by individual banks. Thus, the expansion and contraction of the money supply is not *exogenously* determined by the amount of reserves that the central bank chooses to supply to the economy, but is *endogenously* determined by the inner workings of the economy – by risk appetite and the availability of investment opportunities, which are both integral to the wider economy and outside of the direct control of the central bank.

This focus on the banking sector as the key site of money in the economy extends to questions of how trust in money is generated. Alongside the neo-chartalist examination of the role of taxation in reinforcing legal tender, a branch of Post-Keynesian literature explores how the banking sector, itself mandated and managed by the state, imbues trust in money by stretching out the time horizon of money. Specifically, in denominating credit in state money, the banking system is posited to strengthen the continuing dominance of state money by linking the current economy into the future economy in state money terms. As Paul Davidson argues, the banking system thereby 'enforce[s] the discharge of contractual commitments for future action [which] are essential in providing trust in the future operation of the monetary system' (Davidson 1972: 106).

In each of these variations of Post-Keynesian monetary theory we find a notion of money as chartal money: a token (not a commodity with intrinsic value) that is produced under the auspices of the state – be its authority derived from the state through taxation or through the state-supervised banking system. Either way we have at core a state theory of money, which has been articulated in bitter debate with neoclassical thinkers that echo the lines drawn between metalists and chartalists in the nineteenth century, by which the spontaneous development of money in commodity form was rejected.

In following this lineage, Post-Keynesians declare that money is not and cannot be an ordinary market commodity. Implicit in this proposition is the unique liquidity, safety and stability that is borne by money, which is derived, as Keynes argued in chapter 17 of the *General Theory* (1936), from its connection to the state. This is stated boldly by neo-chartalists, who argue that the term 'money' can only be applied to state money because only state money complies with the defining attributes of money that pinpoint its unique nature. Pavlina Tcherneva, for example, states quite clearly that 'modern money is state money'

(2006: 77). Chartalism, she writes, 'illuminate[s] the tax-driven nature of money and sovereign powers of modern states' (ibid.: 84). This sentiment, although less definitively expressed outside of neo-chartalism, is nonetheless congruent with the agreement of Post-Keynesians of all stripes that money is an object of the state (including the state-supervised banking system), not of the market. In short, commodities can never be a true and full money unless they are imbued with the authority of the state.

This 'money-versus-commodity' dichotomy was further hardened in Post-Keynesian thinking, moreover, through the course of another key set of debates with the neoclassical school on what is known as the 'classical dichotomy'. This debate demonstrates the pivotal role of the 'money-versus-commodity' dichotomy in the broader structures of Post-Keynesian thinking and thus reflects the deeply integrated nature of a state theory of money across Post-Keynesian thought.

At issue is the convention, which is carried through neoclassical theory, of modelling the economy without a specific role for money. For neoclassical theorists, the economy can and should be understood as dichotomous, entailing 'real' economy dynamics in distinction to monetary dynamics: 'real' goods and services circulate in the economy on the one hand, and money circulates in the economy on the other. By this reading, the function of money is only to denominate the 'real' economy, hence change in the monetary sphere (for example, rising money supply) can only change the *nominal* value of goods and services (for example, the price level) but cannot change real variables (such as the quantity or distribution of goods, or investment and employment), which are driven wholly by dynamics in the 'real' economy. According to neoclassical thinking, the economy thus can be modelled in barter terms without deploying variables that represent money and finance as they operate in the real world, given that money cannot change real economic outcomes.[13]

This dichotomous view of economic dynamics is fiercely contested by Post-Keynesian theorists, who see the role of money and finance in the economy as inherently destabilising, a corollary of which is that money must be taken into account when thinking about (and modelling) how the economy works. A key issue for Post-Keynesians is liquidity preference, by which agents shift their wealth into more liquid holdings in response to sentiments of greater uncertainty in the economy. The fact that liquidity preference does not arise in a moneyless barter economy demonstrates how excluding money from the economic model fails to account for important economic dynamics, thereby contradicting the classical dichotomy.

At issue is the way the interest rate on state money is derived, and the way heightened liquidity preference generates higher interest rates as a result of investors' changed preferences, which favour more liquid investments. The higher interest rate that is generated through liquidity preference then reduces investment and output. These effects are compounded by the fact that liquidity preference draws capital out of production. In a monetary economy, an entrepreneur in, for example, the consumer goods sector may minimise the production of goods if she expects the economy is about to move into recession and that medium-term demand for her goods may thus drop sharply (for example, in conditions of greater uncertainty). As she reduces her production of goods, she can hold increasing portions of her current revenue in the bank, thus effectively shifting a portion of her wealth from illiquid to liquid holdings. By putting the money in the bank that would otherwise have been invested in production, the entrepreneur both avoids finding herself encumbered with unsaleable inventory in the face of a drop in demand and is able to invest anew, in whatever sector seems most suitable at the time, when economic conditions are forecast to improve. Yet holding money out of investment in production also carries cumulative implications for unemployment and demand.

In a barter economy, by contrast, neither the interest rate issue nor the abstinence from investment in production arises in the first place: the interest rate on money is irrelevant to a barter economy and there is anyway much less to gain from holding out on investment in production by hoarding wealth in non-money commodities while waiting until economic conditions have improved because non-money commodities are not liquid enough to guarantee a market in the future. That is, the candlestick maker will simply not find buyers for a build-up of candlestick supplies that have been hoarded during a particularly uncertain period, in contrast to state money, which is liquid enough to put to use as soon as a profitable opportunity presents itself.

Just as liquidity preference and the problem of higher interest rates are irrelevant to a barter economy, the existence of liquidity preference in a monetary economy also undermines the classical dichotomy by expressing the interaction of monetary and real dynamics, thus contradicting the efficacy of a notional separation of these two sets of dynamics as mutually exclusive. That is, when economic agents' liquidity preference increases in response to greater uncertainty, we see effects on the 'real' economy (in the form of lower investment, growth and employment), which have been driven by change in the 'monetary' sphere (rising demand for liquidity and thus a rise in bank deposits).

Yet, in declaring the classical dichotomy's separation of the 'real' economy from the monetary sphere a false dichotomy, Post-Keynesian thought relies on the sharpening of another dichotomy: money and commodities. This notional separation hinges on the idea of money as a unique asset amongst other assets, which attracts distinct uses (that is, hoarding) and thereby constructs an economy that is empirically distinct to an economy in which only commodities, not money, circulate. Moreover, the importance of the Post-Keynesian critique of the classical dichotomy to wider Post-Keynesian thinking is reflected in the fact that it reaches into the very core of Keynes' contribution to economic theory.

Central to Post-Keynesian thought is the proposition that, rather than tending towards a natural and inherently beneficial equilibrium, economic dynamics are, in fact, inherently unstable and this instability is derived from the monetary nature of the economy. Specifically, this instability is derived from spikes in liquidity preference that arise amidst declining confidence amongst entrepreneurs. Consequently, as confidence in the economy ebbs and flows, so too does the economy fluctuate in unpredictable cycles, which may push the economy into a 'bad' equilibrium, in which unemployment is high.

Keynes thus argued that the neoclassical school fails to identify the full force of instability in economic processes because their modelling does not take account of the monetary nature of the economy. The distinction between the assumption of self-equilibrating economic dynamics and inherent instability and bad equilibriums remains definitive of neoclassical and Post-Keynesian analysis respectively. This position explains the antithetical perspectives assumed by neoclassical and Post-Keynesian economists, who pursue respectively free markets (because of their self-stabilising nature) and government intervention (to stabilise markets that tend towards instability).

Out of Keynes' refutation of the classical dichotomy then, arises not only a core principle of Post-Keynesian analysis but a cohesive picture of money and monetary relations, which ultimately hinges on a conception of money as chartal. That is, the classical dichotomy is contradicted by the existence of liquidity preference, which represents a 'flight to safety' under heightened uncertainty. This phenomenon sees agents shift their holdings into liquid assets, of which state money is the most liquid. The preference for cash reflects the nature of (state) money as a 'creature of the state', not the market, by which the unique features of money express money's unique relation to the state: state money is uniquely safe and stable in contrast to regular commodities, as per chapter 17 of the *General Theory* (1936). Thus, a flight into cash undermines the classical dichotomy by reflecting the very uniqueness of money amidst other assets that chartalists insist upon.

Moreover, the Post-Keynesian critique of the classical dichotomy and the consequent conceptualisation of money that Post-Keynesianism offers has other facets as well. First, it draws on sociological work that explores the complex social relations in which chartal money is embedded. This work marks out chartal money as the domain of impersonal economic relations that are backed by trust derived from the state's authority, in contrast to the embedded relations of pre-modern barter, in which the value of money is grounded in personal relations that ensure fair exchange. Here again we see a rich body of work on chartalism filling out the Post-Keynesian position on the classical dichotomy with a sociologically nuanced conception of money as distinct to the simpler relations of barter. Second, this positioning of (state) money as bearing social meaning over and above its everyday usefulness as an exchange commodity is reflected in the primacy of the unit of account function of money for chartalists, which is singled out as definitional in contrast to the 'means of exchange' function that is central for neoclassical thinking.

The complexity of money – as more than a neutral representation of the value of a commodity for which it can be exchanged, as uniquely safe and uniquely liquid, and as primarily a unit of account, not a one-dimensional means of exchange – is echoed by Keynes, who writes that 'the age of money had succeeded the age of barter as soon as men had adopted a money of account' (Keynes 1930: 5). Here we have a coherent conception of money that carries from Keynes' description of state money in chapter 17 of the *General Theory* to the intervention in traditional economic thought posed by liquidity preference, to endogenous money theory and the chartalist position on the origins of money. Across all of these pillars of Post-Keynesian thought, money is a product of the state not the market, a social construction that plays a unique role in a complex and unstable economy.

Thus, with each thread of Post-Keynesian theory deepening the distinction between money and commodities, an increasingly resounding rejection of the possibility of the spontaneous development of commodity money is delivered. At issue is the commodity-versus-money distinction, which acts as a lynchpin for Post-Keynesian thought because it sets out the unique attachment to state money that carries right across Post-Keynesian theory. That is, chartalist theory designates a distinct nature of money that, by its definition of money, poses the impossibility of commodity money being money: although value can be stored in various assets, for chartalists these assets cannot be considered to be money. Rather money is subject to distinct monetary dynamics (such as its amenability to being withdrawn from production and saved for future, more certain times) to which commodities and other assets are far less amenable. For chartalists, these peculiar monetary dynamics that distinguish money from commodities ultimately rest in the authority that its state sponsorship sanctions. That is, distinct to ordinary commodities, (state) money is vested with superior authority that marks it out as not merely a medium of exchange but a unit of account, its distinction demonstrated in the distinctly monetary dynamics to which it is subject.

Chartalist Theory and the Rupee

But what if money denominated in that unit of account is risky to hold over time? The rupee challenges the assumption that state money will in all cases be capable of fulfilling the unique role assigned to state money by chartalist theory.

Moreover, the monetary environment in Pakistan challenges the singular definition of money as state money that is offered by chartalist theory. In other words, the chartalist theory of money neither captures the spectrum of money operating in Pakistan nor accounts for the evolution of the relationship between the state and money. As such, the case of Pakistan explicitly challenges chartalist theory as an apparently robust, interdisciplinary response to the puzzle of money's acceptability that is dealt with so poorly by the metalist explanation of standard neoclassical textbooks.

To start with, the key role of state taxation in chartalist theory is ill fitting to circumstances in Pakistan. As described in Chapter 3, social conflict has precluded meaningful increases in Pakistan's extremely low tax base, which has critically compromised the state's ability to raise taxes. Although the state has the power to demand certain payments from constituents as well as the power to determine both the unit of account and the means by which payments may be discharged (Bell 2001: 157), in Pakistan this power is significantly curtailed. Here the state does not dominate economic transactions. Instead, the informal economy dominates the wider economy and even within the formal economy, only a slim minority of citizens pay taxes directly to the state.[14] This predicament undermines the chartalist argument that trust in and acceptability of money is derived from the state's power to tax in that which is designated money, which, for chartalists, offers a 'general theory of money that can be applied equally convincingly to the entire era of state money' (Wray in Bell 2001: 149).

The same argument can be levelled at variations of chartalist theory that identify the banking sector as key to the development of trust in money. In an economy that is largely 'unbanked', the banking sector's state money transactions do not carry deeply into the economy. As research at the International Growth Centre (IGC) suggests, lending for working capital in agriculture (itself employer of some half of the working population) is dominated by informal lending. Moreover, the bulk of such lending is denominated and paid not in state money but in commodity terms.[15] Similarly, the bulk of deposits and lending undertaken by ordinary people are not intermediated by the banking system. As noted in Chapter 3, the Findex survey found in 2014 that although some one-third of the population save, only some 3 per cent do so in a formal financial institution. On the credit side, although almost half of the adult population borrow, only 1.5 per cent use formal financial institutions. This suggests that financial intermediation is occurring outside of the formal banking sector. In these conditions, the stable link between money in the present and money in the future that the banking system offers through deposit and lending services appears to have rather little relevance to the maintenance of trust in state money.

The use of money instruments issued outside the system of state money poses a further challenge to chartalist theory by disrupting its singular definition of money as state money. For chartalist theory, modern money is and only can be state money. As such, chartalist theory cannot account for non-state money instruments except by declaring the economy as pre-modern and identifying non-state money instruments as barter that is engaged in traditional relations of commodity exchange. This explanation is far from adequate for explaining the monetary environment in Pakistan. In Pakistan, complex economic formations engage state money alongside non-state money instruments in an economic environment that is characterised by markers of modernity such as global integration and a regime of monetary governance not dissimilar to the advanced economies.[16]

This suggests that the chartalist view of money is historically contingent rather than a universal or exclusive theory of money. That is, chartalist definitions of money may be an adequate explanation for money in a specific group of economies in a specific era, rather than for money in general. Chartalism relies on a specific institutional formation that, as Gilbert and Helleiner write about territorial currencies, is not 'the natural apex of monetary development, but a fragile, historically specific construction' (1999: 18). This reading suggests that chartalism is challenged by monetary change at the heights of global finance, as well as amongst periphery economies. In any case, this is not to say that the state's designation of state money as legal tender in Pakistan is of no consequence, but rather that a multiplicity of monies operate within the economy and, contrary to the chartalist view, state money is but one of those instruments.

An Infrastructure of Money outside of the State

Yet, if the chartalist explanation of the social foundations of money are ill suited to the Pakistani context, then where does this leave trust in money? As we have seen, the Pakistani state is neither 'the one entity that ... all [citizens] do ongoing business with' (Mehrling 2000: 402) nor is the banking system a dominant intermediary in the economy. Rather, the bulk of citizens neither pay taxes in any substantive way nor have deposits or credit in the banking system. If chartalist theory suggests that broad coverage of taxes and bank intermediation endows state money with the authority to act as the unique definition of money in the economy, then is this where policy attention needs to focus?

To the contrary, this study has focused on the economic environment in which money is embedded, proposing that stability in money and prices is more important to the acceptability of state money and its reproduction as money in the everyday economy than the fiscal authority of the state or breadth of bank intermediation. Specifically, this study links the use of state money to its ability to function as the 'working fiction of the monetary invariant' (Mirowski 1991:

580). This is itself a question not only of stability in money, but of the anchoring of the economy in general and the sense of reliability and predictability in money and the economy that is shared between money users. Building on the discussion in Chapter 2, state money is understood as embedded in an infrastructure of price signals and other macroeconomic indicators that feed into the social status, or legitimacy, of state money by which its role as the 'monetary invariant' is key.

It is thus argued in Chapter 6 that state money can be conceived of as implicated by the intensification of volatility that has been documented in Pakistan across key macroeconomic indicators and relationships as well as in pricing patterns themselves.[17] In such circumstances, the state is not 'representative' (Simmel 1990 [1900]: 177) of trust in the money system. Rather, trust in state money (or its lack of) is embedded in the everyday nominal price signals and the broader infrastructure of macroeconomic indicators that give everyday meaning to the usefulness of money. By this reading, rather than the unit of account or means of exchange functions of money, it is the capacity of money to act as an anchor for the broader economy that is key to the substantive capacity of state money to operate as unique and dominant money. That is, the 'working fiction of the monetary invariant' (Mirowski 1991: 580) is privileged over the legitimacy or authority of the state in providing state money with the everyday legitimacy that is expressed in its everyday use as money.

As described in Chapter 6, this suggests that hyperinflationary responses to relatively moderate monetary conditions are not disproportionate responses to inflation, but proportionate responses to a deeper instability that is not visible in simple inflation statistics. For example, the decline in bank deposits and the muted response of the public to the SBP's efforts to bolster bank intermediation more generally is interpreted in this study as a response to monetary instability in the post-liberalisation period, rather than to any change in the authority of the state as a fiscal power. These shifts in money strategies are read as the kinds of exit strategies that arise where state money's legitimation is seriously compromised (Weber 2016). Money's contestation is thus realised not only where economic agents no longer rely on state money as habit (Carruthers and Babb 1996), but where conscious questioning around the usefulness of state money generates strategies that minimise exposure to state money. This study contends that these strategies have produced new commodity monies that function alongside state money and are embedded in their own social relations of trust. In the informal land market, for example, a sophisticated instrument for holding transactional balances has been developed. More an exposure to market performance than a commodity, the informal land market offers highly liquid money holdings embedded in a highly localised 'trust community' of money (Helleiner 2005).

By this reading, informal land holdings, like any number of other non-state money instruments, go some way in explaining disintermediation in Pakistan. This study thereby offers a fresh perspective where downward trends in conventional monetisation remain little explored in the literature (McLoughlin and Kinoshita 2012) and World Bank survey data cannot pinpoint exactly which instruments are being used for savings and credit practices in developing economies (Demirguc-Kunt and Klapper 2012: 34). The SBP has grappled with the sharp decline in banking sector deposits after 2007 that have stubbornly refused to return to earlier levels, generating huge efforts on the part of the SBP and the international community to improve formal banking sector engagement. Yet, rather than the steep rise in consumption posited by the SBP[18] or the need for greater convenience in deposit products, it is argued here that low deposit rates point to the substantive contestation of money. Assumed away by mainstream theory, new money strategies in Pakistan show how state money is not inviolable.

This proposition has very real implications for the central bank. If new money strategies bring money practices not only outside of the banking system but outside of state money altogether, then the problems of governing money under open markets are compounded in formidable ways. This is taken up in the following chapter not only in terms of monetary policy transmission but the broader implications that this complication of money poses for the financial inclusion agenda. But first, we turn to other theories of money, theories that come not out of the discipline of economics but from anthropology and sociology. These theories offer an alternative theoretical lineage in which money is proffered as fluid and uncertain, and hence in stark contrast to the very distinct definitional bounds of money as state money that is typical of Post-Keynesianism.

Ambiguity and Multiplicity in Anthropological and Sociological Theories of Money

The critique of chartalism extends beyond money in quantitative terms. Chartalism is also challenged by ambiguity within and between different forms of money. The changing nature of state money itself is a case in point. By proposing that only state money can be modern money, chartalism implies a static relationship between the state and money. This approach cannot easily account for change in money as globalisation redefines the conditions of monetary production and governance, as was shown in Chapters 1, 2 and 3.

A key issue addressed in this study is the problem of instability in state money. For Keynes, all commodities have their 'own' interest rate and the potential to be used as money. What makes state money the 'best' rate, however, is its stability, which is rooted in the state's administration of the price of state money and its superior liquidity. Yet, where state money is mired in instability, it may no longer be the preferred unit of account and there may be other highly liquid assets that will be considered and, in some circumstances, circulated instead of state money. In this setting, a new set of issues arises that complicates the relationship between state money and other liquid commodities. Specifically, new issues arise around how those attributes of money that are conventionally associated with the state – issues of trust, enforceability, stability and reciprocity – might arise in non-state social processes. These are more the domain of debates in sociology and anthropology than in the foundational propositions of conventional economics.

Indeed, the anthropological and sociological literature stands quite outside of traditional money theory debates. Engaging the social constitution of money in much more detail than does Post-Keynesian thinking, the anthropological and sociological literature disregards Post-Keynesian theory's neat distinction between money and non-money, giving much more heed to ambiguity in money. Focusing on money's social meaning rather than its economic application, the perspectives on money developed in the anthropological and sociological literature contest earlier conceptions of money and challenge its definitional bounds, thus complicating the one-dimensional representation of money typical of mainstream economics. This literature is briefly discussed here in pursuit of alternative theoretical lineages that develop notions of complexity and ambiguity in money.

Key to the approach to money taken in sociology and anthropology is the conceptualisation of money as a social relationship, rather than an object. While the social nature of money is recognized by Post-Keynesian theory and explicitly so in chartalist theory, the wider sociological and anthropological literature takes this sociality much further. This perspective is drawn from classic anthropological examination of gift-giving societies and develops the basic precepts of an understanding of money as credit.[19] This literature links modern money to 'the gift' (Mauss 1950) through the affirmation of moral claims attached to value involved in exchange, and draws out how money is defined by reciprocal relations of debt (Graeber 2011). This understanding of money lends it to characterisation as language (Parsons 1967) and a 'memory bank' (Hart 2000), by which the shared system of symbolic meanings attached to money use posits money as a source of social memory. Here money is considered as a system of meaning that is implicitly agreed across society. This characterisation of money as a social relation of reciprocity, rather than an object, allows for various instruments to be considered in the definition of money. That is, if money is understood as a social relation, not a 'thing' (Dodd 1994), then any number of commodities and other instruments can be interpreted as money, far beyond the conventional notes, coins and bank deposits of M1.

Moreover, those instruments that can be considered as money are cast as variable, both over time and between different actors. This view opens money up to a degree of localised specificity that contrasts to economists' characterisations of money as homogenous, fungible and neutral. Jane Guyer's (2004) research on Atlantic Africa, for example, finds money to be varied and multiple. Guyer identifies how individual money instruments exhibit different values in different applications, posing 'asymmetrical exchange' in which value scales are defined not by the money object but by the social relationship between those undertaking the transaction. Thus, even within individual monies, heterogeneity prevails.

Within the sociological and anthropological literature on money, moreover, this variation in money extends to the money instruments that make up M1 itself. That is, variability in money is not only applicable to the multiple monies that are identified by anthropologists amongst non-western cultures. Amongst economic actors in the advanced economies, even the money forms that make up M1 are vested with social meaning and these meanings can be multiple. Viviana Zelizer's (1994) work, for example, shows how money is not uniform, but can have different expectations, obligations and restrictions on how it is spent depending on how it is acquired and by whom. By earmarking certain sources of money for certain ends (for example, by spending money differently if it is acquired by tips or a gift in contrast to a regular salary, or if it is a husband's contribution to the family budget or a wife's), the homogeneity of money is disrupted by differentiation within the notes, coins and bank deposits that make up conventional money. Moreover, this kind of differentiation is driven by a more complex process than the 'mental accounting' proposed by behavioural economics.[20] The literature on monetary differentiation emphasizes how earmarking is embedded in the social relationships that differentiate how money is valued and transacted depending on the social relationship between those on either side of a transaction. Here, money is not homogenous, neutral or entirely fungible, but differentiated in very social ways.

The sociological and anthropological literature consequently contests the idea of modern money as a totalising force that is associated with early theorists such as Marx, Simmel, Weber and Polanyi. These theorists saw modern money as superseding embedded economic relations of barter and the 'special purpose monies' that different cultures maintained for different applications. In this literature, exchange in pre-modern societies is characterised by the tight-knit kinship relations in which exchange was embedded. Brass rods exchanged for cattle and as bride money amongst the Tiv of central Nigeria offer the classic example of deeply embedded 'special purpose money' (Bohannon 1959), which catered less to basic economic exchange than to the social function of maintaining certain social spheres and hierarchies. By this reading, the imposition of 'general purpose money' marks the shift to modern money with which disembedded, depersonalising and abstracted economic forms and relations are fostered. With modern money comes calculative rationality in anonymous markets, which erases social ties through the commensuration of disparate values into a single quantitative scale. Here money becomes 'the ultimate objectifier, homogenizing all qualitative distinctions into an abstract quantity' (Zelizer 2011: 379).

By contrast, the anthropological and sociological literature identifies coexistence between modern and traditional forms of money and the potential for money, 'traditional' and 'modern', to acquire new meanings in the context of wider monetary change. This literature shows how 'modern money' is loaded with social meaning, so much so that ostensibly 'general purpose money' becomes 'special purpose money' through differentiation that is derived from everyday earmarking of distinct cash flows. Here money use is not exclusively the domain of calculative rationality. Just as modern monetary societies entail monetary decisions that cannot be defined as the 'utility maximisation' of economic and monetary theory (Ganssmann 2012; Dodd 1994), so too do gift societies entail calculative dimensions (Appadurai 1986).

By contesting the homogeneity imposed on money by the economics discipline, the sociological and anthropological literature on money introduces not only heterogeneity but also fluidity in money that casts money as essentially ambiguous. This literature thereby opens up money to variation and multiplicity, implying indeterminacy rather than the distinct and consistent money of economic theory (Dodd, 1994). That is, this literature shows that there are no hard boundaries around money objects. Not only is money multiple, but it is subject to shifting meaning within and between actors and over time, which complicates any static distinction between money objects and non-money objects and accommodates change within state money by emphasizing the fluidity that accompanies social relations. The anthropological and sociological literature thus offers a perspective on money that is much better suited to the complexity of money in Pakistan's new economy than more conventional notions of money, such as those pertaining to chartalist thinking and to conventional central bank accounting.

Frontier Money and Monetary Theory

This book has argued that in Pakistan, we see a multiplicity of money instruments utilised in new money strategies, in which an array of non-traditional monies sits side-by-side with state money. Here the privilege of state money is observed to be in decline. From this perspective, the sharp distinction between M1 and broader M categories that chartalism implies no longer holds. Rather, state money finds itself on a more even footing with the so-called near monies of M2, M3, and so on.

No longer the money of Keynes' chapter 17, state money has come to share attributes of risk, (il)liquidity and (in)stability in value akin to a series of non-state monies. As set out in Chapter 6, these non-state monies have themselves become more liquid as a response to demand for diverse money instruments. This heterogeneity recalls the contributions to money theory from outside of economics and poses a stark contrast to chartalism's singular, black-and-white definition of what is and is not money. Rather, money has become more complex and more ambiguous, directly undermining chartalism's ring-fencing of money as state money.

Hence, financial innovation in Pakistan entails what appears to be a regression into simplistic barter relations but is more fruitfully understood as developments in money that hedge state money risk; that is, not as primitive or basic economic relations of barter but as financial innovation which actively responds to the risk attached to a liberalised rupee in global markets and thus disrupts a dichotomy between primitive exchange and a modern monetary economy. Specifically, in Pakistan we find the expression of liquidity preference, itself a quintessentially 'monetary' characteristic of a 'monetary economy', played out in terms of non-state money forms that appear as barter. Here Keynes' distinction between a 'barter' and 'monetary' economy, and between money and non-money, is complicated by distinctly 'monetary' processes being expressed in the instruments typical of a 'barter' economy.

This argument at once rejects a chartalist view of money, draws heavily on the multiplicity and ambiguity of sociological theories of money, and is, to some degree at least, reflected in the empirical tracking of money in the M categories. Yet, even though the argument posits an infrastructure of money that lies in large part *outside* the state, the analysis in certain ways maintains a classically Post-Keynesian perspective. That is, by rejecting chartalism but at the same time embracing core tenets of Post-Keynesian theory, the perspective developed throughout this book maintains a seemingly contradictory relationship to Post-Keynesian theory.

To this predicament, the argument put forward in the rest of this chapter is that Post-Keynesian theory is, in principle, well equipped to tackle questions of money and monetary change under conditions of globalisation both at the heights of global finance and amongst peripheral economies. Yet Post-Keynesian theory has, it is contended, faced certain internally generated constraints that have limited its capacity to engage with cutting-edge questions of monetary change. At issue is the overwhelming strength of key strands of Post-Keynesian theory, notably of endogenous money theory and of chartalist accounts of the historical development of money, for which Post-Keynesian monetary theory is most well known. That is, the clearly defined categories and accepted wisdoms that have arisen out of these bold and insightful challenges to mainstream theory (and which have in both cases, arguably, ultimately won the argument) have in ways become a hindrance to the development of Post-Keynesian responses to the kinds of challenges to money that have been exposed most starkly by the recent global financial crisis.

Indeed, this book challenges some of the assumed premises of Post-Keynesian theory. Yet, while it may disagree with much Post-Keynesian analysis, it remains sympathetic to its broad method of analysis. The critical difference here is that some Post-Keynesian propositions (notably the nature of money as a 'creature of the state' and the central role of bank money) are treated as categorical, but, it is argued, they are actually historically and contextually specific: what applied in advanced capitalist economies in the 1950s may well not be apposite in frontier economies in the twenty-first century. Nonetheless, the methodological approach of Post-Keynesianism – its approach to an understanding of money and finance, for example – may still have relevance. This argument is carried forward by first setting out key principles of Post-Keynesian economics before considering how these principles have (or have not) been applied to the analysis of the kind of monetary change that we have begun to see with globalisation.

Principles of Post-Keynesian Economics

Although clear lines of debate separate different strands of Post-Keynesian theory, the principles that constitute the Post-Keynesian perspective imply a broadly coherent (if not homogenous) reading of monetary and economic dynamics. These principles leave Post-Keynesian thinking well positioned to consider complexity in money and the monetary environment. Specifically, notions of fundamental uncertainty and the social embedding of money in Keynesian theory, which feed into a focus on money's safe asset role and the stabilisation function of the central bank, imply a theoretical framework that is well equipped to explore monetary change under open markets.

The prevalence of fundamental uncertainty in open market conditions, for example, is both core to Post-Keynesian thinking and eminently suitable to an analysis of monetary change under globalisation. As distinct from probabilistic risk, fundamental uncertainty pits a constant threat of unknowability and risk that is endemic and systemic, against conventional theory's much narrower concern with pockets of market failure. This persistent unknowability marks out an important role for confidence, or 'animal spirits', that is profoundly more useful to economic thinking than the rational actor, who sits at the heart of neoclassical theory. Fundamental uncertainty points enquiry towards systemic analysis and justifies a broad stabilisation role for the central bank and state policy more generally.

The contrast offered by inflation targeting convention, which is associated with the opposing school of thought known as New Keynesianism or the New Consensus, is instructive. Inflation targeting convention interprets the stability needs of money in the narrow terms of inflation and sees market failure as the exception, not the norm. It therefore relies on self-regulating markets. For Post-Keynesian theory, alternatively, fundamental uncertainty calls for comprehensive regulation of finance in order to actively construct stability in money and the wider economy. Post-Keynesian sensitivity to uncertainty and the links that Post-Keynesian thinking makes between uncertainty and confidence serve to orient Post-Keynesian thinking towards new instabilities generated by open markets and the importance of market sentiments.

The amenability to thinking about globalisation and money thus implied, moreover, is enhanced by the explicitly social nature of money in Post-Keynesian thinking. Carried into the specifics of money theory by chartalist theorists, the social embedding of money in Post-Keynesian macroeconomics is foundational to its key contributions to economic thinking. Here again, Post-Keynesian thinking is well equipped to recognise and interpret the important changes in money that arise with the pressures of globalisation.

Within Post-Keynesian theory, the sociality of money ultimately predicates the inherent instability of the economy, which, in turn, invokes a stabilisation role for the state. Commonly conceptualised in terms of Keynes' distinct ideas about money as 'non-neutral' and his refutation of the 'Classical dichotomy', the Keynesian understanding of money as socially grounded underpins Keynes' most significant contributions to economic thinking. As argued earlier in the chapter, at issue is the flight to safety proposed by Keynes' liquidity preference theory, which reveals how wealth can be periodically held out of investment, causing the economy to run not smoothly at equilibrium but to ebb and flow with the volatile investor sentiments. At its core, liquidity preference theory, itself a key Keynesian contribution to the discipline, is grounded in an understanding of money imbued with social meaning and thus distinct to regular commodities.

From here Post-Keynesianism has developed a sensitivity to the safe-asset role of state money, which is particularly suitable to exploring the question of globalisation and monetary change pursued here. This follows logically from the proposition that money is socially constructed, that uncertainty is a crucially important economic condition and that money is the go-to asset in times of uncertainty. This sensitivity to the safe-asset role of state money focuses policy on securing stability in the banking sector. Moreover, this focus on banking sector stability is invigorated by endogenous money theory, which has become synonymous with Post-Keynesian thought. In evaluating the expansion of money supply, endogenous money theory's focus on decisions made inside the banking sector (rather than the central bank's decision to release or retract central bank reserves) carries attentiveness to money as the safe asset into attention on the integrity of the banking system more broadly.

Within post-Keynesian theory, all this marks out a much broader role for the central bank in stabilising the monetary system by controlling the banking system than more mainstream approaches imply. From a Post-Keynesian perspective, the role of the central bank is not only to control inflation (as it is for inflation targeting theory) but to protect the safety of money so as to maintain trust in money. This consequently demands thorough regulation of banks as key producers of money for the economy in order to defend against potential bank failure and guarantee an order of safety that promises that state money maintains its safe asset status. Similarly, for Post-Keynesians the financial sector more generally needs to be regulated so as to enforce stability, not against the threat of pockets of market failure but against the threat of fundamental uncertainty.[21]

The Post-Keynesian reading of money and central banking thus suggests an alertness to the kind of systemic instability that open markets imply. This suggests that the rapidly changing nature of markets for money and finance discussed in Chapter 1 posit a monetary environment that is ripe for Post-Keynesian analysis. Yet, as the following section argues, the Post-Keynesian literature has had surprisingly little to say about monetary change under globalisation.

Conclusion: Post-Keynesian Theory and Monetary Change

Post-Keynesian thinking offers a more holistic view of money as compared to that offered by more mainstream approaches. Post-Keynesianism would thus appear well equipped to consider the rapid transformation of the monetary landscape that has become visible in the wake of the recent global financial crisis. This proposition is particularly compelling given the glaring weaknesses of mainstream monetary economics that were floodlit by the global financial crisis of 2008. Inflation targeting blatantly neglected financial stability – let alone international spillovers – in favour of a one-dimensional focus on price stability in the lead-up to the crisis,[22] and efforts to insert financial stability into the inflation targeting framework have produced little more than a somewhat unconvincing promise of macroprudential safeguarding. Similarly, the rethinking of the relationship between money, interest rates and prices in the face of the threat of deflation appears to have produced little more than the recalibration of the Taylor Rule[23] to justify lower interest rates. With its weak offerings in the aftermath and its theoretical vulnerabilities harshly exposed, inflation targeting has proved poorly equipped to cope with the challenges posed by the crisis.

By contrast, the far more complex view of money that undergirds Post-Keynesian thinking promises a more nuanced and dynamic perspective on monetary change: money is not a one-dimensional means of exchange, but is embedded not only in an institutional framework that spans the government, the central bank and the banking sector, but also in the social validation that is expressed in social trust in money. This perspective suggests a rich and nuanced response to monetary change from Post-Keynesian quarters. Importantly for the present study, the crucial role of trust in money that is carried through Post-Keynesian thought raises key questions about how that trust can be maintained under global market.

By emphasising that money cannot function without trust, the post-Keynesian view implies the possibility of monetary contestation, akin to that of the sociological literature on money and the international political economy literature on monetary sovereignty. That possibility is conspicuously absent in more conventional policy and theory. From a Post-Keynesian perspective then, we must be attentive to pressures on the social structures that hold trust in money in place and keep monetary contestation at bay.

Specifically, such an attentiveness to the imperative of trust in money raises questions concerning financial innovation, which links into the Post-Keynesian focus on the banking system as a key issuer of money in the economy. Financial innovation suggests a whole new cast of monies along with their attendant institutional issuers. This poses new questions about how the central bank can maintain trust in money when the old contract that provided deposit-taking institutions with a central bank guarantee in exchange for submission to regulation is swamped by alternatives to state money.

Yet these kinds of questions have not featured significantly in Post-Keynesian debates, just as Post-Keynesian thought has failed to engage with money outside of the core, advanced economies. In fact, Post-Keynesian work has had surprisingly little to say about the transformation of money that has become so starkly apparent since the crisis.

More specifically, Post-Keynesian work has been slow to engage on issues relating to the reorganisation of the relationship between the state and money as financial innovation has expanded money instruments and money issuers. One explanation for this is that the controversies generated by endogenous money theory and chartalism alike pushed Post-Keynesian theory into a hardening of those positions. That is, the debates about exogenous-versus-endogenous money, as with the metalists-versus-chartalists debate, became fiercely polarised. These debates generated such a significant literature on the role of the state in sponsoring money and the role of the banking sector in issuing money, that the consideration of money produced by the market and outside of commercial banking lay simply outside of the interests of Post-Keynesian thought. This demarcation of money, by which money is state money (including bank money), has only begun to be broken down in recent years. For example, Post-Keynesian research has only recently begun to consider 'shadow money' as money[24] and to overcome the narrow bounds of circuitist and endogenous money theory in order to incorporate shadow money into Post-Keynesian theories of money creation.[25] Post-Keynesian thinking is yet to seriously engage with money in the periphery.

This hardening of positions may similarly explain how the perspective on money in Pakistan that has been developed in this book at once tracks key Post-Keynesian themes yet contradicts key Post-Keynesian positions. Framed in terms of the capacity of state money to function as the safe asset, this analysis explores the implications for state money of instability in an environment of uncertainty. The analysis thereby focuses on the possibility of monetary contestation, and explores what happens when trust in money fails. By exploring the role of the central bank's guardianship over money beyond simple inflation control, and setting money in its wider social and macroeconomic context, this set of questions remains closely aligned with Post-Keynesian concerns: this book explores money as a social construct under uncertainty and considers the active policy support that money demands where its legitimacy may be impacted by instability in the wider economy in which it is embedded.

Yet the findings identify monetary instruments that lie outside of the kind of money that chartalism posits as the bounded definition of money, and contradicts the focus on the banking sector as the key issuer of money that is proposed by endogenous money theory. The analysis finds money created by the market, not the state, in commodity form and outside of the banking system, all of which offer a version of money in polar opposition to the version that Post-Keynesians have been putting forward in fierce debate with mainstream theorists for decades.

This contrast of an enquiry grounded in Post-Keynesian concerns yet contrary to key theoretical insights in its findings exposes an important set of limitations in Post-Keynesian theory. Whether the polarity of debates that produced the very impressive bodies of literature on chartalism and endogenous money theory can be blamed for holding Post-Keynesian theory back or not, the fact remains that Post-Keynesian theory has, on the whole, remained limited to a narrow geographic and historical focus. Specifically, Post-Keynesian thinking has had very little to say about money and central banking outside of the key currency economies, and has been immensely challenged by recent developments in money. The emphasis on systemic instability and the greater sensitivity of Post-Keynesian thought to the social embedding of the economy situates it well for tackling the complexity of money both at the periphery and under globalisation. It has nevertheless remained inflexible, as if held back by its chartalist and endogenous money moorings, which pin money to the state and the banking system.

Notes

1. Note that Post-Keynesian theory commonly distinguishes between bank money and state money. This study, thus, uses the term 'state money' in a slightly different way. In this study, state money is used to cover bank money and state money since the authority of the state remains at the root of money's authority in either case. That is, for this study, state money is a reference to the chartal nature of bank money and state money, the authority of which is derived from the state. See Bell (2001) for a useful discussion on the relationship between bank and state money and on chartalism more generally.

2. For example, see Dow (2017) on how central banks in the advanced economies took up certain Post-Keynesian prescriptions in the wake of the global financial crisis of 2008.

3. See Krippner (2011), Cetorelli (2014) and Malz (2015) for different perspectives on developments in finance since the post-war years.

4. A very useful review of the M categories, including how the constituent parts of each category have changed over time, is provided by Lim and Sriram (2003).

5. Money supply targeting preceded inflation targeting and was based on an interpretation of inflation as singularly linked to the amount of money in the economy, thus challenging more complex Keynesian explanations of why price rises occur in an economy. Money supply targeting involved quantifying money through the M category monetary aggregates and attempting to adjust the amount of money in the economy in line with the targeted quantity.

6. In fact, as Frederic Mishkin explains, money supply targeting was never really expected to be particularly effective but was adopted by the Fed anyway as a 'smokescreen to obscure the need of the Fed to raise interest rates to very high levels to reduce inflation' (Mishkin 2001: 3). That is, the Fed was well aware that very high interest rates would be contested by the public and especially unions because of the very high unemployment that they implied. Money supply targeting thus offered a discourse that could attack inflation without being centred on raising interest rates. The clear challenge to money supply targeting that was posed by the increasingly complicated movements in monetary aggregates thus put the Fed in an extremely compromised position in its efforts to justify its reliance on money supply targeting. See also Krippner (2011) and Braun (2016).

7. The Pakistani rupee, for example, does not maintain a proportional relationship with national economic growth (the empirical definition) and can be more unstable in value than other instruments, such as stocks, which are disqualified from the functional definition of money due to their instability (Lim and Sriram, 2003: 5). Despite the failure of state money to match either definitions of money, monetary aggregates remain central to policy discourse and practice.

8. See Knapp (1924) and Lerner (1947).

9. This debate is known as the methodenstreit. See Ingham (1996) and Spiegler and Milberg (2013) for a discussion of the continuing relevance of these debates, as well as Bell (2001) on the metalist and chartalist positions.

10. Neo-chartalism is also known as Modern Monetary Theory. See Tcherneva (2006) and Mitchell, Wray and Watts (2019).

11. Although there is still some relatively minor measure of disagreement around neo-chartalists conception of chartal money. See, for example, Rochon and Vernengo (2003).

12. See, for example, Moore (1988), Wray (1990), Chick (1992) and Lavoie (2009).

13. The neoclassical position on the classical dichotomy can be interpreted as a position that defends neoclassical methods. That is, neoclassical methods pivot around mathematical models, which become unwieldy if they involve too many variables. Post-Keynesian analysis, by contrast, recognises a role for an order of social processes which are not amenable to quantification. This echoes the methodenstreit of the nineteenth century, pitting those that want to assess the economy as if a natural science against those who see history and sociology as needing to be incorporated into economic analysis.

14. As explained in Chapter 3, the taxation regime in the post-liberalisation era revolves around a GST, rather than income tax collection, and has a tax-to-GDP ratio that is amongst the lowest in the world.

15. Pakistan's Microfinance Network suggests that less than 15 per cent of the agricultural sector avails credit from the formal sector. Informal credit, in turn, is dominated by arthis, or marketing agents, who, as the IGC study shows, lend more often in kind than in cash. See Qadir (2005) and Haq et al. (2013).

16. Pakistan, for example, is a signatory to Article VIII at the IMF and practises inflation targeting.

17. See Hussein, Saeed and Hassan (2011), Lopez-Calix, Srinivasan and Waheed (2012) and Choudhary and Pasha (2013).

18. In a less impressive analysis, the SBP proposed that declining savings rates implies steep growth in consumption (SBP 2011b: 55). This is discussed further in Chapter 8.

19. Maurer (2006) offers a very useful review of anthropological work on money.

20. See Thaler (1999).

21. See Dow (2017).

22. See the expert report published by the Brookings Institute (2011) on lessons learnt for central banking from the crisis, for example.

23. The Taylor Rule provides central banks with a simple equation that specifies what short-term interest rate should be targeted in order to produce the desired inflation target. Use of the Taylor Rule has been central to the notion of predictability and transparency that is fundamental to the logic of inflation targeting. During the crisis and in the years since, however, the Taylor Rule was effectively abandoned as interest rates were dropped below what the Taylor Rule proposed, demanding the rule be recalibrated to lower interest rates in order to regain its explanatory power.

24. See, for example, Gabor and Vestergaard (2016).

25. See, for example, Michell (2017).

8

Conclusion

Central Bank Challenges: Financial Inclusion with Frontier Money

The sharp deterioration in monetary indicators in 2008 posed significant challenges for the SBP's management of the rupee. The SBP was forced to draw down reserves as the exchange rate depreciated sharply, fed by deterioration in the current account, sharp reversals in the capital account, and formidable speculative activity in foreign exchange markets.[1] The high commodity prices that exacerbated the current account gap also pushed up inflation, which spiked at 25 per cent in August. These conditions characterised what has been termed Pakistan's own home-grown crisis of 2008 (ul Haque 2010).

These conditions were, however, far from monetarily catastrophic. Inflation did not come close to the classic definition of hyperinflation, which is defined as rises in prices of over 50 per cent per month (Cagan 1956). In fact, with 'safe' levels of inflation estimated at around a 10 or 12 per cent threshold for developing economies (in contrast to 2 or 3 per cent for advanced economies),[2] double digit inflation in Pakistan is not in itself necessarily an economic problem. By early 2014, predictions of a firm recovery were materialising with stabilisation in the external payments position, appreciation in the rupee and considerable growth in reserves.[3]

Yet this study identifies monetary practices amongst ordinary people that are characteristic of hyperinflation. The drop in deposits, the shift into 'in kind' stores of value and the expanded use of non-rupee units of account present monetary strategies that are fiercely discordant with the picture painted by monetary statistics. This opens up a set of questions about both the rupee's governability under open markets and about the scope of the rupee's contestation amongst the local population. Taking these points together poses the possibility that in Pakistan's new economy, financial inclusion is being rejected by ordinary, generally poor households at the same time as its potential benefits for monetary governability are being increasingly recognised at the central bank. Might the push for financial inclusion in Pakistan be playing out more as a project to shore up the rupee than an attempt to bring poor households out of poverty?

New Money Practices in Pakistan

The discussion in Chapters 5 and 6 suggests that a series of money practices which counter risk attached to the liberalised rupee have become popular in the post-liberalisation years. For example, although cattle have long offered monetary functions in Pakistan, cattle were reported to have replaced cash in the post-liberalisation environment as the predominant store of value at the village level.[4] The analysis of weekly price movements between 2013 and 2017 suggests that, in comparison to rupee holdings, this portfolio choice improved the affordability of the consumer basket over the period and also offered greater stability and predictability in the affordability of the consumer basket on a week-to-week basis.

More intriguing is the status of wheat. Wheat is extremely liquid: it can be easily sold into the market in small amounts as one-off sales and outside of regular contracts either in exchange for state money or for goods. As such, wheat is a functional means of exchange. More importantly, however, in comparison to the rupee, wheat has been a significantly more reliable commodity against which to denominate the consumer basket over recent years. This shows that, on a week-to-week basis, wheat is much less likely to lose its value against the consumer basket as a whole than the rupee is. In other words, the affordability of next week's consumption is considerably more assured when wheat rather than the rupee is the funding source of next week's consumption. Specifically, the weekly price analysis showed that by stripping out exposure to the rupee, the consumer basket in wheat terms did not experience the inflationary spike that the other commodities in the basket experienced in 2013. The way that the basket as a whole closely tracks the price of wheat suggests a uniquely useful anchoring price for wheat in the economy.

In part, this is because wheat constitutes some 18 per cent of the consumer basket. Yet wheat influences broader prices disproportionately to its contribution to the consumer basket or the size of its market,[5] hence Gazdar and Mallah's description of wheat as 'the primary numéraire in the welfare considerations of a large proportion of Pakistani households' (2013: 36). Indeed, wheat is shown to function as an important anchor for wider pricing patterns in the economy in SBP research.[6] As a corollary, wheat is a good hedge for generalised inflation and a perfect (or matched book) hedge when earned as wage payment set against wheat purchases on the liability side of the household balance sheet. Evidence suggests that wheat is being increasingly used as a store of value asset, in some cases explicitly so as a replacement for bank accounts. Moreover, despite the shift from sharecropping to casualised daily labour contracts, wheat is potentially becoming an increasingly important unit of account and means of denomination and payment for wages.

Alternatively, vacant plots of land offer an unexpected new market for transactional balances that has blossomed in the post-liberalisation period. The plot market has transformed to meet the demand for liquid assets, both by issuing smaller plots and by catering to instant settlement by providing informal transactions. This market is so liquid that it potentially offers derivative exposures to price changes in the market divorced from meaningful ownership of the underlying asset.

With respect to bazaar traders, new money strategies identified in the field interviews include overnight holdings of foreign exchange; smaller and more frequent inventory purchases instead of cheaper, bulk purchases; the diversification of wares out of single commodities; and the uptake of dollar denomination (but not necessarily dollar means of payment), an example of which is found in the carpet industry.

Insofar as these strategies mitigate the risk attached to the liberalised rupee, new money strategies reflect the experience of risk as a substantive concern amongst ordinary people – not just for special interest groups or the state itself, but for the low- and middle-income people, amongst households and in local bazaars, that make up the bulk of the economy on a per capita (if not rupee value) basis.

Moreover, this risk plays out below the radar of conventional statistical indicators. In part, conventional indicators fail to reflect this risk because standard indicators pertain only to the formal sector, and do not capture activity that occurs outside the formal economy. As informalisation has expanded across Pakistan's economy, the limitations of conventional indicators have become more pronounced.

A further reason why conventional indicators do not reflect this risk is because it is both complex and effectively incalculable. Fed by reverberating shocks reacting to yet other shocks, a constant flux of unknowable derivation is generated. In Pakistan's new economy we see uncertainty familiar to Knight, Keynes and Shackle[7] that arises under the distinct conditions of globalised markets. Here monetary flux is both the cause and effect of wider instability, creating an uncertainty that is more than the sum of its parts. Essentially a problem of unstable value, volatility in money is deeply entwined with a new, deeply seated uncertainty that has appeared across economic variables.

This study contends that uncertainty of this nature interacts with public perceptions about state money. State money is implicated in each instance of unstable pricing where it denominates those unstable prices. This may explain why state money itself bears the brunt of wider economic uncertainty, over and above the level of risk carried by state money according to monetary indicators. With state money itself perceived as a key locus of risk, state money is no longer a functional risk-management tool. This is reflected in the predicament of liquidity preference, which has played out in the wake of the 2008 crisis not as a conventional move into the safest and most liquid form of money (for example, an increase in bank deposits) but as a shift out of conventional money (a decrease in bank deposits) and into any number of liquid instruments outside of state money. This study contends that the new open market conditions that have been realised in Pakistan over the last two decades are therefore key to understanding why non-hyperinflationary monetary conditions are prompting hyperinflationary monetary responses in Pakistan's new economy.

In conventional terms, the economy has shifted from being a historically low-inflation economy[8] to an economy of variable and sometimes severe inflation, as the rupee has transformed from its former fixed value in exchange rate and interest rate terms, to marked instability as a floating currency. The liberalisation of financial flows and access to foreign markets is integral to the monetary instability that has ensued. For the SBP, this is primarily a problem of meeting payments booked through the balance of payments without decimating the currency's value. As described in Chapter 3, this predicament was particularly visible during the SBP's kerb purchasing programme in the early years after the float of the rupee. At the level of the street, however, it is not the abstraction of national accounts but the floating of key commodity prices – that which gives everyday meaning to the usefulness of the rupee – that is the most prescient concern. At issue here is access to subsistence.

Yet, the importance of commodity prices flags another set of problems, which play out outside of the focus of conventional analysis. Less immediate but ultimately of greater importance to the SBP is the issue of the rupee's failing governability. This study has argued that the problem of the liberalised rupee is more than a problem of unstable inflation. Rather, it is a problem of uncertainty and is a real, live issue for the rupee and for the central bank that is tasked with governing it – just as it is a very real issue for households, who experience the liberalised rupee as a new burden of risk in everyday exchange.

Money Theory

In terms of money itself, this study has proposed that liberalisation has disrupted the rupee's functioning as money by generating instability both in money and in the wider economy in which money is indelibly couched. In these conditions, instability both in money and in the monetary environment cannot sustain the 'working fiction of the monetary invariant' (Mirowski 1991: 580). This poses a predicament by which trust in state money amongst everyday money users is undermined. Where instability imposes new risk for ordinary people and, in turn, generates new risk management strategies within the domain of money use, these new strategies constitute more than the questioning of habitual reliance on state money. Rather, money becomes the site of active contestation as new money strategies divert money functions away from legal tender and into any number of alternative instruments. In short, trust in state money is undermined by instability, generating material change in money practices that effectively contest the primacy of state money.

For money, we see the decomposition of state money across an array of alternative non-state money instruments in response to the declining capacities of state money to service money demand in all of its guises, including demand for money as the object of liquidity preference. In these conditions, state money has lost its privilege as distinct and exclusive money in the economy, reflecting that state money is no longer uniquely safe but instead has become but one of many risky, liquid money assets. By breaking money down into its constituent functions and spreading those functions across an array of different money instruments, economic agents can undertake monetary transactions while limiting exposure to the rupee, thus matching the distinct money need to the optimal money instrument. Here we see the unravelling of the interlocking monetary attributes that are so central to Keynes' explanation of how state money operates as the superior money object to the exclusion of all other potential monetary instruments. Left behind in the vacant space where the distinct money object used to be is a tangle of different money functions performed by different instruments. In this, we see how the definitional boundaries of money have become blurred as state money's uniqueness has eroded.

Within this monetary ambiguity, we see non-state money forms generated out of market activity. The persistence of wages in kind despite the shift to flexible daily-wage labour, short-term holdings of vacant land purchased in informal markets, overnight holdings of dollars, or transactional balances held in cattle or grain: all can be interpreted as not a necessity in a subsistence moneyless society, but a means to conceive of an alternative commodity money, intentionally separate from state money. This suggests that individuals move in and out of state money as a portfolio choice, juggling a diverse set of assets and liabilities (Collins et al. 2009), attached to each of which is its 'own' interest rate (Keynes 1936) linked to its risk profile pertaining to attributes of liquidity and stability.

The ambiguity and multiplicity that we see in money in Pakistan's new economy consequently relates more to theories of money that lie outside of economics than the state theories of money which have been incorporated into economic theory. More specifically, this perspective conflicts with the binary and static definition of what is and is not money, which chartalist theory binds to the state's sponsorship of money and the banking system. As such, by ring-fencing money as state money, chartalism does not lend itself to exploring how ambiguity and multiplicity in money may arise. This is a question of how state money itself can become compromised in its capacities to function as money, and how markets may respond by cultivating monetary attributes in markets for other liquid instruments. The rise of new forms of commodity money in Pakistan and the degradation of the rupee as safe and stable money emphasises the historical specificity of the singular version of modernity that chartalist theory posits. As others have argued before, this study suggests that money is dynamic, not static; and ambiguous, not distinct and consistent.[9]

Frontier Money and the State Bank of Pakistan

For the SBP, this analysis shifts the focus on money from its familiar chartalist emphasis on the fiscal capacities of the state and the penetration of the banking sector into the economy – towards the safety of state money and the stability of the monetary environment as a whole. For example, in terms of the problem posed to the SBP by stagnating deposits, this reading emphasises the anchoring role of state money (or, more specifically, its lack of) rather than the competitiveness in the banking sector and banking product convenience that have occupied SBP policy. This study has argued that transaction costs associated with state money are not just of the order of 'shoe-leather costs' – the time and effort required to access banking sector products. More important is risk and uncertainty associated with state money. By this reading, SBP policies that loosen documentation requirements or peg the rate of return on savings deposits to the policy rate do not address the problems of a deep-seated risk associated with monetary instability to which new money strategies amongst households attest to.

More specifically, the SBP's focus on the banking sector reflects basic assumptions that the rupee is inviolable as money. The SBP assumes that because 'the ordinary depositor … is generally bound to place his funds with [banks] for the sake of security, transactional access to savings etc' (SBP 2009b: 169), low deposits equate to higher consumption at the cost of lower savings. In 2011, the bank raised concerns about a 'significant behavioural shift' with the apparently sharp increase in the marginal propensity to consume at the level of the consumer. According to SBP calculations, individuals saved on average 30 out of every 100 rupees in the period between 2001 and 2008, but by 2011 were saving only 3 rupees out of every 100 (SBP 2011b: 55).

This reading of savings rates implies that the problem of low deposits lies in the conditions that the banking sector offers to savers, not in the conditions that the rupee offers to savers. By denying the possibility that savings were being held outside of rupee-denominated savings instruments altogether, the SBP here fails to recognise that lower savings in rupees does not necessarily mean more consumption. This interpretation explains the intensive focus on banking sector competitiveness, which drove the low interest rate experiment, as well as the SBP's development of innovative products for release on the market by banks, such as the IPS account, by which the SBP effectively stepped in to produce the kind of innovation that would be expected in a competitive market.

Contrary to the SBP's assumptions, the evidence presented in this study suggests that 'the ordinary depositor' has access to a series of traditional and untraditional money instruments that offer an array of money functions under various conditions of risk and liquidity. Bank deposits are thus but one of many forms of risky money instruments that offer security and transactional access, amidst an array of other attributes of risk and liquidity. This suggests that saving is in large part happening elsewhere, outside of the banking sector.

Monetary instability, itself couched in wider economic instability, is thus much more than the problem of inefficient allocation that a conventional reading from an inflation targeting perspective suggests. Rather, it is of fundamental importance to the rupee and its governability because it can lead to money demand moving outside of the rupee and the formal banking sector even in much less than hyperinflationary conditions. This transfer of monetary transactions outside of the rupee constitutes the contestation of money in very real and tangible ways. Contestation here is akin to the bank runs, inflation scares and outright 'exit' raised by the literature as the outcome of the erosion of trust in money.[10] In Pakistan, we see the nurturing of new liquidities that open up the creation of new commodity monies amidst a wider inversion of liquidity preference theory, by which the rupee is not the object of liquidity preference but the subject of uncertainty. This suggests a run on the rupee that includes the 'unbanked'.

As money, the rupee is observed not as inviolable but as fractured and contested; not 'habitual' or 'taken for granted' as exclusive and homogenous money (Helleiner 2003) but challenged by active strategies that displace state money as money. From this perspective, attending to the shallow markets, uncompetitive banking sectors and exchange intervention that the mainstream economics literature emphasise[11] cannot correct monetary policy transmission without the legitimation of money being first secured. Similarly, in the case of the SBP's deposit problem, enhancing competitiveness in the banking sector as much as creating more consumer-friendly banking products is a second-order concern compared to addressing the riskiness of the rupee. That is, contestability in money analytically precedes the shallow markets, uncompetitive banking sectors and exchange rate intervention that are the focus of mainstream analysis.

Although the SBP is blinkered by assumptions of rupee inviolability, the SBP's own research points towards significant issues in relation to the rupee's capacity to function as the money of conventional theory's monetary policy transmission. Most significantly, large survey-based studies interrogate inflation expectations on the part of households and price setting behaviour on the part of firms. These studies find that the rupee's interest rate does not anchor prices nor inflation expectations.[12] Instead, wheat and energy prices are found to be key drivers of inflation. The exchange rate, itself a proxy for the external account, is also found to be central to inflation expectations and price setting. This body of work supports similar findings in statistical analysis of inflation in Pakistan in other recent studies.[13]

The low interest rate experiment, which began in 2012, implied the same. By cutting the interest rate amidst double digit inflation, the low interest rate experiment demonstrated that the SBP did not, in fact, consider the inflation rate on state money to be a significant driver (if a driver at all) of inflation. Indeed, the interest rate cut neither generated greater inflation nor prompted an increase in private sector credit.[14] Most importantly, however, the low interest rate experiment presented an intriguing contradiction between SBP policy and SBP discourse. By positing high inflation as the result of high global commodity prices and thus assuming inflation to be impervious to an interest rate cut, the experiment effectively brought policy into line with research to demonstrate the recognition that wheat and energy prices play anchoring roles where the rupee itself does not.

Yet this is in clear contradiction to the SBP's commitment to inflation targeting. Inflation targeting denies the tool kit of the pre-liberalisation era, by which an array of different policy tools were brought together to control the monetary environment. For example, price supports and controls were used to slow inflation; regulatory incentives were used to limit the expansion of imports so as to minimise the current account deficit and protect the rupee; and various measures were used to limit speculation, not least of which was control over access to foreign currency. Inflation targeting instead promises 'one tool' and 'one target', seeking to secure the use of only the short-term interest rate on state money to control the monetary environment through a focus on inflation in the consumer price index (CPI) amidst otherwise free market dynamics. The SBP has been very clear in its commitment to inflation targeting. Yet, as the low interest rate experiment reveals, the SBP evidently does not see that one tool as effective on inflation, let alone on stabilising the monetary environment more broadly.

The contradiction implied by this effective admission of dysfunctionality in monetary policy transmission leaves the SBP in ambiguous territory. The bank cannot explicitly recognise the full gamut of complexity in the monetary environment because this would contradict and undermine its own policy and mandate. Inflation targeting hinges on effective expectations management, which requires public confidence in policy. Confidence, in turn, demands that the central bank act *as if* transmission is effective. Just as central banks amongst the advanced economies have long been forced into their own contortions in order to enhance policy credibility,[15] the SBP cannot sustain its commitment to inflation targeting (and thus to open markets) without maintaining the pretence that the rupee is an exclusive and homogenous money.

Yet behind the SBP's self-assured discourse lies a set of problems that take form in the shadow cast by the SBP's own research. If monetary policy pertains only to the regulation of state money, then its traditional policy tools will be undermined by non-state monies that disrupt forecasting and dilute transmission. If monetary policy extends to other money instruments, then where does this mandate end across the spectrum of frontier money? How could policies that stabilise anchor prices be reconciled with central bank independence? And how can state money use be consolidated across the economy if anchor prices are not stabilised?

These questions delineate the in-between space in which the SBP is suspended. After research efforts at the SBP had revealed the importance of key commodity prices such as wheat and electricity in driving inflation, the SBP began collecting an unpublished 'administered price index' in 2012. Yet the prices in the index are not set at the state's discretion but rather have, as discussed in Chapter 3, been increasingly shifted towards global prices as the state's infrastructure of price support mechanisms over key commodities was progressively dismantled. This leaves the SBP demonstrably aware of the crucial role of key commodities in driving inflation, yet able only to use those key prices as inputs into inflation forecasting efforts. That is, as these key anchoring prices have been increasingly relinquished to the market, the SBP is left in an increasingly redundant position – it can use the administered price index to aid forecasting but it cannot actually control those anchoring prices. The SBP is hamstrung: without control over those prices, the interest rate that the SBP sets to meet its forecast (which is anyway undermined by the opacity that accompanies growing informality) is unlikely to have much effect on inflation.

Although conventional analysis is not well equipped to engage with the depth of this predicament, its answer to weak monetary policy transmission nonetheless lies in inflation expectations. In the language of inflation targeting, the central bank needs to entrench expectations, which can be achieved with credible monetary policy. Quite simply, if expectations can be harnessed, then inflation will be brought into line with the central bank's forecast as economic actors enact those price expectations. That is, the market will set prices and demand wages at the inflation rate at which the central bank commits to keeping actual inflation, as long as the central bank's commitment is credible. Credible policy will thus 'perform'[16] the targeted inflation rate by persuading the public that the central bank can and will use monetary policy to shift the economy to its inflation target. Entrenched expectations will thus dampen the impact of inflationary shocks to non-core inflation, if not keep inflation entirely on track despite potential wobbles such as those caused by commodity market shocks.

Certainly this is the position of the IMF, which has long pushed for inflation targeting in its efforts to orient monetary governance in developing economies around open market principles. This ethos finds its way into the conditionalities attached to IMF loans in countless ways. The IMF's insistence on higher interest rates as a condition of new lending in 2013 (which effectively ended the low interest rate experiment) is but one example of how the IMF imposes inflation targeting norms on developing countries.[17] For the IMF, it is paramount that the SBP limit market intervention, such as exchange rate intervention to manipulate the rupee's value or efforts to reduce imports by imposing financial constraints on importers.[18] Instead, the SBP must raise interest rates in the face of rising inflation, and loosen only when inflation is under control, thus relying on 'one tool and one target'. The IMF sees this as the most efficient and sustainable way to manage money and the economy. For the IMF, abstaining from intervention gives markets the chance to generate the correct market signals which will allow markets to equilibrate of their own accord, thus reducing the possibility of well-intentioned interventions creating yet more distortions that demand ever more intervention.

The push for inflation targeting at the SBP is thus congruent with the IMF's position. Expectations management has been a core focus at the SBP in the post-liberalisation years and is evident in SBP research, monetary policy statements and wider discourse with the public. Moreover, expectations management in the shift from inflation targeting 'lite' to inflation targeting is central to the SBP's strategic plan.[19] But the failure of transmission itself demonstrates that the SBP's credibility is sorely undermined: clearly, the price of wheat is much more important to wage demands and price setting than the interest rate on rupees. The SBP's own surveys on inflation expectations amongst the public demonstrate the fact that expectations have very little to do with either the interest rate on state money or the central bank's forecast.[20] In these conditions, it seems somewhat farfetched for the SBP to credibly claim to control inflation with conventional monetary policy.

This predicament is only exacerbated by the proliferating uses of non-state money instruments in money functions in the economy. As alternative money strategies replace conventional money practices, the efficacy of monetary policy is further undermined because central bank command over state money is increasingly diluted amidst rival relations of credit, debt, exchange and denomination. That is, if the banking system is not the beating heart through which money circulates in the economy, then the interest rate on state money will bear little relevance to spending and saving decisions of economic actors.

Moreover, this predicament is further complicated for the SBP insofar as the proliferation of money practices that utilise not the rupee but non-state money instruments reduces visibility in an already opaque data environment. This opacity frustrates the ability of the central bank to formulate policy in response to shifting monetary dynamics because, quite simply, the central bank is unable to reliably observe those monetary and economy dynamics. The central bank simply cannot trust its monetary and economic data. In part, the issue is that liquidity is not concentrated in the banking sector but spread across informal markets and any number of different types of traditionally non-financial assets. But this is not helped by the disruption to monetary and economic indicators alike imposed by informal money markets and not least by the messy netting of flows associated with the *hawala* trade.

Frontier Money and Financial Inclusion

It is in this very complicated monetary governance environment that the appeal of financial inclusion for the central bank itself becomes clear. Regardless of its potential as a tool of poverty alleviation, financial inclusion answers to the need to entrench expectations. If the bulk of households can be brought into the formal banking sector, the relevance of the interest rate on rupees to economic agents at large will expand in meaningful ways at the same time as monetary data are strengthened. That is, if the 'unbanked' can become 'banked' and the 'underbanked' can become 'deeply banked', then a rise or fall in the interest rate is much more likely to feed into consumption, saving and investment decisions across the economy. In a comprehensively 'banked' economy, the function of an interest rate change as a signal of future inflation will have found its footing, and the economy at large will be much more receptive to the central bank's efforts to 'speak to the people' (Braun 2016). Financial inclusion can also bring informal transactions under scrutiny and make the consumption, savings and investment decisions of economic actors much more transparent. It has been argued that growing informality in money and the economy not only drives a sense of uncertainty that undermines trust in state money, but, more directly, poses huge problems for the central bank in conducting monetary policy. Informality obfuscates the knowledge of the economy that is needed by the central bank in order to make the right forecasts of future inflation at the same time as it dilutes the monetary policy transmission that should bring those forecasts to bear on the economy through interest rate manipulation.

By reducing informality and expanding banking sector engagement, financial inclusion can thus be a force for pushing the economy towards more conventional monetary dynamics, at the heart of which is the project of reanchoring the economy in state money. Here financial inclusion attends both to the weakening of the role of the rupee as lynchpin in the economy, by bringing the interest rate on rupees into the household balance sheet, and to the growing problem for forecasting and transmission of monetary policy posed by opacity and informality more generally, by bringing flows through the banking sector.

Indeed, the shunting of the task of entrenching expectations onto the financial inclusion agenda is reflected in the changing terms in which the SBP discusses financial inclusion. The launch of financial inclusion policies in Pakistan had revolved around access to finance as risk mitigation and engine of growth for households.[21] With structural adjustment in the 1990s, the state's insulation of the national economy from the vagaries of global markets had been repealed. Structural adjustment wound down the multi-pronged policy approach that supported stability in money and pricing in the economy. As poverty rose sharply through the decade, the SBP drove efforts to bring financial inclusion into the space vacated by the state, promising access to financial services as the tool with which to reconstruct household stability under open markets. At the SBP, the discourse around financial inclusion was about 'empowering and enhancing the capacity of [the] poor to contribute and participate in economic growth' in a push to 'generate income, [and] improve physical, social, infrastructure, and skills of the vulnerable' (Akhtar 2007). Financial inclusion was presented as a tool with which to confront poor households' risk aversion behaviour, which held them back from taking up potentially viable technologies, production choices and income opportunities (ADB 2000: 8).

By this reading, financial inclusion could thus open new horizons of risk management for households that answer to the imperatives of both economic and social policy: risk mitigation to drive new productivity in household engagement with the economy and risk mitigation as 'a necessary safety net measure for the poor' (Husain 2003; Ministry of Finance 2000: 40). Financial inclusion was thus 'an integral tool of poverty alleviation' (Hussain 2003), central to the enhancement of social capital and a crucial new safety net.[22]

In these early years, informality was only ever referred to as the source market where new customers for the banking system could be found.[23] Moreover, there was no mention of the possibility of improved monetary policy transmission as a result of expanding financial inclusion. Indeed, monetary policy transmission had not been realised as a policy problem until after the boom years had ended.

In the post-liberalisation years, however, the function of financial inclusion in attending to the problem of rupee governability under open markets became increasingly recognised by the SBP. Specifically, the potential contribution of financial inclusion towards minimising informality in the economy became a persistent theme in discourse around financial inclusion.[24] This is made quite clear in the SBP's strategic plan for 2016 to 2020, which explicitly discusses the benefits of financial inclusion in terms of the 'flow-on effects on the transmission mechanism associated with financial inclusion strategies and expansion of the formal sector' (SBP 2015: 9). This very clear statement of financial inclusion's potential capacity to help to normalise the monetary environment underlines a marked distinction with the discourse around financial inclusion prior to the post-liberalisation period, which dwelt solely on the capacity of financial inclusion to alleviate poverty.

Yet, while the benefits of financial inclusion to monetary governability have gained increasing emphasis over its potential for poverty alleviation at the central bank, financial inclusion's usefulness to households has become increasingly undermined. The argument developed across this book is that, in Pakistan's new economy, state money no longer offers the core risk attributes that are fundamental to traditional definitions of money. By this reading, the core unit in which credit and savings products are denominated undermines the usefulness of those products to households and small businesses as state money itself becomes a key locus of risk.

This suggests that the low deposit rates observed in Pakistan in the post-liberalisation years may, in fact, represent a rejection of the financial inclusion agenda amidst broader contestation of the rupee as money. Indeed, the persistently poor response of households to the push for financial inclusion is particularly striking in light of the huge effort and resources thrown at inclusion by the central bank as well as international donors. The SBP has been a pioneer of financial inclusion policy,[25] proving itself both committed and innovative. This unwavering commitment has facilitated huge activity by the private sector as well as other organs of the state to support the broadening of banking sector engagement. Yet take-up amongst the public remains disappointing. Not only has the banking sector failed to maintain the kinds of small deposit levels of the 1990s, but new products like mobile phone banking are being predominantly used only in their most superficial applications: for transferring but not for storing state money.

The problem of monetary policy transmission implies the same: the 'one tool, one target' approach to monetary policy under open markets has failed to gain traction within inflation dynamics in the economy. That is, inflation has not been shown to reliably respond to interest rate changes. This implies that money is not functioning as a lynchpin across economic transactions, a fact implicitly recognised by the SBP's own research on the role of key commodity prices in the economy.

Low deposit rates and the lack of anchoring provided by the rupee thus support the proposition that ordinary people may in fact not *want* to be financially included, not, at least, in rupee terms. This analysis has argued that persistent conditions of uncertainty rooted in Pakistan's open market dynamics has turned liquidity preference on its head by prompting a flight *out* of cash and into alternative liquid instruments, as state money itself becomes a key locus of risk. Here markets respond to new demand for liquidity by evolving, like the land market has, to enhance the money attributes of certain assets. This further erodes the distinction between state money and other instruments, thus further undermining the rupee's governability by undermining its unique role in the economy as money.

On the part of households, this amounts to financial innovation: economic liberalisation exposes household to new risks at the same time as the state's stabilisation policies are wound down. In this new environment of risk, new strategies are adopted to minimise exposure to the new risk attributes of the liberalised rupee. These strategies nurture new money instruments by enhancing liquidity in markets for the variety of instruments that have been described in this study as diverse constituents of frontier money. This juggling of exposures – to the rupee as well as other instruments with varying risk and liquidity profiles – reflects a sophistication in financial practices at odds with the notion of primitive barter that these strategies may be mistaken for. That is, in Pakistan we observe not a regression to barter but the kind of innovation that is called for by exposure to the vagaries of global finance.

Yet it is within the conventional teleology of monetary development that financial inclusion makes the most sense. From the assumed position of stagnancy that barter has long been associated with, financial inclusion offers the (state) money-based tools that allow households to manage risk and leverage human and financial capital so as to shift economic engagement into a new gear. Financial inclusion is offered as a circuit breaker for the simple economic relations of subsistence, which can propel households into prosperity by granting them access to new and more complex techniques of financial manoeuvre.

To the contrary, this study has argued that new money strategies, such as the use of cattle as a store of value instrument, do not necessarily signal a simple economic arithmetic that keeps households tied to a low-risk and low-profit subsistence economy. More specifically, the use of cattle as a store of value does not necessarily signal a lack of access to bank accounts just as low levels of deposits do not signal low levels of savings.

Where the use of non-state money as money reveals sophisticated strategies of financial management, the wind is taken out of the sails of the financial inclusion agenda. More flexible formal financial products may be helpful to ordinary, generally poor households – for example, products that cater to small denominations in credit and savings or include documentary requirements that are more appropriate to local conditions. Yet these kinds of products are not the 'key to ending global poverty' (Driver 2015): such products are not going to catapult households out of poverty by opening the way to more sophisticated financial management techniques because those households already are sophisticated financial players. Ordinary households are riding the vagaries of global liquidity, not as passive subjects but through active risk management strategies that hedge risk in the very tool that the financial inclusion agenda offers households with which to manage risk.

Hence, while financial inclusion was originally crafted as a solution to the problem of new household risk exposures associated with liberalisation, that framing failed to recognise what liberalisation might do to money itself. The SBP neither foresaw the threat to the rupee posed by flourishing economic informality under open markets – and not least the informality in money markets, which was given a huge boost with the SBP's own kerb purchasing programme in the wake of the rupee's float – nor did it apparently recognise the important monetary implications of liberalising key commodity prices, even though the state's repeated reneging on key liberalisation projects demonstrated a persistent hesitancy in releasing control over certain prices in agriculture and energy. The financial inclusion agenda thus failed to foresee that, although financial inclusion with a safe and stable rupee may conceivably offer some means of weathering the vagaries of global markets, financial inclusion with an unreliable and risky rupee is a different matter. That is, financial inclusion with the post-liberalisation rupee does not function as a reliable stand-in for the state's stabilisation policies.

Instead, the problems posed by the post-liberalisation rupee to households are mirrored by the central bank, where the policy tools available to control the post-liberalisation rupee are failing to gain traction in the economy. As the SBP casts around for solutions, the potential benefits of financial inclusion in enhancing the governability of the post-liberalisation rupee have gained increasing salience.

As such, the instability generated by liberalisation has at once undermined the usefulness of financial inclusion for *households* at the same time as it has generated a new set of problems for the SBP. Financial inclusion has ultimately become the solution not, as intended, to the problem for households of exposure to the vagaries of global markets under liberalisation; rather, financial inclusion has become a solution to the problem for the central bank of the *rupee's* exposure to the vagaries of global markets, the scale and complexity of which was unforeseen.

This begs the question of if, and how significant, the discrepancy may be between the intentions of major philanthropic and multilateral interests, which put financial inclusion at the top of the international development agenda, and local stakeholders such as the SBP. That is, organisations like the UN, the World Bank and the Bill and Melinda Gates Foundation may be seeking financial inclusion as a solution to poverty when it is in fact being implemented as a solution to money.

Globalisation and the Teleology of Monetary Development

This study uses the term 'frontier economy' to describe the Pakistani economy, itself interpreted as a subcategory of 'developing economies' in contrast to 'advanced economies'. However, a central theme carried through this work is that we must eschew teleological development thinking in order to gain a better understanding of how globalisation plays out at the periphery of global markets. The language of more- and less-developed economies, and 'frontier economies' alike, implies a continuum of development, at the apex of which sit the advanced economies. Yet, in examining an economy like Pakistan's, it is essential that local institutions are considered in their own conditions and context, and not by reference to their 'immaturity' or 'underdevelopment' or the 'failure' of money, the state, or central banks to exhibit the same institutional formations as those constructed in the advanced economies.

Most importantly, a teleological view of development discounts the historical specificity of the conditions in which money and economic processes evolve. Considering money and local institutions in frontier economies as 'underdeveloped' suggests that they will move 'forward' on a linear path towards the institutional configurations characteristic of the advanced economies. But what of the specific challenges faced by economies that have undergone liberalisation in the context of vast globalised markets that are awash with global liquidity? If monetary policy cannot control money and the economy, must we consider these economies to be 'dysfunctional'? (Mishra 2016)

On the contrary, this study proposes that modern money, including that which is produced in frontier economies like Pakistan, is quite distinct from its Keynesian forebears. The complication to monetary policy that is posed by globalisation in frontier economies is neither an earlier version of what the advanced economies experienced nor some kind of transgression from the norm. Rather, the fractured and unstable monetary environment that prevails in Pakistan is an expression of modern money – no longer contained within a Keynesian economy – where globalisation is experienced within a distinct historical trajectory, and without the benefits of 'key currency' status. In Pakistan, the state's grasp over money may be legitimately considered weak. However, this is not an economic pathology but an expression of modern money: of the liberalised regime of monetary governance, of the openness of the economy to global markets and of the de-anchoring of the international monetary system from gold.

At issue, then, is the question of how the liberalisation of money and accompanying globalisation of markets have transformed money. More specifically, this is a question of frontier money: of what happens when the already complicated attachment of the state to money in a developing economy context meets global markets. In narrow terms, this is about the relationship between the state and money and how that which is traditionally considered money – that is, state money – is challenged by a liberal regime of governance and the globalisation of markets.

From a more abstract perspective, the question of monetary change is about risk and liquidity (Bryan and Rafferty 2006). Beyond the question of currency competition (Helleiner 2003; Cohen 2000; Bowles 2008) are the everyday strategies that utilise liquidity for optimal risk management. Be it in state money, cattle, vacant land, undocumented dollars, grain or inventory, money strategies respond to monetary risk by working within the household portfolio to allocate liquidity against return with respect to risk. In the more insulated Keynesian economies of decades past, state money may have better answered to demand for safe and stable liquidity that could service the full gamut of money functions, not least in balancing risk and return through precautionary and transactional balances. That the domestic market had very limited access to foreign monies and domestic state money was heavily regulated and pegged to gold served to reinforce the reliability of state money to fulfil money functions. Yet in the post-gold environment there is no longer one money instrument that can reliably serve money demand.

By considering money in terms of risk and liquidity, this study has sought to look beyond the confines of state money and step outside of teleological notions of monetary development. In doing so, we find a description of globalised money at the frontier, where state money has lost its privilege and money is multiple, ambiguous, risky and contested. For money users, the study has delved beyond the statistics to identify substantive risk associated with liberalisation that is borne by ordinary people on an everyday basis. Here even the unbanked are found at the forefront of global liquidity, bearing the risk of exposure to global markets and enacting innovative liquidity management strategies in response to new risks. Yet by actively contesting state money in everyday practices, these strategies ultimately undermine the central bank's management of money. By questioning the assumption of state money's integrity, this study suggests that what the 'unbanked' need is not bank accounts, but secure recourse to subsistence.

Notes

1. See SBP (2008a: 4).

2. See, for example, Khan and Senhadji (2001), Sepehri and Moshiri (2004) and Espinoza, Leon and Ananthakrishnan (2010). See Mubarik (2005) for an estimate of the threshold for safe levels of inflation for Pakistan.

3. See, for example, Pasha (2014).

4. See, for example, Waheed (1996).

5. M. A. Choudhury, interviewed by the author on 20 May 2016, in Karachi.

6. See, for example, M. Khan (2015).

7. Frank Knight as well as Keynes and Shackle each have made important contributions to the conceptual distinction between risk, which can be quantified as a probability, and uncertainty (known as Knightian uncertainty), which cannot.

8. See Hasan et al. (1995), Zaidi (2005: 293) and Hamid, Nabi and Nasim (1990: 17).

9. This is the contention of much of the literature on money coming out of sociology and anthropology; see, for example, Dodd (1994) and Zelizer (1994). Making this argument from a political economy perspective, alternatively, is Bryan and Rafferty (2006).

10. Such as Braun (2016) and Weber (2017).

11. See, for example, Mishra and Montiel (2012).

12. See Choudhary, Naeem, et al. (2011), Abbas, Beg and Choudhary (2015), M. Khan (2015) and Choudhary, Faheem, et al. (2016).

13. Such as Khan and Ahmed (2014) and Hanif, Iqbal and Khan (2016).

14. See SBP (2015a: 103).

15. See, for example, Braun (2016) on how central banks have pursued a 'folk theory of money' in order to enhance legitimacy amongst the public.

16. For an account of performativity with regard to monetary policy transmission, see Holmes (2014) and Hall (2009).

17. That is, inflation targeting imposes a framework that identifies a 'correct' inflation rate for the economy in line with broader conditions, including inflation and the output gap. According to this framework, the interest rate had been too low during the low interest rate experiment. By forcing the interest rate up, the IMF was attempting to bring the monetary regime back to inflation targeting norms.

18. These are both recent examples from Pakistan. See respectively *Daily Times* (2018) and IMF (2017).

19. See SBP (2015d).

20. See, for example, Choudhary, Naeem, et al. (2011), Abbas, Beg and Choudhary (2015), M. Khan (2015) and Choudhary, Faheem et al. (2016).

21. See, for example, ADB (2000), Ministry of Finance (2000) and Oxford Policy Management (2006).

22. See Staschen (2014).

23. See, for example, Husain (2001) and Akhtar (2007).

24. See, for example, Dar (2015) and Wathra (2014).

25. See, for example, Statschen (2014) and Anwar (2012).

Appendix

Key stakeholder interviews included those with Ali Choudhary, Director of Research at the State Bank of Pakistan (SBP), Karachi; Mushtaq Khan, former Chief Economist at the SBP; Hanif Akhai, formerly seconded to the SBP on kerb market regulation; as well as Ishraat Husain and Shahed Hafeez Kardar, both former Governors of the SBP. Also Professor Abdul Salam, former head of the Agricultural Prices Commission, Government of Pakistan; Steve Davies at the International Food Policy Research Institute in Islamabad; Mubarak Ali at the Planning Commission, Government of Pakistan; and Mushtaq Gaadi at Quaid-i-Azam University, Islamabad.

References

Aazim, M. (2003). 'SBP Firm to Check Rise of Dollar Kerb Market'. *Dawn*, 30 July.

———— (2014). 'Poor Grain Storage Infrastructure'. *Dawn*, 16 October.

Abbas, H., S. Beg and M. A. Choudhary (2015). *Inflation Expectations and Economic Perceptions in a Developing Country Setting*. Karachi: State Bank of Pakistan.

Acharya, V. V. and L. H. Pedersen (2005). 'Asset Pricing with Liquidity Risk'. *Journal of Financial Economics* 77(2): 375–410.

Adam, C., D. Kwimbere, W. Mbowe and S. O'Connell (2012). 'Food Prices and Inflation in Tanzania'. Working Paper #S-4001-TZA-1, International Growth Centre, London.

Adler, D. (2012). *The New Field of Liquidity and Financial Frictions*. New York: The Research Foundation of the CFA Institute

ADB (2000). *Report and Recommendation of the President to the Board of Directors on Proposed Loans to the Islamic Republic of Pakistan for the Microfinance Development Program*. Manila: Asian Development Bank.

———— (2010). *Pakistan: Agriculture Sector Program II*. Manila: Asian Development Bank.

———— (2014). *Pakistan: Energy Sector Restructuring Program – Performance Evaluation Report*. Manila: Asian Development Bank.

Agenor, P. R. and P. J. Montiel (2008). *Development Macroeconomics*. Princeton: Princeton University Press.

Aglietta, M. (2002). 'Whence and Whither Money?' In *The Future of Money*, 31–73. Paris: Organisation for Economic Co-Operation and Development.

Ahmad, M., C. Cororaton, A. Qayyum and I. Muhammad (2006). 'Impact of Domestic Policies towards Agricultural Trade Liberalization and Market Reform on Food Security in Pakistan'. Paper presented at the International Conference on Trade Liberalization and Food Security in South Asia: The Lessons Learnt. IGIDR/PIDE/IFPRI, New Delhi, 8–9 June.

Akhtar, S. (2006). 'Perspectives on Pakistan's Monetary Policy Developments'. Woodrow Wilson Centre, Washington DC, 4 April.

———— (2007). 'Building Inclusive Financial System in Pakistan'. Paper presented at the Dfid and HM Treasury Financial Inclusion Conference, London, 19 June.

Alleyne, T. and M. Mecagni (2014). *Managing Volatile Capital Flows: Experiences and Lessons for Sub-Saharan African Frontier Markets*. Washington DC: International Monetary Fund.

Alloway, T. and M. MacKenzie (2014). 'Bonds: Anatomy of a Market Meltdown'. *Financial Times*, 18 November.

Amjad, R., G. M. Arif and M. Irfan (2012). 'Explaining the Ten-fold Increase in Remittances to Pakistan 2001–2012'. Working Paper 12/0391, International Growth Centre, London.

Anand, R. and P. Cashin (2016). *Taming Indian Inflation*. Washington DC: International Monetary Fund.

Anderson, J. and W. Ahmed (2016). 'Smallholder Diaries: Building the Evidence Base with Framing Familites in Mozambique, Tanzania, and Pakistan'. *Perspectives 2*. Consultative Group to Assist the Poor, Washington DC.

Anwar, Y. (2012). 'Main Challenges for the State Bank of Pakistan'. Address on the 65th Independence Day, Karachi, 14 August.

Appadurai, A. (1986). 'Introduction: Commodities and the Politics of Value'. In *The Social Life of Things: Commodities in Cultural Perspective*, ed. A. Appadurai, 3–63. Cambridge: Cambridge University Press.

Arby, M. F. (2004). *The State Bank of Pakistan: Evolution, Functions and Organization*. Karachi: State Bank of Pakistan.

Arestis, P. and M. C. Sawyer (2002). 'New Consensus New Keynesianism, and the Economics of the "Third Way"'. Levy Economics Institute Working paper #364, Levy Economics Institute of Bard College, Annandale-on-Hudson.

Armenter, R. and B. Lester (2016). 'Excess Reserves and Monetary Policy Implementation'. Research Department Working Paper #16-33, Federal Reserve Bank of Philadelphia, Philadelphia.

Asghar, U. (2012). *The Analysis of the World Bank Tax Reforms Introduced in the Federal Board of Revenue, Pakistan*. Tokyo: National Graduate Institute for Policy Studies.

Balagamwala, M. and H. Gazdar (2014). 'Life in a Time of Food Price Volatility: Evidence from Two Communities in Pakistan'. IDS Working Paper #2014/449, Institute of Development Studies, London.

Bank of England (2014). 'Money Creation in the Modern Economy'. *Quarterly Bulletin* 54(1): 4–13.

Bell, S. (2001). 'The Role of the State and the Hierarchy of Money'. *Cambridge Journal of Economics* 25(2): 149–63.

Bennett, P. and S. Peristiani (2002). 'Are U.S. Reserve Requirements Still Binding?' *Economic Policy Review* 8(1): 53–68.

Berg, A., R. Portillo and D. F. Unsal (2010). 'On the Optimal Adherence to Money Targets in a New-Keynesian Framework: An application to Low-Income Countries'. IMF Working Paper #10/134, International Monetary Fund, Washington DC.

Bergen, A. (2013). *Rating Change Probabilities: An Empirical Analysis of Sovereign Ratings*. Hamburg: Anchor Academic Publishing.

Bernanke, B. S. (2006). 'Monetary Aggregates and Monetary Policy at the Federal Reserve: A Historical Perspective'. Paper presented at the Fourth ECB Central Banking Conference, Frankfurt, 10 November.

———— (2008). 'Financial Markets, the Economic Outlook, and Monetary Policy'. A speech at the Women in Housing and Finance and Exchequer Club Joint Luncheon, Washington DC, 10 January.

Bhatti, A. and M. Arocha (2014). *Bovine Meat Value Chain Competitiveness Assessment*. Islamabad: USAID.

Black, F. and M. Scholes (1973). 'The Pricing of Options and Corporate Liabilities'. *Journal of Political Economy* 81(3): 637–54.

Bluedorn, J., R. Duttagupta, J. Guarjardo and P. Topalova (2013). 'Capital Flows Are Fickle: Anytime, Anywhere'. IMF Working Paper #13/183, International Monetary Fund, Washington DC.

BIS (2013). 'Sovereign Risk: A World without Risk-free Assets?' BIS Papers #72, Bank of International Settlements, Basel.

———— (2014a). 'Market-making and Proprietary Trading: Industry Trends, Drivers and Policy Implications'. Committtee on the Global Financial System Papers #52, Bank of International Settlements, Basel.

———— (2014b). 'The Transmission of Unconventional Monetary Policy to the Emerging Markets'. BIS Papers #78, Bank of International Settlements, Basel.

———— (2016). *Foreign Exchange Turnover in April 2016: Preliminary Global Results*. Triennial Central Bank Survey. Basel: Bank of International Settlements.

Bohannon, P. (1959). 'The Impact of Money on an African Subsistance Economy'. *Journal of Economic History* 19(4): 491–503.

Borensztein, E., K. Cowan and P. Valenzuela (2013). 'Sovereign Ceilings "Lite"? The Impact of Sovereign Ratings on Corporate Ratings'. *Journal of Banking and Finance* 37(11): 4014–24.

Borio, C. (2011). 'Central Banking Post-crisis: What Compass for Unchartered Waters?' BIS Working Paper #353, Bank of International Settlements, Basel.

———— (2014). 'The International Monetary and Financial System: A Capital Account Historical Perspective'. BIS Working Paper #457, Bank of International Settlements, Basel.

Bowles, P. (2008). *National Currencies and Globalization: Endangered Specie?* New York: Routledge.

Brana, S., M. Djibenou and S. Prat (2012). 'Global Excess Liquidity and Asset Prices in Emerging Countries: A PVAR Approach'. *Emerging Markets Review* 13(3): 256–67.

Braun, B. (2016). 'Speaking to the People? Money, Trust, and Central Bank Legitimacy in the Age of Quantitative Easing'. *Review of Internaitonal Political Economy* 23(6): 1064–92.

Brookings Institute (2011). *Rethinking Central Banking*. Washington DC: Brookings Institute.

Bryan, D. and M. Rafferty (2006). *Capitalism with Derivatives: A Political Economy of Financial Derivatives, Capital and Class*. New York: Palgrave Macmillan.

—— (2016). 'The Unaccountable Risks of LIBOR'. *The British Journal of Sociology* 67(1): 71–96.

—— (2018). *Risking Together: How Finance Is Dominating Everyday Life in Australia*. Sydney: University of Sydney Press.

Bryan, D., M. Rafferty and C. Jefferis (2015). 'Risk and Value: Finance, Labor, and Production'. *South Atlantic Quarterly* 114(2): 307–29.

Bryan, D., M. Rafferty and B. Tinel (2016). 'Households at the Frontiers of Monetary Development'. *Behemoth – A Journal on Civilisation* 9(2): 46–58.

Burki, A. A. and M. A. Khan (2011). 'Formal Participation in a Milk Supply Chain and Tachnical Inefficiency of Smallholder Dairy Farms in Pakistan'. *The Pakistan Development Review* 50(1): 63–81.

Burki, S. J. (2007). *Changing Perceptions, Altered Reality: Pakistan's Economy under Musharraf*. Karachi: Oxford University Press.

Cagan, P. (1956). 'The Monetary Dynamics of Hyperinflation'. In *Studies in the Quantity Theory of Money*, ed. M. Friedman, 25–117. Chicago: University of Chicago Press.

Callon, M. (2007). 'What Does It Mean to Say That Economics Is Performative?' In *Do Economists Make Markets? On the Performativity of Economics*, ed. D. A. MacKenzie, F. Musiesa and L. Siu, 311–57. Princeton, NJ: Princeton University Press.

Carruthers, B. G. and S. Babb (1996). 'The Color of Money and the Nature of Value: Greenbacks and Goldin Postbellum America'. *American Journal of Sociology* 101(6): 1556–91.

Cashman, J., J. Olderman, Y. Pan, M. Terrieux, A. Yu, D. Zhang and Z. Shahnoza (2016). *The Financial, Economic, Social and Political Impact of Quantitative Easing in the United States*. New York: Columbia University.

Cetorelli, N. (2014). 'Hybrid Intermediaries'. *Federal Reserve Bank of New York Staff Reports* 705. Federal Rserve Bank of New York, New York.

Chakravarty, S. (1956). 'Non-Monetized Economy and Development'. *The Economic Weekly* 8(24): 703–05.

Chandavarkar, A. G. (1977). 'Monetization of Developing Economies'. *Staff Papers* 24(3): 665–721.

Chaudhry, M. G. and S. A. Sahibzada (1995). 'Agricultural Input Subsidies in Pakistan: Nature and Impact'. *The Pakistan Development Review* 34(4): 711–22.

Chen, J., T. Mancini-Grifoli and R. Sahay (2014). 'Spillovers from United States Monetary Policy on Emerging Markets: Different This Time?' IMF Working Paper #14/240, International Monetary Fund, Washington DC.

Cheng, I. H. and W. Xiong (2014). 'Financialization of Commodity Markets'. *Annual Review of Financial Economics* 6(1): 419–41.

Chick, V. (1992). 'The Evolution of the Banking System and the Theory of Saving, Investment and Interest'. In *On Money, Method and Keynes: Selected Essays*, ed. P. Arestis and S. Dow, ch. 12. New York: St. Martins Press.

Choudhary, M. A., A. Faheem, M. N. Hanif and F. Pasha (2016). 'Price Setting and Price Stickiness: A Developing Economy Perspective'. *Journal of Macroeconomics* 48: 44–61.

Choudhary, M. A., S. Khan, F. Pasha and M. Rehman (2016). 'The Dominant Borrower Syndrome'. *Applied Economics* 48(49): 4773–82.

Choudhary, M. A, S. Mahmood, S. Khan, W. Ahmed and G. Zoega (2013). 'Sticky Wages in a Developing Country: Lessons from Structured Interviews in Pakistan'. Discussion Papers in Economics #02/13, University of Surrey, Surrey.

Choudhary, M. A., S. Naeem, A. Faheem, N. Hanif and F. Pasha (2011). 'Formal Sector Price Discoveries: Preliminary Results from a Developing Country'. SBP Working Paper #42, State Bank of Pakistan, Karachi.

Choudhary, M. A. and F. Pasha (2013). 'The RBC View of Pakistan: A Declaration of Stylized Facts and Essential Models'. Discussion Papers in Economics #03/13, University of Surrey, Guildford.

Chowdhury, A. H. M. N. (1969). 'Some Reflections on Income Redistributive Intermediation in Pakistan'. *The Pakistan Development Review* 9(2): 95–110.

Coddington, A. (1975). 'Creaking Semaphore and Beyond: A Consideration of Shackle's "Epistemics and Economics"'. *The British Journal for the Philosophy of Science* 26(2): 151–63.

Cohen, B. J. (1998). *The Geography of Money*. Ithaca: Cornell University Press.

——— (2000). 'Money in a Globalized World: From Monopoly to Oligopoly'. In *The Political Economy of Globalization*, ed. N. Woods. Basingstoke: Palgrave MacMillan.

Collins, D., J. Morduch, S. Rutherford and O. Ruthven (2009). *Portfolios of the Poor: How the World's Poor Live on $2 a Day*. Princeton: Princeton University Press.

Credit Suisse (2016). *The Next Frontier*. Zurich: Credit Suisse Research Institute.

Dabrowski, M. (2006). 'Rethinking Balance-of-payments Contraints in a Globalized World'. Studies and Analyses Case No. 330, Centre for Social and Economic Research, Warsaw.

Daily Times (2018). 'SBP Imposes 100% Cash Margin on Imports of 131 Items'. 17 July.

Damodaran, A. (2010). 'Into the Abyss: What If Nothing Is Risk Free'. Working Paper, Stern School of Business, New York University, New York.

Dar, I. (2015). 'Keynote Address by Finance Minister. Islamabad, Launch of National Financial Inclusion Strategy'. SBP, 22 May.

Davidson, P. (1972). 'Money and the Real World'. *The Economic Journal* 82(325): 101–15.

——— (1993). 'The Elephant and the Butterfly: Or Hysteresis and Post Keynesian Economics'. *Journal of Post Keynesian Economics* 15(3): 309–22.

Dawn (2002). 'SBP Updating Forex Manual'. 2 January.

―――― (2013). 'Alarming Picture: Capital Flight'. 3 October.

Demirguc-Kunt, A. and L. Klapper (2012). 'Measuring Financial Inclusion: The Global Findex Database'. Policy Research Working Paper #6025, World Bank, Washington DC.

Dodd, N. (1994). *The Sociology of Money: Economics, Reason and Contemporary Society*. Cambridge: Polity Press.

Dorosh, P., E. B. Alonso, S. Malik and A. Salam (2016). 'Agricultural Prices and Trade Policies'. In *Agriculture and the Rural Economy in Pakistan: Issues, Outlooks and Policy Priority*, ed. D. J. Spielman, S. J. Malik, P. A. Dorosh and N. Ahmad, 255–90. Philadelphia: University of Pennsylvania.

Dorosh, P., M. K. Niazi and H. Nazli (2006). 'A Social Accounting Matrix for Pakistan, 2001–02: Methodology and Results'. PIDE Working Papers #2006:9, Pakistan Institute of Development Economics, Islamabad.

Dorosh, P. and A. Salam (2006). 'Wheat Markets and Price Stabilisation in Pakistan: An Analysis of Policy Options'. PIDE Working Paper #2006:5, Pakistan Institute of Development Economics, Islamabad.

―――― (2007). 'Distortions to Agricultural Incentives in Pakistan'. Agricultural Distoritions Working Paper #33, World Bank, Washington DC.

Dow, S. (2017). 'Central Banking in the Twenty-first Century'. *Cambridge Journal of Economics* 41: 1539–57.

Du, W. and J. Schreger (2016a). 'Local Currency Sovereign Risk'. Harvard Business School BGIE Working Paper #17-024. *The Journal of Finance* 71(3): 1027–70.

―――― (2016b). 'Sovereign Risk, Currency Risk and Corporate Balance Sheets'. Harvard Business School BGIE Working Paper #17-024, Harvard University, Cambridge, MA.

Draghi, M. (2012). 'Speech by Mario Draghi, President of the European Central Bank at the Global Investment Conference in London 26 July 2012'. Available at https://www.ecb.europa.eu/press/key/date/2012/html/sp120726.en.html (accessed 1 September 2019).

ECB (2012). *Virtual Currency Schemes*. Frankfurt: European Central Bank.

Eichengreen, B. J. (2011). *Globalizing Capital: The History of the International Monetary System*. Princeton: Princeton University Press.

El-Qorchi, M., M. Maibo and J. F. Wilson (2003). 'Informal Funds Transfer Systems: An Analysis of the Informal Hawala System'. IMF Ocassional Article #222, International Monetary Fund, Washington DC.

Espinoza, R. A., H. L. Leon and P. Ananthakrishnan (2010). 'Estimating the Inflation–Growth Nexus: A Smooth Transition Model'. Working Paper #1076, International Monetary Fund, Washington DC.

Fair, C. C. (2008). 'US–Pakistan Relations: Assassination, Instability, and the Future of US Policy'. Testimony given at the House Foreign Affairs Committe, Subcommittee on the Middle East and South Asia, Rand Corporation, Arlington, VA, 16 January.

Fair, C. C. and S. J. Watson, eds (2015). *Pakistan's Enduring Challenges*. Philadelphia: University of Pennsylvania Press.

Faruqee, R. and J. R. Colemand (1996). 'Managing Price Risk in the Pakistan Wheat Market'. World Bank Discussion Paper #334, World Bank, Washington DC.

FII (2015). *Pakistan: Quicksights Report, FII Tracker Survey Wave 2*. Washington DC: Financial Inclusion Insights/InterMedia.

Fraser, J. M. (2005). 'Lessons from the Independent Private Power Experience in Pakistan'. Energy and Mining Sector Board Discussion Paper #14, World Bank, Wshington DC.

Friedman, M. and A. Schwartz (1963). 'The Relative Stability of Monetary Velocity and the Investment Multiplier in the United States, 1897–1958'. New York: National Bureau of Economic Research.

Gabor, D. and S. Brooks (2017). 'The Digital Revolution in Financial Inclusion: International Development in the Fintech Era'. *New Political Economy* 22(4): 423–36.

Gabor, D. and J. Vestergaard (2016). 'Towards a Theory of Shadow Banking. Institute for New Economic Thinking'. Institute for New Economic Thinking, April.

Ganssmann, H. (2012). *Doing Money: Elementary Monetary Theory from a Sociological Standpoint*. New York: Routledge.

Gazdar, H. (2015). 'Food Prices and the Politics of Hunger: Beneath Market and State'. *IDS Bulletin* 46(6): 68–75.

Gazdar, H. and H. B. Mallah (2013). 'Inflation and Food Security in Pakistan: Impact and Coping Strategies'. *IDS Bulletin* 44(3): 31–37.

Geertz, C., H. Geertz and L. Rosen (1979). *Meaning and Order in Moroccan Society: Three Essays in Cultural Analysis*. Cambridge: Cambridge University Press.

Gera, N. (2007). 'Impact of Structural Adjustment Programmes on Overall Social Welfare in Pakistan'. *South Asia Economic Journal* 8(1): 39–64.

Ghumman, M. (2009). '40 Percent Increase in Power Tariff Likely This Year'. *Business Recorder*, 29 September.

Gilbert, E. and E. Helleiner (1999). *Nation-states and Money: The Past, Present and Future of National Currencies*. London: Routledge.

Gokarn, S. and B. Singh (2011). 'External Factors and Monetary Policy: Indian Evidence'. BIS Working Paper #57, Bank of International Settlements, Geneva.

Golec, P. and E. Perotti (2017). 'Safe Assets: A Review'. ECB Working Paper #2035, European Central Bank, Frankfurt.

Graeber, D. (2011). *Debt: The First 5,000 Years*. New York: Melville House Publishing.

Guyer, J. I. (2004). *Marginal Gains: Monetary Transactions in Atlantic Africa*. Chicago: University of Chicago Press.

Haider, A., Q. M. Ahmed and Z. Jawed (2014). 'Determinants of Energy Inflation in Pakistan: An Emprical Analysis'. *The Pakistan Development Review* 53(4): 491–504.

References   233

Hall, R. B. (2009). *Central Banking as Global Governance: Constructing Financial Credibility*. New York: Cambridge University Press.

Halligan, L. (2009). 'Why I Believe Tim Congdon Is on Losing Side of Monetary Easing Argument'. *The Telegraph*, 2 January.

Hamid, N., I. Nabi and A. Nasim (1990). *Trade, Exchange Rate, and Agricultural Pricing Policies in Pakistan*. Washington DC: World Bank.

Hanif, M. N., J. Iqbal and I. N. Khan (2016). 'Global Commodity Prices and Inflation in a Small Open Economy'. SBP Working Paper #76, State Bank of Pakistan, Karachi.

Haq, A., A. Aslam, A. A. Chaudhry, A. Naseer, K. Muhammad, K. Mushtaq and M. S. Farooqi (2013). 'Who Is the "Arthi": Understanding the Commission Agent's Role in the Agriculture Supply Chain'. Working Paper March 2013, The International Growth Centre, London.

Hart, K. (2000). *The Memory Bank: Money in an Unequal World*. London: Profile Books.

———— (2009). 'Money and Anthropology: Object, Theory and Method'. Available at http://thememorybank.co.uk/2009/04/28/money-and-anthropology-object-theory-and-method/ (accessed 1 September 2019).

Hasan, M. A., A. H. Khan, H. A. Pasha and M. A. Rasheed (1995). 'What Explains the Current High Rate of Inflation in Pakistan?' *The Pakistan Development Review* 34(4): 927–43.

Helleiner, E. (1994). *States and the Reemergence of Global Finance: From Bretton Woods to the 1990s*. Ithaca: Cornell University Press.

———— (2003). *The Making of National Money: Territorial Currencies in Historical Perspective*. Ithaca: Cornell University Press.

———— (2005). 'Structural Power in International Monetary Relations'. EUI Working paper RSCAS #2005/10, European University Institute, Florence.

Hericourt, J. and S. Poncet (2013). 'Exchange Rate Volatility, Financial Constrains, and Trade'. Policy Research Working Paper # 6638, World Bank.

Holmes, D. R. (2014). *Economy of Words: Communicative Imperatives in Central Banks*. Chicago: Chicago University Press.

Hossain, A. (1990). 'The Monetarist versus the Neo-Keynesian View on the Acceleration of Inflation: Some Evidence from South Asian Countries'. *The Pakistan Development Review* 29(1): 19–32.

Hove, S., A. T. Mama and F. T. Tchana (2015). 'Monetary Policy and Commodity Terms of Trade Shocks in Emerging Market Economies'. *Economic Modelling* 49: 53–71.

Human Rights Watch (2004). *Soiled Hands: The Pakistan Army's Repression of the Punjab Farmers' Movement*. London: Human Rights Watch.

Husain, I. (2001). Remarks delivered by Dr. Ishrat Hussain, Governor, State Bank of Pakistan at the Asia Pacific Microcredit Summer held at New Delhi, 3 February. Available at http://www.sbp.org.pk/about/speech/2001/asiapacific-3-2-01.pdf (accessed 1 September 2019).

—— (2003). Remarks delivered as Chief Guest at the launching ceremony of the Financial Sector Strengthening Program of the Swiss Agency for Development and Cooperation, Islamabad, 26 Feburary. Available at https://www.bis.org/review/r030311f.pdf (accessed 1 September 2019).

Hussain, Z. (2017). 'A Political Census'. *Dawn*, 22 March.

Hussein, S., A. Saeed and A. Hassan (2011). 'The Financial Accelerator: An Emerging Market Story'. Working Paper #41, State Bank of Pakistan, Karachi.

Hyder, S. N. (2012). 'IMF Stand-By Arrangement for Pakistan and Its Inconclusive End: What Went Wrong?' Worlking Paper #126, Sustainable Development Policy Institute, Islamabad.

IFPRI/IDS (2016). *A User's Guide to Data from Round 2 of the Pakistan Rural Household Panel Survey (PRHPS) 2013*. Washington DC: International Food Policy Research Institute.

IMF (2001). *Staff Report for the 2000 Article IV Consultation and Request for Stand-By Arrangement*. Washington DC: International Monetary Fund.

—— (2005). *Staff Report for the 2005 Article VI Consultation*. Washington DC: International Monetary Fund.

—— (2006). *Staff Report for the 2006 Article VI Consultation*. Washington DC: International Monetary Fund.

—— (2012). 'Safe Assets: Financial System Corenerstone?' In *Global Financial Stability Report: The Quest for Lasting Stability*, 81–122. Washington DC: International Monetary Fund, April.

—— (2015). 'Evolving Monetary Policy Frameworks in Low-Income and Other Developing Countries'. Washington DC: International Monetary Fund.

—— (2016a). 'Consumer Price Index, All Items'. International Financial Statistics, available at http://data.imf.org/ (accessed 30 June 2017).

—— (2016b). 'Eleventh Review under the Extended Arrangement and Request for Modification of Performance Criteria and Extension of the Extended Arrangement'. Washington DC: International Monetary Fund.

—— (2017). 'IMF Executive Board Concludes Article IV Consultation with Pakistan'. Press Release 17/227. Available at https://www.imf.org/en/News/Articles/2017/06/16/pr17227-imf-executive-board-concludes-article-iv-consultation-with-pakistan (accessed 1 September 2019).

Ingham, G. (2004). *The Nature of Money*. Cambridge: Polity Press.

Irfan, M. (2011). 'Remittances and Poverty Linkages in Pakistan:Evidence and Some Suggestions for Further Analysis'. PIDE Working Papers #2011/78, Pakistan Instute for Development Economics, Islamabad.

Irwin, D. A. (2017). 'The Missing Bretton Woods Debate over Flexible Exchange Rates'. NBER Working Paper #23037. National Bureau of Economic Research, Cambridge, MA.

Islam, N. (1972). 'Foreign Assistance and Economic Development: The Case of Pakistan'. *The Economic Journal* 82(325): 502–30.

Ito, H. and M. Chinn (2014). 'Notes on the Chinn-Ito Index – A de jure Measure of Financial Openness'. Available at http://web.pdx.edu/~ito/Chinn-Ito_website.htm (accessed 21 October 2019).

Jahan, S. (2017). 'Inflation Targeting: Holding the Line'. *Finance and Development*. Available at https://www.imf.org/external/pubs/ft/fandd/basics/target.htm# (accessed 1 September 2019).

Jahan, S. and D. Wang (2016). 'Capital Account Openness in Low-income Developing Countries: Evidence from a New Database'. IMF Working Paper #16/252, International Monetary Fund, Washington DC.

Jalil, A. and Y. Ma (2008). 'Financial Development and Economic Growth: Time Series Evidence from Pakistan and China'. *Journal of Economic Cooperation* 29(2): 29–68.

Jan, A., A. Haider and K. Hyder (2013). 'On the (Ir)Relevance of Monetary Targeting in Pakistan: An Eclectic View'. SBP Working Paper #62, State Bank of Pakistan, Karachi.

Jones, S. (2007). 'Pakistan's Dangerous Game'. *Survival* 49(1): 15–32.

Judson, R. (2012). 'Crisis and Calm: Demand for U.S. Currency at Home and Abroad from the Fall of the Berlin Wall to 2011'. Board of Governors of the Federal Reserve System, International Finance Discussion Papers, IFDP 1058, Washington DC.

Kafeel, O. (2015). 'Mobilizing Micro Savings through Mobile Wallets: Part 1'. MicroNote #28. Pakistan Microfinance Network, Islamabad.

Kar, D. (2010). *The Drivers and Dynamics of Illicit Financial Flows from India: 1948–2008*. Washington DC: Global Financial Integrity.

Karim, S. (2014). 'Trade Policy Reforms in Pakistan'. Research Papers #7-2014. Southern Illinois University, Carbondale, IL.

Kessides, I. N. (2013). 'Chaos in Power: Pakistan's Electricity Crisis'. *Energy Policy* 55: 271–85.

Keynes, J. M. (1930). A Treatise on Money. New York: Harcourt, Brace and Co.

—— (1936). *The General Theory of Employment, Interest and Money*. New York: Harcourt, Brace and Company.

Khalid, A. (2014). 'Pakistan's Parallel Foreign Exchange Market'. *The Lahore Journal of Economics* 19(September): 1–16.

Khalid, A. and T. Nadeem (2017). 'Bank Credit to Private Sector: A Critical Review in the Context of Financial Sector Reforms'. SBP Staff Notes 03(17).

Khan, A. K. and S. A. Khan (2011). 'Foreign Direct Investment and Economic Growth in Pakistan: A Sectoral Analysis'. PIDE Working Paper #67, Pakistan Institute of Development Economics, Islamabad.

Khan, A. S. (2014). 'Pakistan's Food Security from Wheat Value Chain Perspective'. Ph.D. thesis, Centre for Development Studies, University of Aukland.

Khan, H. A. (2012). *The impact of Privatization in Pakistan*. Lahore: Ferozsons.

Khan, M. (2015). 'PKR and Price-Setting Behavior'. Staff Notes 02/15. State Bank of Pakistan, Karachi.

Khan, M. A. and A. Ahmed (2014). 'Revisiting the Macroeconomic Effects of Oil and Food Price Shocks to Pakistan Economy: A Structural Vector Autoregressive (SVAR) Analysis'. *OPEC Energy Review* 38(2): 184–215.

Khan, M. A. and A. A. Burki (2005). 'Wheat Market Reforms, Marketing Margins and Food Security in Pakistan.' Paper presented at South Asia Regional Conference of International Association of Agricultural Economists and IFPRI on 'Globalization of Agriculture in South Asia: Has It Made a Difference to Rural Livelihoods?' International Association of Agricultural Economists, Hyderabad, India, 23–25 March.

Khan, M. H. (1994). 'The Structural Adjustment Process and Agricultural Change in Pakistan in the 1980s and 1990s'. *The Pakistan Development Review* 33(4): 533–91.

Khan, M.u.H. and F. Hussain (2005). 'Monetry Aggregates in Pakistan: Theoretical and Empirical Underpinnings'. SBP Working Paper #07, State Bank of Pakistan, Karachi.

Khan, M. S. and A. S. Senhadji (2001). 'Threshold Effects in the Relationship between Inflation and Growth'. *IMF Staff Papers* 48(1): 1–21.

Khan, M. Z. (2013). 'Another Attempt to Reform Tax Administration'. *Dawn*, 3 March.

Khan, Z. (2008). 'Labour Leaders Vent Their Rage on Govt'. *Dawn*, 11 May.

Kharal, A. (2012). 'FIA Books 13 Dealers for Money Laundering'. *The Express Tribune*, 18 January.

Khwaja, A. I., A. Mian and Z. Bilal (2008). 'Dollars Dollars Everywhere, Nor any Dime to Lend: Credit Limit Constraints on Financial Sector Absorption Capacity'. *Review of Financial Studies* 32(12): 4281–323.

Kinder, M. (2010). 'Background Note: Multilateral Missteps in Pakistan's Energy Sector'. Center for Global Development, Washington DC.

Knapp, G. F. (1924 [1905]). *The State Theory of Money*. London: MacMillan.

Knight, F. H. (1921). *Risk, Uncertainty and Profit*. Boston: Hart, Schaffner & Marx; Houghton Mifflin Co.

Krippner, G. (2011). *Capitalizing on Crisis: The Political Origins of the Rise of Finance*. Cambridge, MA: Harvard University Press.

Krugman, P. (1989). 'The Case for Stabilizing Exchange Rates'. *Oxford Review of Economic Policy* 5(3): 61–72.

Kumar, K. and D. Radcliffe (2015). 'Mobile Money in Pakistan: From OTC to Accounts, Part 1'. 8 January. Consulting Group to Assist the Poor, Washington DC. Available at http://www.cgap.org/blog/mobile-money-pakistan-otc-accounts-part-1 (accessed 1 September 2019).

Kuran, T. (1986). 'The Economic System in Contemporary Islamic Thought: Interpretation and assessment'. *International Journal of Middle East Studies* 18: 135–64.

Kustin, B. (2015). *Islamic (Micro) Finance: Culture, Context, Promise, Challenges*. Seattle: Bill and Melinda Gates Foundation.

Laidler, D. (1969). 'The Definition of Money: Theoretical and Empirical Problems'. *Journal of Money, Credit and Banking* 1(4): 508–25.

Lane, P. R. and G. M. Milesi-Ferretti (2005). 'Financial Globalization and Exchange Rates'. IMF Working Paper #05/03, International Monetary Fund, Washington DC.

Laumas, P. S. (1990). 'Monetization, Financial Liberlization, and Economic Development'. *Economic Development and Cultural Change* 38(2): 377–90.

Lavoie, M. (2009). *Introduction to Post-Keynesian Economics*. London: Palgrave MacMillan.

Lechner, F. and J. Boli, eds (2015). *The Globalization Reacher*. New York: John Wiley & Sons.

Leong, R. (2015). 'U.S. Officials Eye Risks from High Frequency Trading in Bonds. *Reuters*, 4 August.

Lerner, A. P. (1947). 'Money as a Creature of the State'. *American Economic Review* 37(2): 312–17.

Lim, E. G. and S. Sriram (2003). 'Factors Underlying the Definitions of Broad Money: An Examination of Recent US Monetary Statistics and Practices of Other Countries'. IMF Working Paper #03/62, International Monetary Fund, Washington DC.

Loening, J. L., D. Durevall and Y. A. Birru (2009). 'Inflation Dynamics and Food Prices in an Agricultural Economy: The Case of Ethopia'. Policy Research Working Paper #4969, World Bank, Washington DC.

Lopez-Acevedo, G. and R. Robertson, eds (2012). *Sewing Success? Employment, Wages and Poverty following the End of the Muli-fibre Arrangement*. Washington DC: World Bank.

Lopez-Calix, J. R., T. G. Srinivasan and M. Waheed (2012). 'What Do We Know about Growth Patterns in Pakistan?' Policy Paper Series on Pakistan #05/12, World Bank, Washington DC.

MacKenzie, D. (2006). *An Engine, Not a Camera*. Cambridge, MA: MIT Press.

Mahmood, Z. (1999). 'Pakistan: The Impact of Liberalisation on Poverty'. Working Paper #43, Sustainable Development Policy Institute, Islamabad.

Malik, N. (2001). 'Pakistan's Rupee Sinks under IMF's "Rescue"'. *Asia Times*, 24 February.

Malik, S. J., H. Nazli, A. Mehmood and A. Shahzad (2014). 'Issues in the Measurement and Construction of the Consumer Price Index in Pakistan'. Pakistan Stragety Support Program Working Paper #20, International Food Policy Research Institute, Washington DC.

Malik, S. J., H. Nazli and E. Whitney (2014). 'The Official Estimates of Poverty in Pakistan: What Is Wrong and Why? – Illustrations using the Government of Pakistan's Household Integrated Economic Survey 2010–11'. Pakistan Strategy Support Program Working paper #26, International Food Policy Research Institute, Washington DC.

Malz, A. (2015). *Financial Risk Management: Models, History, and Institutions*. Hoboken, NJ: John Wiley & Sons.

Mankiw, G. N. (2008). *Principles of Macroeconomics*. Mason, OH: South-Western Cengage Learning.

Markowitz, H. M. (1952). 'Portfolio Selection'. *Journal of Finance* 7(1): 77–91.

——— (1959). *Portfolio Selection: Efficient Diversification of Investment*. New York: John Wiley & Sons.

Maurer, B. (2006). 'The Anthropology of Money'. *Annual Review of Anthropology* 35: 15–36.

Mauss, M. (1954). *The Gift*. New York: Norton.

McLoughlin, C. and N. Kinoshita (2012). 'Monetization in Low- and Middle-Income Countries'. WP/12/160, International Monetary Fund, Washington DC.

Meenai, S. A. and J. A. Ansari (2010). *Money and Banking in Pakistan*. Karachi: Oxford University Press.

Mehrling, P. (2000). 'Modern Money: Fiat or Credit?' *Journal of Post Keynesian Economics*. 22(3): 397–406.

——— (2012). 'The Inherent Hierarchy of Money'. In *Social Fairness and Economics: Economic Essays in the Spirit of Duncan Foley*, ed. L. Taylor, A. Rezai and T. Michl, 394–404. New York: Routledge.

Meltzer, A. H. (2011). 'Ben Bernanke's '70s Show'. *Wall Street Journal*. 5 February.

Menger, C. (1892). 'On the Origins of Money'. *Economic Journal* 2(6): 239–55.

Michell, J. (2016). 'Do Shadow Banks Create Money? "Financialisation" and the Monetary Circuit'. Working Paper #1605, Post Keynesian Economics Study Group.

Michell, J. and J. Toporowski (2014). 'Critical Observations on Financialization and the Financial Process'. *International Journal of Political Economy* 42(4): 67–82.

Ministry of Finance (2001). *Debt Committee Report*. Islamabad: Government of Pakistan.

——— (2000). 'Development Policy Letter from Pakistan's Finance Minister to the ADB'. In ADB, *Report and Recommendation of the President to the Board of Directors on Proposed Loans to the Islamic Republic of Pakistan for the Microfinance Development Program*. Manila: Asian Development Bank.

——— (2008). *Pakistan Economic Survey 2007–08*. Islamabad: Government of Pakistan.

——— (2015). *Pakistan Economic Survey 2014–15*. Islamabad: Government of Pakistan.

Ministry of Finance/SBP (2015). *National Financial Inclusion Strategy: Pakistan*. Islamabad: Government of Pakistan/State Bank of Pakistan.

Miraj, N. (2015). 'Real Estate Abroad: Govt Ponders Steps to Curb Flight of Capital'. *The Express Tribune*. 11 May.

Mirakhor, A. and I. Zaidi (2004). 'Foreign Currency Deposits and International Liquidity Shortages in Pakistan'. IMF Working Paper #04/167, International Monetary Fund, Washington DC.

Mirowski, P. (1991). 'Postmodernism and the Social Theory of Value'. *Journal of Post Keynesian Economics* 13(4): 565–82.

Mishkin, F. S. (2001). 'From Monetary Targeting to Inflation Targeting: Lessons from Industrialized Countries'. Policy Research Working Paper #2684. World Bank, Washington DC.

—— (2010). *The Economics of Money, Banking and Financial Markets*. Boston: Pearson Education.

Mishra, P. (2016). 'Monetary Transmission in Developing Countries: Some Evidence from India'. BIS-CAFRAL Asian Research Network Workshop. 22 March.

Mishra, P. and P. Montiel (2012). 'How Effective in Monetary Transmission in Low-Income Countries? A Survey of the Empirical Evidence'. IMF Working Paper #12/143, International Monetary Fund, Washington DC.

Mitchell, W., L. R. Wray and M. Watts (2019). *Macroeconomics*. London: Macmillan International Higher Education.

Moe, T. G. (2014). 'Shadow Banking: Policy Challenges for Central Banks'. Working Paper #802, Levy Economics Institute, Annandale-on-Hudson, NY.

Moody's Investors Services (2012). 'Sovereign Default Recovery Rates, 1983-2012H1'. New York, 30 July.

Moore, B. (1988). *Horizontalists and Verticalists: The Macroeconomics of Credit Money*. Cambridge: Cambridge University Press.

Moreau, R. (2006). 'Promise in Pakistan'. *Newsweek*, 26 March.

Mubarik, Y.A. (2005). 'Inflationa and Growth: An Estimate of the Threshold Level of Inflation in Pakistan'. *SBP Research Bulletin* 1(1): 35–44.

Mustafa, U., W. Malik and M. Sharif (2001). 'Globalisation and Its Implications for Agriculture, Food Security, and Poverty in Pakistan'. *The Pakistan Development Review* 40(4): 767–86.

Nabi, I. (1997). 'Outward Orientation of the Economy: A Review of Pakistan's Evolving Trade and Exchange Rate Policy'. *Journal of Asian Economics* 8(1): 142–63.

Nakaso, H. (2013). 'Financial Markets without a Risk-free Sovereign'. *Sovereign Risk: A World without Risk-free Assets?* BIS Papers #72. Basel: Bank of International Settlements.

Naqvi, N. H., A. H. Khan, A. M. Ahmed and R. Siddiqui (1994). 'Inflation in Pakistan: Causes and Remedies'. Pakistan Institute of Development Economics, Islamabad.

Nenova, T., C. T. Niang and A. Ahmad (2009). *Bringing Finance to Pakistan's Poor: Access to Finance for Small Enterprises and the Underserved*. Washington DC: World Bank.

Naseemullah, A. and C. E. Arnold (2015). 'The Politics of Developmental State Persistence: Institutional Origins, Industrialization and Agrarian Change'. *Studies in Comparative International Development* 50(1): 121–42.

Nasim, A. (1995). *Determinants of Inflation in Pakistan*. Karachi: State Bank of Pakistan.

Nasir, J. (2012). 'IMF Programs in Pakistan (1988–2008): An Analysis'. *Criterion Quarterly* 6(4).

Nurkse, R. (1937). *International Currency Experience*. Geneva: League of Nations.

Oxford Policy Management (2006). *Poverty and Social Impact Assessment: Pakistan Microfinance Policy.* Oxford: Oxford Policy Management.

Pakistan Bureau of Statistics (2015). *Labour Force Survey 2014–2015.* Islamabad: Pakistan Bureau of Statistics.

Pakistan Times (2013). 'Why Raise Electricity Tariff Every Other Day?' 31 January.

Palley, T. I. (2011). 'Quantitative Easing: A Keynesian Critique'. *Investigacion Economica* 70(277): 69–86.

Pagliari, M. S. and A. H. Swarnali (2017). 'The Volatility of Capital Flows in Emerging Markets: Measures and Determinants'. IMF Working Paper #17/14, International Monetary Fund, Washington DC.

Parish, D. (2006). *Evaluation of the Power Sector Operations in Pakistan.* Manila: Asian Development Bank.

Park, C. and R. V. Mercado (2015). 'Financial Inclusion, Poverty, and Income Inequality in Developing Asia'. ADB Economics Working Paper Series #426, Asian Development Bank, Manila.

Park, D., ed. (2013). *Sovereign Investment: Volatility, Diversity, Sustainability.* London: Central Banking Publications.

Parsons, T. (1967). *Sociological Theory and Modern Society.* New York: Free Press.

Pasha, H. A. (2014). *Economic Review of 2013–14 and Outlook for 2014–15.* Lahore: Institute for Policy Reforms.

Pasricha, N. and K. Revzi (2013). *After Watan: The Contributions of a G2P Payments Program to Building a Branchless Banking Industry.* Islamabad: Mennonite Economic Development Association.

Pesnani, R., M. Saleem and S. Rahooja (2008). *Fuel Price Trends: An Analytical Review.* Karachi: State Bank of Pakistan.

Players Captial Group (2014). 'Understanding Liquidity and What It Means to You'. Available at www.playerscapital.net/liquidity (accessed 1 September 2019).

Qadir, A. (2005). *A Study of Informal Finance Markets in Pakistan.* Islamabad: Pakistan Microfinance Network.

Qureshi, J. A. (2016). 'The Pakistan Remittances Initiative and Remittance Flows to Pakistan'. Pakistan Strategy Support Program Working Paper #35, International Food Policy Research Institute, Washington DC.

Radice, H. (1984). 'The National Economy: A Keynesian Myth'. *Captial and Class* 8(1): 111–40.

Rafique, N. (2015). 'Pakistan–US Relations: Reset After 2011'. *Strategic Studies* 35(3): 43–70.

Rana, P. I. (2008). 'Amnesty Scheme Lacks Assets Value Formula'. *Dawn,* 4 July.

Rana, A., A. Settle and G. A. Khan (2010). *Analysis of Federal Budget 2010–2011.* Islamabad: UNDP/SDPI.

Rana, S. (2019). 'Govt to Pay Rs 3.6 Trillion on Defence, Debt Servicing'. *The Express Tribune*, 7 February.

Rashid, A. and F. Husain (2010). 'Capital Inflows, Inflation and Exchange Rate Volatility'. Working Paper #2010:63, Pakistan Institute of Development Economics, Islamabad.

Rashid, N. (2015). 'Interpreting the Financial Inclusion Numbers in Pakistan. CGAP, blog, 14 September. Available at http://www.cgap.org/blog/interpreting-financial-inclusion-numbers-pakistan (accessed 1 September 2019).

Rasmussen, S. (2018). 'Pakistan Enigma: Why Is Financial Inclusion Happening So Slowly?' CGAP. Available at https://www.cgap.org/blog/pakistan-enigma-why-financial-inclusion-happening-so-slowly (accessed 1 September 2019).

Reinhart, C. M. and M. A. Savastano (2003). 'The Realities of Modern Hyperinflation'. *Finance and Development*, June, 20–23. Available at https://www.imf.org/external/pubs/ft/fandd/2003/06/pdf/reinhard.pdf (accessed 1 September 2019).

Rehman, A., L. Jingdong, A. A. Chandio and I. Hassain (2017). 'Livestock Production and Popultion Census in Pakistan: Determining Their Relationship with Agricultural GDP using Econometric Analysis'. *Information Processng in Agriculture* 4: 168–77.

Ricks, M. (2012). 'Money and (Shadow) Banking: A Thought Experiment'. *Review of Banking and Financial Law* 31: 731–48.

Rochon, L. and M. Vernengo (2003). 'State Money and the Real Rorld: Or Chartalism and Its Discontents'. *Journal of Post-Keynesian Economics*. 26(1): 57–67.

Rodrik, D. (2015). 'Managing Capital Flows in Frontier Market Economies'. Keynote Speech at the Conference on 'Managing Capital Flows: Lessons from Emerging Markets for Frontier Economies', International Monetary Fund, Mauritius, 2 March.

Salam, A. (2001). 'Support Price Policy in Pakistan: Rationale, Practices and Future Options'. APCom Series #196, Agricultural Prices Commission, Government of Pakistan, Islamabad.

——— (2009). 'Distortions in Incentives to Production of Major Crops in Pakistan: 1991–2008'. *Journal of International Agricultural Trade and Development* 5(2): 185–208.

Salam, A. and M. M. Mukhtar (2008). 'Public Intervention in Pakistan's Wheat Market: The Story of Two Agencies'. In *From Parastatals to Private Trade: Lessons from Asian Agriculture*, ed. S. Rashid, A. Gulati and R. Cummings Jr. Baltimore: The John Hopkins University Press.

Sayeed, A. and Z. F. Abbasi (2015). 'The Role of Central Banks in Supporting Economic Growth and Creation of Productive Employment: The Case of Pakistan'. Employment Policy Department Working Paper #171, International Labour Organisation, Geneva.

SBP (2001a). *Annual Report 2000–2001*. Karachi: State Bank of Pakistan.

——— (2002a). *Annual Report 2001–2002*. Karachi: State Bank of Pakistan.

—— (2002b). *Prudential Regulations for Banks*. Karachi: State Bank of Pakistan, 4th edition, 31 January.

—— (2003). *Annual Report 2002–2003*. Karachi: State Bank of Pakistan.

—— (2004a). *Financial Markets Review FY04*. Karachi: State Bank of Pakistan.

—— (2004b). 'SBP Board of Directors Clarifies the Position regarding Foreign Exchange Purchases'. State Bank of Pakistan, Karachi, 21 June.

—— (2005a). *Annual Report 2004–2005*. Karachi: State Bank of Pakistan.

—— (2005b). *Financial Sector Assessment 2005*. Karachi: State Bank of Pakistan.

—— (2006). *Annual Report 2005–2006*. Karachi: State Bank of Pakistan.

—— (2007). *Annual Report 2006–2007*. Karachi: State Bank of Pakistan.

—— (2008a). *Annual Report 2007–2008*. Karachi: State Bank of Pakistan.

—— (2008b). *Financial Stability Review 2007–2008*. Karachi: State Bank of Pakistan.

—— (2009a). *Annual Report 2008–2009*. Karachi: State Bank of Pakistan.

—— (2009b). *Financial Stability Review 2008–2009*. Karachi: State Bank of Pakistan.

—— (2009c). 'Refinancing Facility for Modernization of SMEs: Rice Husking Mills'. IH&SMEFD Circular #17 of 2009, State Bank of Pakistan Karachi..

—— (2009d). 'Scheme for Modernization of Cotton Ginning Factories'. IH&SMEFD Circular #14 of 2009, State Bank of Pakistan, Karachi.

—— (2009e). *The State of Pakistan Economy: Second Quarterly Report for FY10*. Karachi: State Bank of Pakistan.

—— (2010a). *Annual Report 2009–2010*. Karachi: State Bank of Pakistan.

—— (2010b). *Financial Stability Report 2009–2010*. Karachi: State Bank of Pakistan.

—— (2010c). 'Investor Portfolio Securities Account (IPS)'. FSCD Circular #18 of 2010. State Bank of Pakistan, Karachi.

—— (2011a). *Annual Performance Review of SBP BSC - FY11*. Karachi: State Bank of Pakistan.

—— (2011b). *Annual Report 2010–2011*. Karachi: State Bank of Pakistan.

—— (2011c). 'New Microfinance Strategic Framework to Promote Financial Inclusion in Pakistan: Yaseen Anwar'. State Bank of Pakistan, Karachi, 2 December.

—— (2011d). 'State Bank Revises Branchless Banking Regulation to Bring Low Income Segment of Society into Financial Loop'. State Bank of Pakistan, Karachi, 20 June.

—— (2012). *Annual Report 2011–2012*. Karachi: State Bank of Pakistan.

—— (2013a). *Annual Report 2012–2013*. Karachi: State Bank of Pakistan.

—— (2013b). 'Export Finance Facility for Locally Manufactured Machinery (EFF-LMM)'. IH&SMEFD Circular #04 of 2013, State Bank of Pakistan, Karachi.

—— (2013c). 'Prime Minister's Youth Business Loans Scheme'. IH&SMEFD Circular #10 of 2013, State Bank of Pakistan, Karachi.

—— (2013d). 'Revised Prudential Regulations for Small and Medium Enterprise (SME) Financing'. IH&SMEFD Circular #08 of 2013, State Bank of Pakistan, Karachi.

———— (2013e). 'SBP Links Minimum Rate of Return on Saving Deposits with Repo Rate'. State Bank of Pakistan, Karachi. 27 September.

———— (2013f). *The State of Pakistan Economy: Third Quarterly Report for FY13*. Karachi: State Bank of Pakistan.

———— (2014). *Annual Report 2013–2014*. Karachi: State Bank of Pakistan.

———— (2015a). *Annual Report 2014–2015*. Karachi: State Bank of Pakistan.

———— (2015b). 'Guidelines on Low Risk Bank Accounts with Simplified Due Diligence – Asaan Account'. BPRD Circular #11 of 2015, State Bank of Pakistan, Karachi.

———— (2015c). *Handbook of Statistics of Pakistan Economy 2015*. Available at www.sbp.org. pk/departments/stats/PakEconomy_Handbook/index.htm (accessed 1 September 2019).

———— (2015d). *SBP Vision 2020: Strategic Plan 2016–2020*. Karachi: State Bank of Pakistan.

———— (2016). 'Branchless Banking Regulations'. State Bank of Pakistan, Karachi.

———— (2017). *Annual Report 2016–17*. Karachi: State Bank of Pakistan.

Schaefer, D., A. Ross and D. Strauss (2013). 'Foreign Exchange: The Big Fix'. *Financial Times*.

Schipke, A., ed. (2015). *Frontier and Developing Asia: The Next Generation of Emerging Markets*. Washington DC: International Monetary Fund.

Scholte, J. A. (2017). *Globalization: A Critical Introduction*. New York: Palgrave Macmillan.

Schularick, M. and A. M. Taylor (2012). 'Credit Booms Gone Bust: Monetary Policy, Leverage Cycles and Financial Crises, 1870–2008'. *American Econonmic Review* 2012: 1029–61.

Sepehri, A. and S. Moshiri (2004). 'Inflation-Growth Profiles across Countries: Evidence from Developing and Developed Countries'. *International Review of Applied Economics* 18: 191–207.

Settle, A. (2012). 'Foreign Agricultural Land Acquisition in Pakistan: Government Policy and Community Responses'. Land Deal Politics Initiative Working Paper #7, University of the Western Cape, Cape Town.

———— (2018). 'Liberalisation, Financial Risk, and Formal Financial Participation in Pakistan: Hyperinflationary Microeconomic Responses to Moderate Volatility in a Developing Economy'. *New Political Economy* 23(3): 348–65.

Shackle, G. L. S. (1972). *Epistemics and Economics: A Critique of Economic Doctrines*. Cambridge: Cambridge University Press.

Sharif, M., Z. Altaf, H. Shah and N. Akmal (2009). 'Value Chain Analysis of the Meat Sector in Pakistan'. SSI Working Paper#02-09, National Agricultural Research Centre, Islamabad.

Siddiqui, S. K. (2014). 'The Regulation of Hawala and Other IVTS in Post 9/11 Years: A Case Study of Pakistan's Hawala Regulation 2002'. Ph.D. thesis, School of Law, University of Wollongong.

Simmel, G. (1990 [1900]). *The Philosophy of Money*. London: Routledge.

Singh, B. (2009). 'Changing Contours of Capital Flows'. *Economic and Political Weekly* 44(43): 58–66.

Singh, M. and P. Stella (2012). 'Money and Collateral'. IMF Working Paper #12/95, International Monetary Fund, Washington DC.

Social Sciences Institute NARC (2003). 'Action Plan for Livestock Marketing Sytems in Pakistan'. TCP/PAK/0168, Food and Agricultural Organisation, Islamabad.

Spiegler, P. M and W. Milberg (2013). 'Methodenstreit 2013? Historical Perspective on the Contemporary Debate Over How to Reform Economics'. *Forum for Social Economics* 42(4): 311–45.

Sriram, S. S. (2000). 'A Survey of Recent Empirical Money Demand Studies'. *IMF Staff Papers* 47(3): 334–65.

Staschen, S. (2014). *Inclusion, Stability, Integrity, and Protection: Observations and Lessons for the I-SIP Methodology from Pakistan.* Washington DC: Consultatative Group to Assist the Poor.

Stone, M. R. (2003). 'Inflation Targeting Lite'. IMF Working Paper #03/12, International Monetary Fund, Washington DC.

Storchak, S. (2013). 'Risk-free Assets: An Unreachable Dream or a Must'. In *Sovereign Risk: A World without Risk-free Assets?* BIS Papers #72. Basel: Bank of International Settlements.

Strahan, P. (2008). 'Liquidity Production in 21st Century Banking'. NBER Working paper #13798, National Bureau of Economic Research, Cambridge, MA.

Syed, B. S. (2015). 'Concern over Delay in Disbursement of US Coalition Support Fund'. *Dawn*, 4 Februry.

——— (2016). 'US Finds Action against Haqqani Network Inadequate'. *Dawn*, 20 August.

Taylor, E. (2013). *Materializing Poverty: How the Poor Transform Their Lives.* New York, Rowman and Littlefield.

Taylor, J. B. (2011). 'A Two-track Plan to Restore Growth'. *Wall Street Journal*, 28 January.

Tcherneva, P. R. (2006). 'Chartalism and the Tax-driven Approach to Money. In *A Handbook of Alternative Monetary Economics*, ed. P. Arestis and M. Sawyer, ch. 5. Cheltenham: Edward Elgar.

Thaler, R. (1999). 'Mental Accounting Matters'. *Journal of Behavioural Decision Making* 12(3): 183–206.

The News (2009a). 'Kerry-Lugar Bill Is an Insult, Army Tells US Military'. 7 October.

——— (2009b). 'Powered by Pride, Pakistan Set to Reject Kerry-Lugar Bill'. 6 October.

——— (2011). 'No Let Up in Capital Flight despite Ban'. 23 July.

Thompson, E. (2011). *Trust Is the Coin of the Realm: Lessons from the Money Men of Afghanistan.* Karachi: Oxford University Press.

Tobin, J. (1958). 'Liquidity Preference as Behavior towards Risk'. *Review of Economic Studies* 25: 65–86.

Treynor, J. L. (1961). 'Market Value, Time, and Risk'. Unpublished manuscript, no. 95-209.

Ul Haque, I. (2010). 'Pakistan: Causes and Management of the 2008 Economic Crisis'. TWN Global Economy Series #22, Third World Network, Penang.

———(2011). 'The Capital Account and Pakistani Rupee Convertibility: Macroeconomic Policy Challenges'. *The Lahore Journal of Economics* 16(September): 95–121.

UNCTAD (2012a). *Development and Globalization: Fact and Figures 2012*. Geneva. United Nations Conference on Trade and Development.

——— (2012b). 'Don't Blame the Physical Markets: Financialisation Is the Root Cause of Oil and Commodity Price Volatility'. UNCTAD Policy Brief #25, United Nations Conference on Trade and Development, Geneva.

UNDP (2011). *Towards Human Resilience: Sustaining MDG Progress in an Age of Economic Uncertainty*. New York: United Nations Development Programme.

Unicef (2011). *District Development Profile 2011: Zhob*. Quetta: United Nations Children's Fund Provincial Office.

Usmani, A. A. (2003). 'Exchange Companies Ready to Replace Money Changers'. *Economic Review* 1: 9–11.

Usmani, B. (2008). 'Lights Out for Pakistan'. *The Guardian*, 3 November.

Waheed, S. (1996). 'Household Savings in Rural Pakistan: Empirical and Conceptual Issues'. Ph.D. thesis, Faculty of Agricultural Sciences, Georg-August Universitaet, Goettingen.

Walsh, J. P. (2011). 'Reconsidering the Role of Food Prices in Inflation'. IMF Working Paper #11/17, International Monetary Fund, Washington DC.

Wathra, A. M. (2013). 'Welcome Address', Internaitonal Branchless Banking Conference, Islamabad, 17 November.

Weber, B. (2016). 'Bitcoin and the Legitimacy Crisis of Money'. *Cambridge Journal of Economics* 40: 17–41.

Woodruff, D. (1999). *Money Unmade: Barter and the Fate of Russian Capitalism*. Ithaca: Cornell University Press.

World Bank (2002). *Pakistan Development Policy Review: A New Dawn?* Report #23916-PAK. Washington DC: World Bank.

———(2003). *Implementation Completion Report for a Second Structural Adjustment Credit*. Report #25156. Washington DC: World Bank.

——— (2004). *Implementation Completion Report (SCL-39650) for a Ghazi Barotha Hydropower Project*. Repot #28781. Washington DC: World Bank.

——— (2006). *Pakistan: Household Use of Commercial Energy*. Report #320/06. Washington DC: World Bank.

——— (2012a). *Global Economic Prospects: Managing Growth in a Volatile World*. Washington DC: World Bank.

———(2012b). *Implementation Completion and Results Report (IBRD-72640 IDA-40070 TF-54392) for a Tax Administration Reform Project*. Report #ICR00002147. Washington DC: World Bank.

——— (2014a). 'Account at a Financial Institution (% Age 15+), Saved Any Money in the Past Year (% Age 15+), Saved at a Financial Institution (% Age 15+), Borrowed Any Money in the Past Year (% Age 15+), Borrowed from a Financial Institution (% Age 15+)'. Global Financial Inclusion, available at www.data.worldbank.org (accessed 20 June 2017).

——— (2014b). 'Domestic Credit to Private Sector (% of GDP), Bank Deposits to GDP (%)'. Global Financial Development, available at www.data.worldbank.org (accessed 30 June 2017).

——— (2015). 'Portfolio Investment, Net (BoP, Current US$), Foreign Direct Investment, Net (BoP, Current US$), Tax Revenue (% of GDP), Personal Remittances Recieved (Current US$)'. World Development Indicators, available at www.data.worldbank.org (accessed 30 June 2017).

WTO (1995). 'Pakistan: February 1995'. Trade Policy Reviews: First Press Release. World Trade Organization, Washington DC.

Wray, R. L. (1990). *Money and Credit in Capitalist Economies: The Endogenous Money Approach*. Aldershot: Edward Elgar.

——— (2012). *Modern Money Theory: A Primer on Macroeconomics for Sovereign Monetary Systems*. Hampshire: MacMillan.

Zaidi, A. S. (2005). *Issues in Pakistan's Economy*. Karachi: Oxford University Press.

——— (2015). *Issues in Pakistan's Economy*. Karachi: Oxford University Press.

Zaman, F. (2017). 'Census 2017: How Can Flawed Results Have Any Credibility?' *Dawn*, 17 September.

Zia, U. and M. Zia (2015). *Wheat Value Chain Governance: Sindh and Punjab*. Islamabad: Cynosure Consultants.

Zelizer, V. (1994). *The Social Meaning of Money*. New York: Basic Books.

——— (2011). *Economic Lives: How Culture Shapes the Economy*. Princeton: Princeton University Press.

De Zeeuw, M. (1996). 'The Household Integrated Economic Survey of Pakistan 1990–91: Internal and External Consistency'. *The Pakistan Development Review* (Spring): 71–84.

Index